"Most of us think of Mai to live...Jim Moore's pain those Pollyanna deceits a inal perversion, dark doings, incest, drug use and a decidedly unromantic look at how the sex drive dominates these so-called quiet, little towns.... There's drunkenness, there's small-time police corruption and there's big-time miscarriage of justice. There's venality in high places, a sloppy tolerance of community criminals and even the grimly unethical behavior of the law enforcement agencies charged with maintaining order.

"Better than *The Beans of Egypt Maine*, this book written in laconic police-report prose, reveals our small towns for what they are, not what we so hopefully imagine them to be. Readers are convinced from the start that this is a guy who knows what he is talking about and can back it up with documentary evidence."
—John Cole, *Lewiston Sun-Journal*

"...residents who were here at the time will tell you the sexual assault and murder of 12-year-old Sarah Cherry of Bowdoinham in July of 1988 was Maine's crime of the decade, if not the century.... [*Human Sacrifice*] is a shattering documentation of law enforcement at its most casual and our legal system at its worst."
—Lael Morgan, Publisher, *Casco Bay Weekly*

"Mr. Moore's book raises many questions. The State of Maine should, without delay, order a thorough and open-minded investigation that would hopefully produce sufficient new evidence for the State to determine that justice requires a new trial."
—Stanley Tupper, former Maine Congressman

Human Sacrifice
On the Altar of Injustice

James P. Moore

Blackberry Books
Nobleboro, Maine

BLACKBERRY BOOKS
617 East Neck Road
Nobleboro, ME 04555
chimfarm@gwi.net
207–729–5083

Copyright © 2002 by James P. Moore.
First Edition: 2002
Second Edition: August 2006, July 2017

All rights reserved.

ISBN 978-0-942396-98-0

Cover photograph of the Knox County Court House
   by Douglas K. Lee
Editing by Bernie Huebner
Layout by Jennifer Bunting
Printed and bound by Maple Vail, Kirkwood, New York

The brutal murder of little Sarah Cherry horrified Maine. The police—consumed with a natural rage and driven by press and public for a quick solution—fell into the easy trap that Sherlock Holmes warned against more than a century ago:

> It is a capital mistake to theorize before one has data. Insensibly one begins to twist facts to suit theories, instead of theories to suit facts.
> —*A Scandal in Bohemia* (1891)

Contents

Author's Note	ix
Introduction	xi
Personae	xii
1. The Fear	1
2. The Search	23
3. The Arrest	39
4. Thomaston	53
5. Gearing Up	72
6. The Prosecutor's Case	88
7. The Hidden Key	103
8. Dechaine's Defense	117
9. Elation	140
10. A Cynical Volunteer	171
11. Comes The Dawn	180
12. And In This Corner....	197
13. Bradford Rules	204
14. Reverse The Clock	226
15. State Secrets	238
16. Friendship And Blood	263
17. Myth-Conception	282
18. What Really Happened?	304
19. Who Killed Sarah Cherry?	310
20. "Cheer Up, Things Could Be Worse"	329
Afterword	345
What The Jury Never Heard	348

Exhibits

Contemporaneous notes of Detective Mark Westrum	392
Trial testimony of Detective Alfred Hendsbee	393
Contemporaneous notes of Detective Hendsbee	395
Chronology, investigation of Jason Fickett re the "A.A." case	396
Report of Detective Steven Drake regarding footprints	397
Report of Detective Hendsbee regarding footprints	398
Registered sex offenders within 10 miles of Bowdoin, Maine	399
Report of Detective Hendsbee regarding the tracking dog scenting deer	400
Report of Deputy Sheriff Daniel Reed	402
Statement concerning false allegation by ex-prosecutor Eric Wright	403
Report of Maine State Police expert regarding tire tracks	404

Report of Detective Hendsbee regarding no need
of key to lock truck   405

Final Report of state psychologist MacLean   406

Medical Examiner's Report   407

An analysis of the leaflet distributed by Rev. Dorr
at the Democratic Convention   408

American Bar Association Standards for Prosecutors   410

Attorney General Rowe's assignment to commission
to investigate   411

Letter to AG Rowe requesting results of the year-long
study   413

Response from AG Rowe   414

Photographs   415

Author's Note

THIS STORY IS DRAWN DIRECTLY from police files, court records, trial transcripts, contemporaneous media reports, and recorded interviews with individuals involved: detectives and uniformed officers, prosecutors, members of the Maine Medical Examiners' staff, doctors, scientific experts, private attorneys, knowledgeable members of the legal community, suspects, the defendant, his family, and his friends. Their kindness in sharing their knowledge, points of view and expertise is appreciated. My thanks, too, to Julie Zimmerman, who authorized me to draw on verse by a prison inmate, published in her book, *Trapped Under Ice*. The assistance of Richard A. Leo, Professor of Criminology, University of California at Irvine, is deeply appreciated for his generous sharing of his own research and that of others in his field.

My special thanks to author/teacher/poet/mentor and friend Gary Lawless who convinced me that I should write this book.

Gratitude is due those who were kind enough to read the manuscript for this book and offer their suggestions, advice and insights. Among them: Kate Cone, J. D. and Jo Ann Kocher, U.S. Treasury Department (ATF), Retired.

My greatest and eternal gratitude is to my wife, JoAnne, who has encouraged me in all of my undertakings and endured all the hardships of a wife—first of a federal agent who was too often late for dinner or working for weeks away from home, now of a writer-husband whose mind is often elsewhere even when he seems to be present.

Introduction

THIS IS A STORY OF INJUSTICE: an innocent man bulldozed into life imprisonment and kept there by a legal community that doesn't give a damn. Americans really need to know that every story doesn't have a happy ending. And it could happen to anyone.

The terrible story began when a beautiful, innocent child approaching the adventure of adolescence was desecrated and discarded in a lonely wood. A tidal wave of outrage overwhelmed the public. Officials charged with protecting us from such nightmares were swept into a state of desperation.

Human Sacrifice chronicles the chilling series of events that led the State of Maine to railroad an innocent man—a thirty-year-old college-educated farmer never before even suspected of a crime—into life imprisonment. In Maine, life imprisonment means "until you're dead."

Cops ignored the evidence. Prosecutors concealed evidence. It was four years before the travesty of the trial was established, but it took twelve years, even after the truth was known, to uncover the treachery behind the authorities' willful determination to fight every effort at freeing their victim.

On the positive side, this is also the story of an attorney who lives the lawyer's code in the highest tradition, a woman who wouldn't let the power of the state diminish her dedication to a friend, and a man who cultivated inner resources of mind and spirit to a degree that merits our admiration.

But federal law has changed, reducing our rights for the convenience of the courts, ensuring a future where more of us will join the ranks of those consigned to life behind bars, or execution. And this book reveals a reality that renders all of us vulnerable: that some unknown number among our established legal community harbors a casual indifference toward violations of their self-professed ethics by colleagues.

Since the 2002 publication of the first edition, events have continued to unfold. For the reader already familiar with the story told in *Human Sacrifice*, and wishing only an update and overview of the evidence, together with pertinent documents, one may go directly to the section entitled "What The Jury Never Heard" at the end of the book.

—J.P.M

PERSONAE

THE BENCH
Judge Carl O. Bradford, presiding

THE DEFENSE
Dennis Dechaine
Nancy Dechaine, his wife
Tom Connolly, lead attorney
Carol Waltman, Dennis's lifelong friend and advocate
George Carlton, co-counsel

THE PROSECUTION
Eric Wright, assistant attorney general
Alfred Hendsbee, Maine state police detective
Mark Westrum, Sagadahoc County sheriff's department detective
Tom Bureau, Maine state trooper, canine officer
Dr. Ronald Roy, state medical examiner

THE VICTIM
Sarah Cherry, age twelve
Debra Cherry, Sarah's mother
Chris Crosman, Sarah's stepfather
Jackie Crosman, Sarah's stepsister
Jessica Crosman, Sarah's stepsister

OTHERS

Maureen Senecal, Chris Crosman's first wife and mother of Jackie and Jessica

Doug Senecal, married to Maureen

John and Jennifer Henkel, hired Sarah to babysit the day she was abducted

Richard Bruno, boarder at the Dechaine farm

Jason Fickett, resident of Bowdoin

1

The Fear

THE NEAR-NINETY-DEGREE HEAT along mid-coast Maine on the afternoon of Wednesday, July 6, 1988, drove many into air-conditioned theaters. The year's films included *Gorillas In The Mist* and *Funny Farm* and *Rain Man* and a sequel to Rodney Dangerfield's ridiculous *Caddyshack*. In retrospect, some saw the day's oppressive weather as an omen of the dread that was about to descend on the sparsely settled town of Bowdoin.

John Henkel left his house shortly after 8:00 A.M., picked up babysitter Sarah Cherry, and arrived back home at 8:45. He led the girl up the stairs to the family living quarters on the second floor, took a quick shower and departed for his job as a goldsmith in Freeport. Wife Jennifer Henkel gave Sarah some last-minute instructions for the care of ten-month-old Monica. She'd had some misgivings about young Sarah—twelve years old, and this was only her second baby-sitting job—but the owner of the day care center Mrs. Henkel usually used, on vacation this week, had assured her that honor student Sarah was serious and responsible.

Jennifer Henkel was thirty-six, a consultant for the state's Department of Education. She hadn't expected to work today—hadn't planned on needing a sitter—but an assignment came up unexpectedly. She told Sarah she'd be home by four. At ten minutes after nine, she descended the stairs and pulled the door of the *au naturel* cedar home tightly shut. It tended to go ajar if it wasn't pulled hard. She backed her white Subaru across the graveled clearing to the trees where the family's two barking hounds were tethered, turned her car and headed out. The Henkels' 200-foot earthen driveway led through a screen of trees that nearly obscured the house from the highway. She paused at the "No Hunting" and "Private Road" signs, turned on to black-topped Lewis Hill Road, and drove to Augusta.

Sarah Cherry was a pretty, wholesome country girl of twelve. She earned excellent school grades and still had time for the things she loved—sports and the outdoors and children. Today, Sarah was excited. Until six months ago she, herself, had been cared for by babysitters any time her parents were away from the house. This was her second babysitting job, her first experience being left alone to care for an infant. But she was secure in her home life and in herself, and she was a responsible child. And optimistic. It was summertime, and next September she'd begin the adventure of Junior High School.

It was a beautiful day. Warm and sunny. Sarah was happy.

❖

The afternoon was half-gone. Jennifer Henkel was glad to be nearly home, grateful for the breeze coming through the window to relieve the eighty-one-degree temperature, and pleased to be arriving sooner than she'd told Sarah to expect her. When she'd phoned at noon, the girl was preparing the baby's lunch and cooking hot-dogs for herself. Everything was fine.

The mongrel hounds, 200 pounds of dog, barked as she passed them. They always barked—at everyone. She parked in front of the garage, stepped from the car, and then she saw some papers on the ground, a notebook and some sort of a receipt. Probably dropped by the meter reader, she thought. She picked them up and headed for the house. The door leading to the upstairs living quarters was ajar.

Jennifer Henkel glanced at her watch—it was 3:20 P.M.—and called out as she climbed the steps, "Sarah? Sarah, I'm home."

There was no answer.

Surely the girl wasn't napping.

The TV was on in the living room overlooking the driveway, its volume turned low so as not to disturb the baby. A few toys were scattered on the floor. Sarah's jacket lay in a chair beside the couch. Her glasses rested on the rocking chair near the door. Her sneakers and socks were beside the rocker.

"Sarah? Are you here?" The mother hurried to the nursery. Monica was asleep in her crib, breathing softly. Jennifer went from room to room throughout the house.

But Sarah wasn't there.

Anxious now, Mrs. Henkel yelled, "Sarah!"

No answer.

No sound but the low murmur of the television and the drone of summer insects, outside, wafting through the screened windows

She telephoned her husband at work. "I came home and Sarah's not here. The baby's fine, but...."

"Call around," Paul told her. "Maybe she's visiting a friend, or maybe she went home."

Jennifer Henkel telephoned kids who knew Sarah. She phoned Sarah's mother, Debra Crosman. Then she called the sheriff's department.

By the time Deputy Leo Scopino arrived at the Henkel house, Debra was there with Jennifer in the living room. The officer noted the girl's description—blonde, blue eyes, five feet tall, ninety-three pounds, wearing blue jeans and a purple tanktop. Then he asked the questions policemen always ask when a child is missing. "She have any arguments with anybody last night?"

"No," Debra replied. "Nothing like that."

"Has she ever run away before?"

"Never," Debra was wringing her hands. "And she hasn't run away this time. Sarah's a very good girl. Very obedient. Very responsible. Something's happened to her."

Down in New Mexico, hikers had recently discovered the remains of an apparent teenager slain by stab wounds and a shotgun blast but things like that didn't happen in Bowdoin. Maine invariably ranks around forty-seventh among the states in violent crime.

Not that some cops don't relish the prospect of something more exciting than spousal abuse and traffic cases, but Scopino saw no sign of a struggle and this wasn't a house anyone could approach unnoticed. The hounds sounded an alert when anything moved. The windows to either side of the TV set looked down on the driveway.

And nothing was missing.

Just Sarah.

"Does she use liquor or drugs?"

"No, no," Debra insisted, growing more distraught. "I tell you, something's happened to her." She pointed to the socks and sneakers on the floor. "Sarah's feet are very tender. She'd never go out barefoot." Debra brought herself to add, "Not willingly."

Scopino examined the items Jennifer Henkel found on the driveway—the notebook, and a repair estimate for a Toyota pickup showing its owner's name: Dennis Dechaine. He went downstairs to his cruiser and radioed a request for a 10-28 to get the vehicle's complete description and color. Then he broadcasted descriptions of Sarah Cherry and Dechaine's red Toyota pickup.

More deputies came. Others scoured the roads for the Toyota. The state police were notified, their assistance requested.

Harry Buttrick was a tall, stout, balding man with glasses, an engineering technician retired from the Portsmouth Naval Shipyard. Now he worked part-time at a hardware store. He and his wife, Helen, had spent the afternoon in Falmouth watching their twelve-year-old granddaughter play in an "important" all-star softball game against the Durham team. On the way home, they stopped to buy groceries, but it was a brief stop because there was a TV show beginning at nine that Harry wanted to watch. It was 8:45 P.M. when he wheeled his white station wagon off the macadam Litchfield Road onto the unpaved Dead River Road in the northeast corner of Bowdoin.

Helen said, "Look."

Harry looked. A tall, dark-haired, thirty-ish man wearing a pale blue T-shirt and Dickeys was crossing the lawn toward the old farmhouse where Helen Buttrick's mother lived. But no one was home there, so Mr. Buttrick stopped the car.

"Hello there," he called to the man, "is there something you need?"

"I lost my truck," the man replied. "I parked it and went in the woods, fishing. Now I can't find where I left it."

Harry told him, "Get in. I'll see if I can help you." He knew a couple places where people fished. It shouldn't take long.

The man rode with them to their white mobile home, helped carry the groceries inside and asked for a glass of water. Helen brought a canister from the fridge, poured him a glass and watched him drink it. He seemed a nice enough fellow, polite and respectful, nothing out of the ordinary except for his concern over having lost his truck. He told them he lived in Yarmouth, worked at L.L. Bean's, and that he'd been fishing.

But he didn't live in Yarmouth; he lived in the adjoining town of Bowdoinham. And he wasn't employed by L.L. Bean; he worked his own farm. Nor had he been fishing. He'd been doing drugs—amphetamines he'd injected into his arm that morning and again in the afternoon.

He also said his name was Dennis Dechaine. That was true.

He was finishing his second glass of water when Harry

glanced at his watch and said, "We'd better get going." It was still light out, and he still hoped to see that TV show.

Dechaine described where he remembered driving before he'd parked his truck in a short lane off the road—paved highway, an overpass above the turnpike, then dirt road—and Harry Buttrick recognized the description: the Hallowell Road from Litchfield toward the Dead River Road. But they cruised this route up to Litchfield Corner, then back again, without spotting the truck. They'd been driving for about forty-five minutes and they were back on the Dead River Road when they saw a sheriff's patrol car coming toward them. Harry told Dechaine, "Maybe they can help you." He blinked his lights and stopped.

Harry didn't know it but after he'd departed with Dechaine, Helen had switched on her police monitor—a common appliance among rural residents who liked to keep up on what was happening around their town—and she'd heard the alert for a red Toyota pickup registered to one Dennis Dechaine. She'd phoned the sheriff's dispatcher.

Dechaine left Harry Buttrick's station wagon and climbed into the back seat of the cruiser. Heavy-set, middle-aged Deputy John Ackley was at the wheel. Beside him in the front seat sat Detective Mark Westrum of the sheriff's department—thirty-ish and red-haired with a neatly trimmed pale-red mustache. Both officers had been called out to aid in the search; both had been briefed about the girl and the papers found in the Henkel driveway.

Ackley asked, "What's your name?"

"Dennis Dechaine."

"Where do you live?"

"In Bowdoinham. On the Old Post Road."

Ackley radioed to the other officers, gathered about a mile away in an open space beside the intersection of Dead River Road and Lewis Hill Road. They'd all examined the notebook and repair estimate. They all knew the situation. "We have him," Ackley informed them. Then he asked Dechaine, "Where do you think you left your truck?"

It took about two minutes to reach the open space where the other deputies waited. Except for Detective Westrum, all of the officers, like Ackley, wore the chocolate brown uniform of the Sagadahoc County Sheriff's Department. Detective Westrum left the cruiser to talk with Deputy Daniel Reed. Dechaine waited in the cruiser with Ackley.

Ackley asked, "Is your truck locked?"

"No. In fact, I left the keys in it."

A few minutes later, Westrum and Reed returned.

Westrum looked closely at the slender young farmer. Dechaine's eyes were open wide. He looked nervous. Reed advised Dechaine of his Miranda rights. Westrum recorded the time—9:30 P.M.—then he walked away, leaving Reed and Dechaine alone.

Reed asked, "Where's your truck, Dennis?"

"I parked it in the woods to go fishing. Then I got lost in the woods and I couldn't find it."

"Did you catch anything?"

"No."

"Where's your fishing gear?"

"Well, once I realized I couldn't find my truck, I ditched the pole."

Reed pointed through the cruiser's rear window to the Lewis Hill Road. "Have you been on this road today?"

Dechaine turned and looked back. "No."

Reed showed him the notebook and repair estimate. "Are these yours?"

"No. I've never seen them before."

"Then how do you explain this? Your name's on this estimate."

Dechaine looked at the papers again. "Well, I guess they are mine."

"Do you carry them in your truck?"

"I...well I may have. I'm not sure."

"Where do you keep them in your truck?"

"On the passenger seat."

"Well tell me this—how could these have been found in a driveway off the Lewis Hill Road if you haven't been on that road today?"

"I don't know."

"Someone saw your truck going down this road today."

"I think I did go down this road once, looking for a fishing hole."

"Did you enter anyone's driveway?"

"I...I think maybe I did."

"It was a long driveway with a house that set back from the road."

"I never saw a house."

"We're looking for a twelve-year-old girl that's been missing since this afternoon."

"Oh my God, you think I did *that*?"

"Did you go all the way in that driveway?"

"No, all I did was turn around. I met two older people and I asked them where I could find a fishing hole. They told me to follow this road out to the end and take a right."

"So how did these things end up in the driveway?"

"Probably when I got out to take a piss. They must have fallen out."

"You just told me all you did was turn around."

"No!" Dechaine answered angrily now. "I told you I stopped and took a piss."

"Do you always take a piss in people's driveways in the middle of the day?"

"It wasn't the middle of the day. I worked at the farm 'til five o'clock. Then I came out to fish. And I didn't piss in the driveway, I went off into the woods."

"If you dropped these things at the end of the driveway, how did they get up to the house?"

"Whoever grabbed the girl saw them and put them in the driveway to set me up."

Reed got out of the car, leaving Dechaine alone in the back seat, and walked over to recount his conversation to Detective Westrum.

Westrum got Dechaine out of the cruiser, gave him the Miranda warning again and had him sign the form acknowledging he'd been given his rights. Dechaine said he'd prefer not to answer any more questions until he'd talked to a lawyer. Westrum patted his suspect down and found nothing, but his flashlight showed a scratch on Dechaine's upper left arm and a dirty handprint on the shoulder of his T-shirt. He deposited his suspect in another cruiser and went back to search where Dechaine had been sitting. On the floor beneath the front passenger seat, the detective found a set of keys for a Toyota pickup truck.

❖

Sarah's mother, powerless to simply sit and wait, telephoned neighbors, friends, anyone who might relieve her agonizing terror with some happy solution to the mystery of her missing daughter. Then she worried that she might have missed a call from someone trying to reach her with news while her line was busy. Husband Chris tried to comfort her. Family members who'd gathered at the house suggested any solution they could imagine—Sarah followed some little animal into the woods and got lost; she tripped and hurt herself and she'll be found in the morning and she'll be fine—anything except the hideous images that wouldn't be blocked, wouldn't go away. They prayed.

❖

Detective Westrum drove the half-mile up the Dead River Road and interviewed the Buttricks. Then he and Deputy Reed spent the better part of an hour driving Dechaine around in a vain effort to find the Toyota.

It was just after midnight when Sheriff Haggett and State Police Detective Al Hendsbee arrived at the scene. Westrum briefed both of them. The suspect had lied to the Buttricks about where he lived and where he worked. He'd lied about the truck keys. His papers were found in front of the house from which the girl had vanished, and he acted nervous as hell. But where was that truck? And the girl, where was she? Was she alive?

Sarah Cherry had been missing for at least eight-and-a-half hours. It was dark. Prospects looked grim. In Maine, every homicide except those occurring in its largest cities comes under the jurisdiction of the state police and the state's attorney general and, while there was always hope, this began to look like murder. State Police Detective Al Hendsbee had been contacted by telephone at 11:30 P.M. and assigned to the hunt.

Hendsbee looked so ordinary—medium height, dark hair, slight paunch—he'd have fit most people's conception of a country storekeeper. Minutes after his arrival, deputies located Dechaine's pickup just off the Hallowell Road about forty feet down a disused logging road, a quarter-mile from Dead River Road.

Detective Hendsbee conducted his examination without touching the vehicle, noting snow tires on the rear, regular tires on the front wheels; a bag of Blue Seal grain in the truck bed; a missing right-front headlight and bondo—that gray material used to fill dents and holes in damaged vehicles—on the right fender. Its doors were locked. Hendsbee shone his flashlight through the window. There was no key in the ignition. The cab was dirty, papers were scattered on its floor and across the passenger seat. There was an impression in the papers, as if someone had sat on them. Some leafy sort of plant growth was stuck in the door as if it had been caught there when someone shut it, but that couldn't have happened here. The ground here was covered with pine needles—very little vegetation and none high enough to have been caught in the door. The detective took photos of the Toyota, front and rear.

Then Trooper Tom Bureau handed him the items found in the Henkels' driveway. Hendsbee leafed through

Dechaine's notebook and examined the estimate from Roland's Body Shop in Brunswick dated two weeks ago. It bore Dechaine's name with a description of the pickup and the notation, "Damage on the right front, truck is totaled."

Trooper Bureau produced a paper bag containing Sarah's jacket, socks and sneakers left at the Henkel home. At this point, Hendsbee's official report states:

0120—Tr. BUREAU and I ran the track with his canine unit from the Toyota pickup truck. The first track was run in the wooded area from where the Toyota pickup was located. The canine went into the woods and crossed the roadway. Another track was run across from the pickup truck was [sic] located across the road. The dog scented the area and ran across a deer track at which time started following the deer track. Tr. BUREAU thought he was chasing a deer when we heard a noise in the woods and pulled the dog off. The dog was then taken back to Tr. BUREAU's cruiser.

It was 2:40 A.M. when Hendsbee sat beside Dechaine in the back seat of the cruiser. He noted that the suspect's gray sneakers and green pants were wet, and he observed a round bruise on Dechaine's left bicep. The detective introduced himself and asked whether Mr. Dechaine would like to talk to him.

"Well, I don't want to say anything that could incriminate me in anything."

"The questions I'll be asking will be about what you've been doing yesterday up to when you met the deputies."

Dechaine agreed to talk with him.

"Look, I want to advise you of your rights again because I understand that when you talked with the sheriff's people, you said you wanted a lawyer." Hendsbee read the warning aloud from the Miranda card. He seemed a kindly man, unlike the aggressive Reed. Dechaine acknowledged that he understood his rights and agreed to talk without having a lawyer present.

"How long have you been here?"

"Since nine-thirty or ten o'clock."

"Are you under arrest?"

"Well, not that I know of. Nobody's said I am."

"You're not wearing handcuffs, right?"

"Right."

Al Hendsbee was experienced. Establishing and recording the fact that his suspect was not in official custody was important, legally, because the necessity of affording an attorney didn't come into play, technically, until a suspect has been arrested or otherwise deprived of his freedom to leave, or until investigators acknowledged that their suspicions had centered on him. At this point, Hendsbee chose to consider him a witness.

Dechaine told how he and his wife had just arrived home late yesterday, Tuesday, from a weekend-through-Tuesday Fourth of July holiday gathering with his family and friends in Madawaska, 320 miles to the north. He began his account of Wednesday at around 8 A.M. when he'd gone to the West Gardiner Beef Company. Then, he said, he went back home for a while, then drove around the rest of the day looking for fishing holes. He didn't believe he'd come down the Dead

River Road to Lewis Hill Road because there was a bridge over a stream and he couldn't recall seeing any water from the road anyplace he'd driven. Later, he'd parked his truck and gone into the woods and gotten lost. When he finally found his way to a road, he'd met a man who helped him search for his truck. He admitted lying about where he lived because, he said, he was embarrassed to admit he'd gotten lost so close to home. As for the truck keys, he'd found them in his pocket after telling the officers he'd left them in the pickup. He hid them to prevent their being found if he was searched, making it seem he'd lied again.

"Has anybody else used your truck today?"

"Well, I suppose they could have. I might have left the keys in it some of the places I got out to look for fishing holes."

"How do you think your papers got next to the house where this girl is missing from?"

"I don't know. I have a flower business in Brunswick and I leave papers around there. I've got papers in my truck. If anybody wanted to steal them, they could. If you ask me, somebody must have stolen those papers and put them there to frame me."

"How far did you go in school, Dennis?"

"Six years' college, out in Washington State. I've got an associate degree in agriculture and a B.A. in French."

"You married?"

"Yep. My wife's name's Nancy. We've been married five years."

"Can she account for any of your time today?"

"No, she was at work when I left the house. She doesn't

even know where I am now. Gosh, I'd like to call her and let her know."

"I'll take you to a phone pretty soon and you can call her and tell her you're okay. Now I want to ask you something. Do you mind if we take your truck to our lab in Augusta and have it searched? It'll help us either clear you, or we'll find evidence that you took that girl. It'll either tie you in with her, or clear you from the case."

Dechaine said, "Sure, I've got no objection."

"Would you sign a consent paper for us to take the truck?"

"Okay."

"You understand now, it's your truck, you're not under arrest and you don't have to let us take it if you don't want to."

"No, by all means, take the truck and do what you have to do, process it or whatever."

"How about a polygraph? Would you be willing to take a lie detector test some time in the next day or two?"

"Okay, but can we do it on the weekend? I have things to do the next couple days, but I want to do whatever I can to help clear my name."

"Fine. How about going with me over to the Bowdoinham police station where you can clean up and phone your wife, let her know you're okay, and let me take some pictures of you if that's okay. And you can sign the consent there, for us to search your truck. Besides, I want to call the attorney general's office to see what they say."

Dechaine agreed. That would be fine.

"Dennis? Look, Dennis, if you did take that girl, we'd like

to know where she is so we can get her and bring her back to her parents. You know, two wrongs don't make a right and, well, if you did harm her somehow, whether you meant to or not, it would be good for you to tell me and get it off your chest so it won't bother you. If you don't, it'll bother you every time you think of her and you'll get goose pimples on the back of your neck."

Dechaine sat staring at the front of the car.

Hendsbee noted goose bumps on his arms.

"If you did take her, Dennis, tell me so we can bring her back home."

"I didn't take her. I wouldn't do anything like that."

"Well, the ball's in your court. You know whether you did it or not, so any time you want to talk to me, I'd appreciate a call."

"Yeah, well okay. But I didn't take her."

It was 3:20 in the morning when Hendsbee, Dechaine and Detective Westrum began the drive to the Bowdoinham police station. They arrived there at 3:45 A.M. Hendsbee telephoned Assistant Attorney General Mike Wescott and brought him up to date regarding the investigation. Dechaine washed up, signed a consent form to search the truck and posed for photos. He willingly removed his shirt and allowed pictures to be taken of his right side and his back. There were light scratch marks, although it didn't appear that the skin was broken. Dechaine said he couldn't be sure, but he thought he got those marks walking through bushes in the woods. There were muddy handprints just over each of his shoulders; he thought they got there when he reached over his shoulder to swat at bugs. He demonstrated, reaching over his left shoulder with his right hand, then reaching over his right shoulder with his left hand.

Hendsbee asked, "How about that polygraph, Dennis? The weekend would be fine. We'll probably be through with your truck by then, so you could have your wife drive you up to take the test—or I'd come pick you up if you like—and you can drive your truck home then."

"Well, let me get back to you on that, okay?"

"Sure, Dennis. Whatever you say."

Dechaine's wife, Nancy, had come home from work late that Wednesday afternoon. She spoke briefly with their boarder, Richard Bruno, about his day. Richard mentioned he hadn't seen Dennis all day—unusual, but not totally out of the ordinary. Dennis had arranged to pick up some frozen chickens from the place where they had their birds slaughtered and, indeed, the birds were in the freezer.

Nancy began to prepare supper. Short, blonde and attractive with a medium build she usually concealed beneath the somewhat shapeless dresses favored by back-to-land folks, she hadn't a care in the world.

Then two sheriff's deputies came to the door and asked for Dennis.

Nancy told them he wasn't home.

"Does he own a red pickup?" one of them asked.

Nancy said, "Yes."

"Has he had any work done on it recently?"

"No. Someone hit it a while back while it was parked and he's gotten some estimates but.... What's this all about?"

"We can't say," the deputy told her. "A receipt was found in a driveway that had his name on it. Look, when he comes home would you have him call Mr. Reed? The number's 443-9711."

Not long after they left, Reed telephoned the house to ask whether there was a work number or any other phone where Dennis might be reached.

Nancy told them no, there wasn't. She was growing concerned now. Her anxiety increased later in the evening when a friend who happened to be a Bowdoinham policeman stopped by to see Dennis. He seemed nervous.

Nancy asked him, "Please, tell me what's going on."

The officer said, "I can't talk."

Around 4:00 A.M., Dennis called the house. Nancy asked, "What's going on?"

"I'll tell you when I get home."

Relieved that Dennis seemed all right, Nancy went upstairs to bed.

Hendsbee dropped Dechaine off at his home at 4:20 Thursday morning. He looked haggard when he trudged upstairs to the bedroom.

"What's happened?" Nancy asked. "Are you all right?"

"Nance, I've been questioned as a suspect in a kidnapping."

She held him and assured him, "You're an innocent man. You needn't be afraid. Try to get some sleep."

They lay there holding one another. An hour passed. Neither found sleep. Nancy began to rub his back.

He said, "I have to tell you something. I'm ashamed and—and I'm embarrassed, and I know you'll be upset but you remember when we went down to Boston? Some guy offered me some street speed and I bought it. Yesterday morning I went out to get high."

He showed her the mark on his arm from the hypodermic needle. She noticed now how his eyes were dilated. He told of remembering he'd lost his truck, and coming out of the woods, and a man offering to help him find the truck. And he kept asking himself, "Could I have kidnapped a child? I can't remember my day."

Detective Al Hendsbee spent the next few hours conferring with troopers and sheriff's deputies, adding up the meager facts they possessed, speculating on where the girl might be, whether she was alive.

Daylight came and Dechaine still couldn't sleep. Nancy got up, did a few chores and readied herself to go to her job at a surveying firm. "Don't worry," she told him. "The girl will be found and she'll be fine."

But he could only recall brief bits of Wednesday—driving back roads, parking the truck, entering the woods, shooting up. He remembered fleeting visions of shimmering leaves and wildly waving grasses but most of the day...most of the day.... He thought about those papers the officers said were found outside the house from which the girl vanished, and he recalled their certainty that he was involved. Cops knew things. They were trained and experienced in these matters. And they were so confident. Dechaine told Nancy, "I have a feeling I might have done something awful while I was on that drug but—I can't remember. I can't remember."

❖

The police had their own problem.

The sequence of successful law enforcement starts with a crime; then the evidence; charge a defendant; hold a trial; get a conviction. But they can't get a conviction without a trial; can't hold a trial without a defendant, can't charge a defendant without evidence, can't find evidence without a crime.

So far, they couldn't prove a crime.

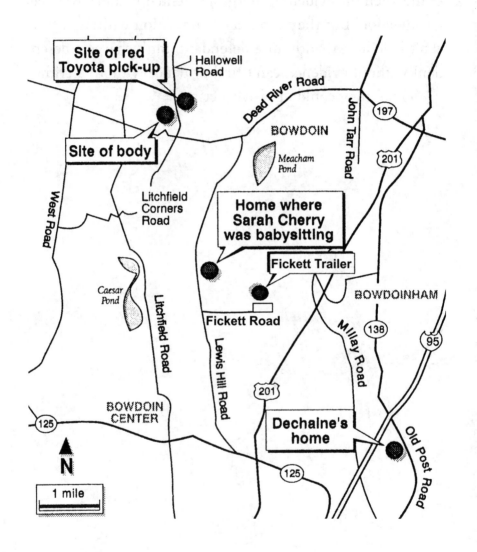

2

The Search

WEDNESDAY EVENING'S SIX O'CLOCK NEWS mentioned Prince Charles's visit with survivors of the Piper Alpha oil rig disaster—166 dead, 149 still missing. And 250 feared dead following a passenger train derailment in India. And a federal judge's order that Oliver North's trial regarding Iran-Contra begin in September. But the lead story on every Maine television station that night was the mystery of the missing baby-sitter.

The eleven o'clock news showed her photo. "Have you seen Sarah Cherry?"

Thursday's newspapers headlined the story on front pages with a picture of the sweet, blond twelve-year-old girl wearing a white dress and a happy smile.

Summer tourists were shocked. Maine was the quiet retreat they'd chosen for respite from crime and congestion. Mainers were absolutely appalled. Bowdoin was such an ordinary little town: 2,207 urban escapees and suburban yuppies, a few perhaps hiding from something or someone, and sixty-six welfare families with incomes below $15,000 (a mere eight Bowdoin families acknowledged incomes exceeding $100,000)—98.8 percent white, with three

African Americans, thirteen Native Americans, and a few other minorities—people attracted by cheap land and low taxes where they could build a house or park their mobile home amidst forty-nine square miles of placid fields and forest.

Fewer than 2 percent of Bowdoin's population was older than sixty; 1,052 had jobs; only seventeen worked at the traditional Maine occupations of farming, fishing or forestry. Most were high school graduates; 43 percent had some college. Two-thirds of them were employed outside Sagadahoc County—they lived half-an-hour from the state capital at Augusta, forty-five minutes from Maine's two largest cities, Portland and Lewiston. For these people, privacy and the intimacy with nature compensated for the commute to work.

Now volunteers swarmed to Bowdoin to join police and game wardens in their search—civilians from adjacent Bowdoinham and surrounding towns, Coast Guard and Navy personnel from nearby bases. Nearly two hundred of them assembled, waiting for search assignments at the state police command center—a thirty-foot Silver Bullet van hooked to power and telephone lines in an open space at the intersection of Lewis Hill Road and Dead River Road. Scores more combed the woods and byways on their own, amidst sweltering near-ninety-degree temperatures. A Civil Emergency van offered searchers sandwiches and cold drinks. National Guard helicopters swooped in to cruise at tree-top level with heat-sensing detectors that pick up body heat. An ambulance stood by in the hope Sarah would be found alive.

On Thursday morning, Nancy Dechaine went to work and asked around for the name of a good lawyer. Her boss recommended an affable attorney who'd done some work for their company. His name was George Carlton. Nancy and Dennis went to his office in Bath shortly before noon. The lawyer suggested that he and Dennis confer alone. Nancy waited in Carlton's outer office.

A short time later, Dennis drove home. Nancy went to work, but she couldn't focus on her job so she left her office and they spent the rest of the day together. Nancy noted her husband's frustration at his inability to recall the events of Wednesday. Dechaine, himself, was consumed by the dread that grew from his uncertainty.

Jennifer Henkel's husband John told Detective Hendsbee he was extremely upset about Sarah being missing. Normally, he said, his wife takes the children to a day care center but the person running the center went on vacation this day. He'd known Sarah for several years and termed her "real responsible and a real intelligent young girl for her age." The decision to use her had been made at the last minute. He suggested the police check an old road that goes off from his house—perhaps they'd find her there.

Detective Hendsbee sat down with Sarah's parents. Like a sympathetic old uncle, easy to talk with, he exuded sympathy but he had to know everything about Sarah, and about them. Debra Crosman was an attractive, thirty-three-year-old brunette; husband Chris, five years older, was tall and fit with dark hair and a mustache.

Debra said that Jennifer Henkel had phoned to ask whether Sarah baby-sat because she'd been called out to work unexpectedly and her usual baby-sitter was already booked.

Sarah's age on the day she vanished was twelve years, one month, and one day. At school, she'd been involved in the chorus and she played baseball. A "super-protected child," according to mother Debra, Sarah was never left alone for more than the half-hour when her parents were either going to or coming home from work. She'd been told never to answer the phone or the door when she was by herself, never to let anyone know she was home alone, and she was an extremely obedient child. With school out, she'd spent much of her time at the home of Debra's mother, Margaret Cherry, in nearby Lisbon Falls. Sarah's activities were well supervised. She wasn't even allowed to ride her bike along the roadside. Problems with her feet caused her to wear shoes or sneakers any time she ventured outdoors. She never left the house unless accompanied by an adult.

❖

The girl's real father, Gilbert Austin, lived in Lisbon with a girlfriend and worked at the Bath Iron Works. State Police Detective Steven Drake verified that he'd been at work from 7:30 in the morning until 4:00 P.M. that day. Austin hadn't seen Sarah since Father's Day. He told the detective about that last visit. They'd chatted about a fire at the Bowden Center Store in Bowdoin Center, and about school. She showed him her report card and he gave her a dollar for each "A" she'd earned. He described his daughter as "very mild-mannered, very well-behaved," and very close to grandmother Margaret Cherry.

Debra and Gilbert had never married. She'd left him after a falling out, taken Sarah with her, and later married Chris Crosman.

Husband Chris informed Hendsbee that his ex-wife, Maureen, had married Doug Senecal of Phippsburg. And Senecal had been investigated by the sheriff's department. In fact, Senecal had been indicted for sexually abusing Chris and Maureen's oldest daughter, Jackie, but Jackie took off to California. So the case hadn't come to trial.

This would be Sarah's second baby-sitting job and she'd been instructed to tell no one she'd be doing it. She had told one friend, Julie Wagg, but Julie was away on vacation in Virginia this week.

Sarah's other friends were contacted. None knew anything helpful.

❖

Officers knocked on every door along Lewis Hill Road where the Henkels lived, the Hallowell Road where Dechaine's Toyota was found, and the Dead River Road linking those two. Homes in this area are far apart, most beyond the view of neighbors, accessed by long driveways and screened by trees from the sights and sounds of the road. One resident after another, away at work or occupied inside the house most of the day, had observed nothing. But there were some potential leads.

A thirty-five-year-old woman named Rhonda, camping in the woods behind the Henkel house, had seen two men driving a brown Subaru station wagon through the trails on the afternoon in question. A sixty-seven-year-old woman named Dorothy said she'd heard gunshots coming from a direction in line with the Henkel house between one and one-thirty when she was trying to take a nap. A thirty-three-year-old man named Robert looked at a photo of Dechaine's damaged Toyota and told the officer he'd seen this vehicle on Tuesday, the day before Sarah's disappearance; it went by twice and it had one headlight out. Its driver was a dark-haired man wearing a greenish T-shirt.

A neighbor named Lois told Detective Roy Brooks she'd seen a small red pickup that looked like a Toyota on several days recently. The last time she saw it was yesterday, Wednesday, at about 4:15 P.M. heading west, but it had been going so fast she couldn't tell how many people were in it. The driver was a man, but she couldn't identify him.

A nearby resident reported seeing a red pickup truck driven by a man speeding past his house, coming from the direction of the Henkel house that afternoon. State Police Detective Patrick Lehan switched on a tape recorder and asked him, "Okay, Gary, now I showed you a photograph of a red pickup truck with a headlight out, could you tell me when you saw that?"

"Around three or three-thirty in the afternoon."

"Where was that?"

"It was on the Dead River Road heading east. As I was coming at it on the bridge, the second bridge, it was heading—going by me at about forty, forty-five miles an hour."

"Okay, you mentioned you saw it earlier that day?"

"About an hour, an hour-and-a-half earlier that afternoon, going by my house pretty fast."

"And you live on...?"

"Lewis Hill Road."

"You also mentioned that a friend of yours near the bridge saw that vehicle. Or he believes it was that vehicle."

"Yeah, that's what he told me."

"Could you tell me about that?"

"He said he heard this vehicle stop up the road past his house, and just at the time he was getting ready to leave he heard somebody shouting, like to him it sounded like 'Hurry, hurry.' And by the time he had reached the road to check it out he saw somebody getting into a red pickup truck and heading west."

Detective Lehan took down the name and phone number of Gary's friend, Ralph Jones, and asked Gary whether he could describe the driver.

"Not much, except he looked like he had short sandy brown hair, blond, and I couldn't tell what he was wearing or anything like that. I was going, you know, going by so quick, things happened fast, but I do recall the hair as being light-colored, not real dark, and short."

A man came to the command post with a fishing pole he'd found alongside the Lewis Hill Road—an orange "Snoopy" child's pole about three feet long. A twenty-seven-year-old volunteer from Litchfield found two sets of bare footprints—one small, one large—along a dirt lane called the Fickett Road. Detective Steven Drake took a few minutes to phone Debra Crosman about the possibility that the school had taken Sarah's fingerprints as part of some program, but that turned out to be a false hope. Mrs. Crosman promised to get him Sarah's hairbrush so they'd have a sample of the girl's hair. Then he and Detective

Hendsbee tracked those bare footprints to a blue and white trailer bearing the name "Fickett." Another searcher came to say he'd found some footprints around a mudhole along with a shirt, a chain and some broken glass; a tree nearby had its bark scarred. It was growing dark. The shirt the searcher had found was dirty, red and white; the chains were old discarded tire chains; the broken glass looked like pieces of a mirror. There were tracks of truck tires, too.

"We're losing the light," Hendsbee told Detective Drake. "I'll have the wardens check all this out in the morning."

A woman telephoned the command post to say she'd heard that Dechaine once lived in Washington State. She thought the police should check into a possible connection with the notorious Green River murders out there.

Meanwhile, technicians and scientists at the state police lab had vacuumed the interior of Dechaine's Toyota pickup. Agency spokesman Lt. Arnold told television reporters, "We go through [the truck] with a fine-toothed comb and microscopically examine anything that might pertain to the crime."

Reporter Linda Holstein told viewers, "Lt. Arnold says in some cases microscopic evidence can point the finger at one person, in others it can prove that a prime suspect couldn't have committed the crime. He's not saying in which way the evidence is shaping up in this case...."

The inventory of items removed from that truck was lengthy and detailed: paper bags; an inspirational paperback, *There Is A Place Where You Are Not Alone*, by Hugh Prather; matchbooks, a pencil, one wrapper from a Good Humor King Cone; bottle caps, broken sunglasses, a Tuborg beer bottle, loose wire, empty cigarette packs, a Vantage pack containing two cigarettes, tissues, a cassette tape; three one-dollar bills, two quarters, four dimes, five nickels, ten pennies; a Styrofoam cup, a yellow memo pad, a jackknife, one length of yellow rope, two lengths of white rope—the list went on with 155 separate entries, some of them including several related items.

Experts processed results from the search of the Henkel home: no blood, no hairs or fibers that couldn't be accounted for; two fingerprints they couldn't identify.

It was nine-thirty that night when Detective Al Hendsbee decided it was time to knock off for the day. He'd been called out on this case at 11:20 the previous night and he needed some rest. His final act before quitting was a phone call to game warden Bill Allen, asking him to follow up on those footprints around the mudhole and the Fickett Road.

The warden said he'd take care of it in the morning. "And, hey Al, we're bringing in some of our scent dogs tomorrow. See if we can pick up some trace of Sarah along the roadsides."

Detective Hendsbee interviewed Susan Norris. A small red pickup truck had pulled into her driveway. She noticed it because she was expecting someone who'd phoned to say they'd come to see a tractor she'd advertised for sale. The red truck hesitated for a moment, then turned around and drove away.

"Did you notice the driver?"

"Yes, I saw him through his windshield. He was average size, dark hair cut the regular way, and wearing glasses. He wore a T-shirt, it wasn't white but I'm not sure of the color, but there was a child with him. A child or a small woman, light hair, maybe light brown, and curly. I noticed the tailgate, there was some damage there."

A woman living across the road from Dechaine's farmhouse told Detective Drake he'd lived there for about nine months and he was an excellent neighbor, a man who minded his own business. "I buy eggs from him. He seems like a nice guy." But he had a tenant living there—whom she thought looked "a little like Clark Kent"—and she thought that man acted a bit strange. She remembered that the tenant told her that Dennis had gone for the weekend to visit his family in Madawaska.

The Dechaine home on the Old Post Road in Bowdoinham was a large, two-and-a-half-story white frame house with blue shutters. An open porch on one side faced a circular driveway; inside that circle, a large tree grew beside a vegetable garden. Off to the side and back away from the road a bit further, a brown cedar-shingled barn stood at the end of a sheep pasture. A sign on the side porch proclaimed, "Basswood Farm."

Detective Hendsbee and State Police Lieutenant Peter McCarthy arrived there a few minutes after two on Thursday afternoon. McCarthy stayed in the car while Hendsbee went to the house. Dennis and Nancy were sitting together on the porch.

Dechaine told the detective he'd hired a lawyer, George Carlton. "He'll be representing me so, if you want any information, you'll have to go through him."

"What about the polygraph, Dennis? Are you still willing to take that test?"

"Well, okay, if it's all right with my lawyer."

Hendsbee turned to Nancy. "Are you aware of what's going on here?"

She looked at Dennis, then said, "Well, bits and pieces."

"I'll fill you in if you like."

Dechaine interrupted, "Look, my lawyer said what Nancy knows now is all she should know, so don't discuss the case with her, okay?"

Hendsbee nodded, and left the house. State Police Detective Graves called him to relate that he'd received some information from a psychic.

After pondering what he knew—about himself, and facts the police had given him, and the bits of memory he could retrieve—Dechaine told Nancy he couldn't have kidnapped a little girl. Whoever had done it had somehow obtained those papers with his name on them and planted them in that driveway to frame him.

But how could any frame-up artist have had the good fortune to choose a patsy with no alibi for the day, a man whose drug-clouded memory precluded the normal, cogent denials of guilt? And, while Dechaine offered a frame-up as the only possible explanation for his frightening situation, the authorities saw this as the absurd and desperate bid of a man with no innocent explanation for the damning evidence.

In any investigation, the point where a suspect is designated guilty in official minds is the point where Phase Two commences. The investigative mission shifts from "solve the crime" to "nail the perp." Primary resources are now aimed at finding and documenting every piece of evidence to prove guilt beyond a reasonable doubt.

Richard A. Leo, Professor of Criminology at the University of California at Irvine, has written:

> The blood sport attitude that often develops in high profile criminal prosecutions—"get the guilty party no matter what"—sometimes causes significant harm to innocent individuals who the police and prosecutors have identified as guilty....

From this moment on, any other suspect popping up, or thrust at the detectives, must be eliminated. But the process of accomplishing this is seen as a bothersome chore to be achieved with the least diversion of energy from the main task—like the gardener plucking pesky beetles from a plant he's intent upon cultivating.

The prosecutor's need is to receive from the detectives a clean case, uncomplicated by distractions some defense lawyer might use to divert jurors from a just and swift verdict of guilty.

❖

A man named Bruce approached police to say he'd been out for a drive with his girlfriend on Wednesday and he'd seen two young girls on the Dead River Road at around three-thirty or four o'clock. One, who looked to be about twelve, wore a pink leotard-type swimsuit and she was wet as if she'd been swimming. She just stood on the culvert above the river and gazed downstream, as if daydreaming. The other girl, maybe six or seven, was riding a twenty-inch bicycle toward the girl on the culvert.

When dusk fell on Thursday without Sarah Cherry being found, Nancy Dechaine felt sure the girl had been abducted. Nancy was equally certain that the kidnapper was, by now, far from the area.

❖

Thermometers had hit ninety before noon on Thursday. Friday dawned with every promise of continuing the heat wave.

At eight that morning, Detective Hendsbee met Assistant Attorney General Eric Wright at the district court in Bath. The two men began the process of obtaining search warrants for Dechaine's truck and his residence.

Wright, a slim angular man with spectacles, a shock of jet-black hair over a pale, triangular face and a habit of pursing his lips when he pondered, was now in charge of the case on behalf of the state. Detractors likened his appearance to Jerry Lewis's film portrayal in *The Nutty Professor*, but Eric Wright was a formidable foe in any courtroom. At the moment, while he believed Dechaine's written consent to search his truck was legally sufficient, prudence dictated the additional authority of a search warrant. He also believed that Sarah was dead and he was confident that Dechaine had killed her. But no one could guarantee they'd ever find the girl. Wright told ranking state policemen, "We'll try him for murder whether we find the body or not. We've won murder trials without a body before."

Meanwhile, Warden Barry Woodward had formed a

group of eighteen volunteers from the Brunswick Naval Air Station in a line along shimmering, dusty Hallowell Road. Sergeant Bill Allen of the Warden's Service instructed the perspiring men to do a close-quartered search through the dense forest, "and don't leave any spot not looked at." They began in the northeast corner of the wooded area and walked west to the end. Then they moved south and trudged back through trees with wilted leaves, drooping in the heat, to Hallowell Road. They made seven passes in this manner and then, halfway through the eighth pass, one of the searchers yelled out. Warden Woodward ran to where the sailor stood, pointing.

Sergeant Allen was summoned. He knelt beside the body, put his hand on the girl's forehead. It was cool to the touch. Allen shouted, "Sarah! Sarah?"

There was no response.

It was 11:00 A.M. before Judge Clifford O'Rourke signed the two warrants prepared by Wright and Hendsbee. Twenty minutes after noon, when Hendsbee returned to the command post at Lewis Hill Road and Dead River Road, State Police Captain Reynold LaMontagne informed him that a body had been found in the woods, a few hundred yards across Hallowell Road from where Dechaine's truck had been parked.

Hendsbee was led to the scene. A large area around the body was surrounded with yellow flagging tape. He could tell, even from that distance, that the body was that of a small, blond child. She lay on a knoll beside a small stream almost entirely covered with leaves and branches, with only the top of her head exposed.

Dr. Ronald Roy of the state medical examiner's office arrived and examined the body at two o'clock. Rigor mortis appeared to be passing off. There were small stab wounds on the girl's chest and on her head. She lay on her side, knees bent, her jeans pulled down to her knees, no panties. Sticks had been inserted into her rectum and vagina. A blue scarf was wound tightly about her neck and wrapped across the face holding a dark blue bandanna, a gag, in the girl's mouth. Yellow plastic rope bound her wrists.

When the corpse was moved, Dr. Roy saw a considerable amount of blood beneath where her head had lain. Police covered her hands with paper bags to preserve any evidence that might remain under her fingernails. The body was placed in a blue plastic bag and strapped to a stretcher. Television cameras captured the police van leaving for the Kennebec Valley Medical Center in Augusta.

Dr. Roy began his autopsy at 3:30 P.M. He concluded that Sarah Cherry had died of strangulation. That scarf had constricted her neck to a diameter of two-and-a-half to three inches.

❖

Most of the search parties had disbanded. A few score volunteers milled around the command center where an officer made announcements to the press.

Until now, the biggest local news this year had been the issuing of a license allowing a decoy shop in adjoining Bowdoinham to make wood-carved reproductions of the Federal Migratory Bird Hunting and Conservation stamp.

Fear and trepidation always occur when a child disappears anywhere but one can only comprehend the addition of mind-numbing shock in this case by realizing what life was like for the people who live in this area. The town of Bowdoinham sits on the banks of Merrymeeting Bay, a placid 9,000 acres of water fed by six rivers. Its banks, where many residents have their homes, consist of mudflats, beaches, bulrushes, and wild rice, forests, and fields where farmers raise strawberries, carrots, peas and apples.

Bowdoinham's population had nearly tripled over the preceding two decades. And still, that heavily forested 22,176 acres with its 2,192 residents remained a place where bean suppers, beano games and barbecues brought folks together, where every passing car had a familiar face and one resident said, "We always leave our doors open so friends can come in and out."

There were no open doors in Sagadahoc County that night. Few in Maine.

3

The Arrest

On Friday, Nancy Dechaine was still unable to focus on her work. She came home around one o'clock to find Dennis and their boarder, Richard Bruno, sitting on the side porch. Dennis told her the girl's body had been found—a radio newscast said it was discovered near the spot where his truck had been located.

"They'll arrest me," he said. "I'm the only suspect."

She sat beside him and they held one another. He told her again and again, it was simply inconceivable to him that he could have killed a child.

Around three o'clock, Detective Hendsbee and Lieutenant Peter McCarthy drove up. Dechaine got up from where he'd been sitting next to Nancy and approached Hendsbee. "I heard the news and I know why you're here."

Nancy recalls Dennis saying, "Al, I don't know how I could have killed her. I *couldn't* have done such a thing. I can't even kill my own chickens."

But Hendsbee reports Dechaine's next words as, "I can't believe that the guy I know would do such a thing. The real me isn't like that. I know me, and I couldn't do anything like that. It must be someone else in me that's doing this."

Hendsbee says he just stood on the step, shocked at what he was hearing.

Dechaine said, "Well, do what you've got to do. I just can't believe I could do that."

"I'm here to serve a search warrant," Hendsbee told him.

Lieutenant McCarthy came forward and read Dechaine the contents of his printed Miranda card.

Dechaine said, "I'd like to get a lawyer's advice before I say anything else."

Hendsbee showed him the search warrant. "Here's the things I'm looking for, Dennis. Some of these things are pretty small and this is a big house. Can you help me?"

"Sure, I'll help you."

Hendsbee began by asking for items that weren't required by the warrant. "One thing I need is your sneakers. Another thing," the detective turned to Nancy, "I'd like to start with the dirty clothes. Where do you keep your dirty laundry?"

Nancy said, "Well, I washed clothes yesterday. It's still out there, hanging on the line."

Prosecutors would see the act of doing the laundry as removing evidence.

Hendsbee went to the back yard and retrieved a blue T-shirt and green trousers from the line. He returned to the house where Dennis handed him the gray sneakers he'd worn on Wednesday.

Hendsbee acknowledged that the clothing wasn't listed on the warrant but Dechaine said, "Take them, sure." Then he said, "I just can't believe I could do something like this. I couldn't have killed a girl. I can't even kill the chickens I raise for meat. I take them to a butcher shop and have them do it."

Lieutenant McCarthy stood nearby, writing down everything Dechaine said.

Dechaine telephoned lawyer Carlton and told him what was happening. Carlton asked to speak with the detective.

Hendsbee got on the phone and Carlton asked whether it was still possible to make arrangements for the polygraph examination. Then he requested he be notified and be allowed to be present if Dechaine was going to be arrested.

More detectives arrived.

Hendsbee began his search in the living room while Dechaine and his wife stood by. Dechaine kept saying, over and over, "I couldn't have done something like that. It's not the real me. I'm a person that likes to help people, I've made my life doing that." At one point, he said he sometimes gets sharp pains in his head that cause his eyes to scrunch up. He'd had one of those pains just the other day while he was driving but he hadn't lost consciousness or control of himself. He knew exactly where he was when the pain hit him, and afterwards, too.

Detectives Drake and John Cormier moved their search from the upstairs bedroom to the library. While they were there, they heard Nancy enter the bedroom and telephone a man named Joe, asking Joe to come and buy all their farm animals and all the grain as soon as possible.

Like most people, the Dechaines never thought about it before, but it doesn't matter whether you're guilty or innocent. Becoming a suspect isn't cheap.

Drake opened the door to the room occupied by the tenant, Richard Bruno. Bruno would say later, "I had to set them straight on the search warrant not covering my room." He refused to allow a search and denied them permission to photograph his room. The officers respected his wish because he was right, and he knew the law. Bruno rented the room at $65.00 a month, a fact that rendered his space legally a separate premises, not covered by a warrant specifying Dechaine's residence.

Hendsbee was searching the dining room when Assistant Attorney General Wright arrived at 3:45. They conferred. Five minutes later, Hendsbee placed Dennis Dechaine under arrest for the murder of Sarah Cherry. He ordered Detective Cormier to transport the prisoner to the Sagadahoc County Sheriff's Office..

Hendsbee resumed his search of the dining room. He noted Dechaine's fishing license on the hutch where Nancy had laid the papers Dechaine handed her from his wallet before he was taken away. Then Hendsbee and Wright prepared an affidavit for a search warrant specifying the shirt and pants, even though Dechaine had already consented to their taking. Prudence. Wright wanted to be doubly certain that everything they had was legally nailed down.

Captain LaMontagne telephoned the house and spoke with Detective Drake. "The girl's panties are missing. Look for them while you're there."

Hendsbee asked Nancy, "Do you folks have any blue bandannas?"

"I think we have two." She led him upstairs to a drawer filled with various bandannas, and handed him three blue ones. "I have a lot of these, I really don't know how many."

"Does Dennis ever use them? Wear them around his neck or his head when he'd working outside?"

"No, I'm the only one that uses them. Why?"

"Does Dennis have any knives?"

"Not that I can recall, why?"

"How about in the truck? Does he have any knives in the truck?"

"Well there's a little teeny one he keeps on the keychain. You should know. You have the keys, don't you?"

"There's no knife on the keychain."

At this point, Nancy came to a full realization that Hendsbee was adept at his job, a job she saw now as "to extract information from me under the guise of trust. He had been working to make me believe he was trustable and wanted to help me."

In truth, Hendsbee was simply being courteous and sympathetic as he went about his duties.

Nancy said, "I liked you and I felt you were being exceptionally kind and understanding but now I feel you've betrayed me. I don't want to say anything else."

Hendsbee assured her he wasn't wearing a tape recorder, "but I'll have to report that Dennis had a knife on his keychain."

"I don't want to talk any more about this. Look, I've been living with Dennis for ten years and we've been married for five years and he's telling the truth when he says he can't even kill his own chickens, never mind a human being."

❖

At the jail, Nancy was permitted a few minutes with her husband. She would write, later, "Dennis was ashen and very frightened when I arrived. He told me he was sorry to have put me through this and that he loved me. He assured me that, if he had committed this crime, it [sic] was not in his right mind. I knew this. He is a gentle, kind, giving and loving man. I believe in this man."

While Dechaine was being printed and photographed, lawyer George Carlton stopped by and spoke with Lieutenant McCarthy in the lobby. Told that his client "is busy right now," Carlton asked McCarthy to inform Dechaine that he'd been there but "there's nothing I can do now."

The minute deputies finished fingerprinting and photographing Dechaine at the Sagadahoc County Court House, Sheriff's Detective Westrum began talking to him. He relayed Carlton's message.

Dechaine just nodded.

Westrum left, then came back a few minutes later and took the prisoner to the men's room so he could wash off the fingerprint ink. "You want a drink? Some coffee?"

"No thanks." Dechaine stood there, washing his hands and shaking his head, and then he looked over at Westrum. Detective Westrum's report of what followed states:

> At 1730 hrs. Dechaine looked up at me and said to me, "I don't know what ever made me do that." Dechaine sobbed for a moment and said "I can't believe it happened." I then took Dechaine to the booking room where he sat down. I sat in a chair diagonal to him. After approx. 45 seconds Dechaine then said to me "It should

never have happened." Dechaine then said, shaking his head, "Oh my god why did I do this?" Dechaine then sobbed to himself for several minutes while still seated in the chair.

Dechaine then said to me, "I'm sorry, I forgot your name." Once I reminded him, Dechaine then called me by my first name, Mark.

Dechaine, after a few more minutes said to me, "Mark, I went home and told my wife I had done something bad and she just laughed at me." Dechaine continued to sob and then said, "I told her I wouldn't kill myself besides that's the easy way out." I then offered Dechaine a cigarette which he smoked for several minutes. Dechaine then said to me "Mark, please believe me, something inside me made me do that." During this time Dechaine was looking directly at me sobbing "Please believe me."

Westrum's report states he then informed Dechaine that he didn't have to say anything, that he wasn't there to make Dechaine say anything and he didn't have to.

Dechaine was silent for a short period and said "I knew they were coming after me and I was waiting.... It was something inside me that made me do that...I can only look forward now, that's all I have left...." Dechaine kept looking at me and asking "Why would I do this" My reply to Dechaine was "I can't answer that question and I don't know." Dechaine asked me that several times....Dechaine then got up from his chair and walked around saying "Why."

Before this conversation with Westrum, Dechaine had already asked to speak with his lawyer. Anything said *in response to questioning* after that would be legally inadmissible in court. But Westrum's report took pains to convey that there had been no questioning. Everything Dechaine said was uttered spontaneously, on his own, without being asked anything. The state could use it in court. Westrum's version continues:

> When Dechaine sat back down he looked up at me and said "I didn't think it actually happened until I saw her face on the news and then it all came back I remember it.... What punishment could they ever give me that would equal what I've done...." he reached out and grabbed me tightly for approx. 2 minutes saying "Why Mark Why" "I wished I had never gone down that road that day.... Why couldn't my truck have broke down somewhere instead.... I told my attorney I remember being on a dirt road and coming out of the woods but nothing else.... I had it all.... This shouldn't have happened to me, why did I let this happen.... I'm Dennis Dechaine. I love life. I had everything. I love my wife. I love my farm. I love my garden. We wanted children some day and have a family."

The search of Dechaine's home yielded nothing of value to the prosecution. Hendsbee and Prosecutor Wright drove to the home of Judge Paul McDonald for an amended warrant extending the search into the night. When they stopped by at the sheriff's department, Westrum told them, "He's confessed to me."

Detective and prosecutor returned to the Dechaine home where they officially seized the sneakers, the newly washed clothes Dechaine had worn on Wednesday, samples of rope they found here and there, and a small Swiss Army penknife found in a planter box. They prepared an inventory of items taken and left a copy at the scene.

It was nearly eleven o'clock when the officers finally went home.

The next day, and for weeks afterward, newspapers would headline these events:

GIRL SLAIN, SUSPECT ARRESTED
SEARCHERS FIND BODY OF MISSING YOUNGSTER
CRIME LAB EXAMINES PICKUP
POLICE REPORT SHOWS SARAH MAY HAVE
FOUGHT HER KILLER
STUNNED NEIGHBORS LIVE WITH FEAR

In the weeks that followed, newspapers would run photos of Dechaine being escorted in and out of courtrooms. Television stations would air that same file footage along with fresh on-the-street interviews each time any new trickle of information or rumor could be found to talk about.

❖

Nancy, like her husband, was unsure of anything. The police seemed so positive. There was evidence. Dennis couldn't remember. Lawyer Carlton wasn't encouraging.

In a moment of despondent gloom, she'd write in a letter to Carlton that she had "absolutely no doubt in my mind that he was unaware of what he was doing. Carelessness is not part of a smart man's murder...the receipt. He wore no gloves; he made no (or a feeble) attempt to hide the body of the child; he eventually stopped (with the man who offered to help him find his truck) an official to ask if he'd seen his truck. These moves are ludicrously stupid for a man trying to cover or escape suspect [sic] in a murder. The officials said he was nervous. He was nervous because he was full of drugs. Hendsbee did state to me that, as he was questioning Dennis on the night of July 6 and into the early morning of July 7, he noticed Dennis's attention faltered and his eyes drifted into space often."

At ten on Saturday morning, Hendsbee began answering his phone messages. Deputy Darryl Maxey of the Lincoln County Sheriff's Office wouldn't be back on duty until four in the afternoon. Dechaine was lodged in their jail because Sagadahoc County had no jail, so Hendsbee returned a call from a private investigator named Ron Morin.

Morin lived in Madawaska, three hundred miles north of Bowdoinham on the Canadian border, the town where Dechaine had grown up. According to police reports, he told Hendsbee he'd once located a corpse with the aid of a psychic and now, that same psychic was getting vibes about the Cherry case. She said they'd arrested the right person and she had thoughts that the suspect was now saying that it shouldn't have happened. "He keeps repeating it to himself. It shouldn't have happened."

When Hendsbee finally reached Deputy Maxey, the jail guard reported the suspect as having said, when he was brought in, that "You people need to know that I am the one that murdered that girl and you may want to put me in isolation." Guard Brenda Dermody, who was at the booking station at the time, confirmed Maxey's report.

❖

Dechaine was arraigned on Monday morning amidst tight security due to threats against him. Reporters and spectators were scanned with metal detectors before entering the courtroom and none were permitted to occupy the first three rows of seats. Dechaine was charged with kidnapping, gross sexual assault and murder. The penalty for homicide in Maine ranges anywhere from twenty-five years to life imprisonment and in Maine, where parole was outlawed years ago, "life" means "'til you're dead."

Newspapers reproduced Detective Hendsbee's five-page affidavit detailing justification for the arrest—Sarah's disappearance; the discovery of Dechaine's papers near the scene; his initial denial that those papers were his; Dechaine's proximity to the place where the girl's body would be found; scratches on his body; the muddy handprints; the lie he'd told officers about his truck keys when he was first interrogated; the absence of a penknife which had allegedly been on that key ring; and the discovery of Sarah's body with knife wounds and blood beneath her fingernails close to where Dechaine's truck was found.

Carlton pleaded his client Not Guilty. Dechaine was bound over for a probable cause hearing unless prosecutors obtained a grand jury indictment first, and he was transferred to the state prison, where they had facilities for high-risk inmates.

Assistant Attorney General Eric Wright was quoted by *Brunswick Times Record* reporter Melinda Lake as stating, "I'm satisfied that when all of you hear the case, the evidence is sufficient to show Dechaine caused the murder of Sarah Cherry." He confirmed reports that Dechaine's notebook and a receipt were found in the Henkel driveway along with "other documents" he wouldn't specify. Wright also declined to say what evidence had been found in Dechaine's truck.

❖

More than two hundred family members, friends and neighbors attended Sarah's funeral the next morning. The closed casket was decorated with nearly thirty bouquets, her photograph, and a flower centerpiece with a stuffed Koala bear.

The Reverend Robert Dorr spoke of "Sarah's world with God, a world filled with heavenly teddy bears.... She explored life, she challenged and enjoyed life.... She was always bouncing from one thing to another but she was thorough, a good student...."

Mother Debra and stepfather Chris Crosman seemed to be bearing up well under the emotional strain. Many followed the funeral cortege to Auburn where little Sarah Cherry was laid to rest.

Sheriff Haggett spoke with Hendsbee on the phone, saying he wanted to be kept advised of the progress. There were rumors floating all over town. Haggett repeated one alleging that Sarah had previously had consensual sex with

Dechaine. While most malicious gossip lives and grows despite its absurdity, this one was squelched by science: the autopsy showed Sarah was a virgin when her killer attacked her.

Another rumor, according to Haggett, held that Doug Senecal, the man under indictment for molesting his stepdaughter, had been in on the murder with Dechaine.

An employee of the state's Department of Human Services (DHS) contacted Hendsbee to relay allegations by a woman claiming to know Senecal. According to the DHS employee's informant, aside from the allegations of sexual abuse, the family was very violent. Senecal had behaved strangely since the death. Not sad, but strange. His whole family attended Sarah's funeral but Senecal stayed home. He just said, "Life goes on."

The DHS worker had had calls from this woman before and, "she sounds crazy at times but her information is usually true."

❖

State Police Detective Drake interviewed people to verify Senecal's account of his actions on the fatal Wednesday, and came away satisfied Senecal wasn't involved.

It would be February 7, 1989, before Hendsbee talked to Rose Knodt, John Henkel's employer. She said that on that day, seven months ago, Henkel came to work at his usual time, around ten in the morning, and remained until about 3:30 when his wife phoned to say that Sarah had disappeared. "John's lunch is usually made right at the business" which was located at the rear of the Knodt house.

Hendsbee's reports don't say why it took him seven

months to verify Henkel's alibi. A waitress from the Corsican Restaurant in Freeport telephoned Hendsbee back in early July to say that she knew Dechaine and his wife through their business selling flowers and produce in Brunswick. "He's a real nice guy, a real likeable fellow. He wouldn't hurt anybody."

The waitress also knew John Henkel as a regular customer at the Corsican. According to Hendsbee, she said:

> [Henkel] was a real weird pervert...would harass the waitresses and other help in the restaurant to a point where none of the female waitresses wanted to wait on HENKEL.... One time, she recalls, JOHN told one of the waitresses that he knew she was not at home that night because he went by the house. Another time, he told the waitress that he knew she did not have a published phone number and wanted to know why it was unpublished. All the people in the restaurant used to feel real creepy about HENKEL.

4

Thomaston

THE FIRST COMMITTEE TO LOOK into means of punishing criminals in Maine made their report to the legislature on January 23, 1823:

> The state prison should be so constructed that even their aspect might be terrific and appear like what they should be, dark and comfortless abodes of GUILT and WRETCHEDNESS; that no mode of punishment ever has been or ever can be adopted so good as CLOSE CONFINEMENT in a SOLITARY CELL, in which, cut off from all hope of relief during the time for which the prisoner shall have been sentenced....

That institution was built in Thomaston, Maine. When it burned in 1923, it was rebuilt—this time with a library, wood shop, an upholstery shop and other comparative amenities. But the dank segregation unit where Dechaine was held bore a chilling resemblance to that original recommendation. Dechaine sat in his cell and wrote:

> Today, incredulity breaks like

> A fever and reality sets in.
> I am a prisoner.

He had been there for five days when, on July 13th, the minutes from a hearing before the prison's Administrative Segregation Panel stated:

> Inmate will be held in Segregation due to the nature of the alleged crime and the resulting threats received from reliable informants in the general inmate population.
> Capt. Mahoney

Inmate's Reply: "Absolutely not. Whoever comes to my sphere long enough to speak to me, leaves a friend." He feels people will judge him not on the basis of alleged crime, but on his personality.

"The heat, ventilation are intolerable. If I treated my animals that way I'd be in trouble with the Humane Society." He protests this deprivation, esp. since he has not been convicted of any crime.

"My wife is being made a victim." He protests this. He has not had phone calls, outside exercise etc. "Nothing to give me any sense of human dignity.... I don't want to be confrontational. I have not [sic] a violent individual, but I am capable of explaining my character. Death in the defense of my character is more acceptable than being deposited in that hell hole.... If more attention isn't paid to basic human dignity, eventually my own human pride will erode."

Panel's Decision and its reason(s): (made out of presence of inmate and solely upon evidence produced at hearing) This panel feels that there is potential danger to this man from the general population at this time because of the nature of the alleged crime, and that he therefore should be maintained on Ad Seg status. It is felt however that the present conditions of confinement, protection are too stringent and that he could be appropriately confined on the Southside of the Seg unit. With full privileges. He should be afforded opportunity to communicate with his family.

The one bright spot in the drear and despondency of his days became mail call. Publicity motivated dozens of strangers to send spiritual suggestions. Friends attempted cheeriness with lighthearted accounts of happy events in the free world—family picnics, sailing along the coast, watching whales and porpoises and those funny-looking puffin birds. Friend Ann Brandt-Meyer, an attorney, offered legal advice and her colleagues' estimates of local defense lawyers. A few, bewildered by what they read in the papers or saw on TV, would send letters like the friend who wrote, "I want you to know that whatever may have happened, or whatever may happen in the future, we will always love and support you."

On July 13th, a letter from wife Nancy:

First, I love you and I'm thinking about you. It looks like I can't call you so you must call me collect. Do it!...The prison said you cannot have visitors until you're "checked out" and have a physical. They say this may take a week to 10 days....

Baby, you must find some serious strength in yourself to endure this. I will make every effort to see you and talk w/ you. You are my heart and soul. I am taking care of myself and am doing just fine.

Much love. I love you, I love you. Nancy

Dechaine's older brother Phil had raised him from the age of fourteen, after their parents had both died. On July 14th, Phil sat at the kitchen table in his northern Maine home so distant, so remote from the greed and crime, the poverty and naked pragmatism that creates most of the world's despair, and he wrote:

Dennis,
Hope this finds you holding up well or as well as possible under the circumstances. By now you must feel terribly isolated and alone. Don't, we're still here, thinking, praying for you/us for strength to go through this together!

It's amazing how many people out there are calling to lend support for you. The list would be unmanageable. *All* have been giving us support, standing by you through thick and thin and offering to continue as long as necessary....

I called Thomaston and they've pretty well outlined their visiting procedures and hopefully will send the necessary paperwork to allow us visits. The process, I'm told, takes 8–10 weeks....

Love, Phil

Letter from brother Phil Dechaine, July 25th, in part:

> I think we're both having the same nightmare, waiting to wake up. In the past few weeks I've been through every emotion ever invented and a few that haven't, knowing that what I'm going through is a drop in the bucket compared to what you're experiencing. When I feel frightened, you must feel terrified. When I'm depressed, you must be despondent etc. Somehow I wish I could relieve you of your burden, make your days brighter and offer you more support than is now possible. I do need to see you. Unfortunately, we've been denied visiting privileges until our forms are processed, which they claim takes 4 to 6 weeks more. *J'espere que sait la verite....*
>
> Love you always,
Phil

Another letter from Phil, July 29th, in part:

> Dear Dennis,
> Fr. Ron stopped in tonight to offer his support. Pretty nice of him but he's three weeks too late. We haven't been getting much support in town. I felt hurt by what I perceived as shunning, but that's not the case. Most simply don't know how to react to the situation....

And, two days later:

> Just talking to you [on the phone] was terrific yesterday, even if the news was not so hot. It's reassuring to know

that you're keeping your spirits up. Somehow your strength rubs off on me and it's getting easier to keep mine up, too....

                                  Love you always,
                                  Phil

And on August 4th:

Dear Dennis,
On the subject of your financial needs, I've contacted the credit union for a second mortgage on this place. They'll loan the remainder of 80 percent unmortgaged value, and they use the tax bill as a guide. The value of this property is $26,890 and I owe $16,466. That means they will allow a loan of $5,057. The process is simple....

                                  Love,
                                  Phil

It was August 16th, and Dechaine had been locked away for thirty-nine days before Deputy Warden Arthur Kiskila officially informed him that he'd be allowed five hours of visits per week—two two-hour visits on weekdays; one one-hour visit on weekends.

Dechaine happened to be friends with the son of Professor Orlando Delogu of the University of Maine School of Law. The son relayed the professor's recommendation of a Portland attorney he had mentored as a student, one Professor Delogu considered, "young, aggressive and bright. He's one lawyer who takes on defendants he believes deserving of a defense even if they can't pay what the case merits, whereas that would be difficult for the "hot shit' attorneys.

"Besides," Delogu would add later, "Tom Connolly wins enough of those 'impossible cases' in a state that's not unduly sympathetic with criminal defendants."

Professor Delogu telephoned Connolly, and asked him to "look into the case."

❖

Some Mainers knew Connolly as the lawyer who'd defended an assortment of controversial clients. One was the half-Korean son of an abusive soldier-father, Ernie Allard, who'd murdered his girlfriend and disemboweled her.

Prosecutor Eric Wright had charged Allard with First Degree Murder. He now knew Connolly as the lawyer who'd convinced the jury to come back with a manslaughter conviction for Allard. Worse yet, from Wright's point of view, Connolly won because Wright had felt sure the defense would be going for an insanity defense. Wright countered that tactic by playing for jurors a tape recording of Ernie Allard's long, rambling confession. But that confession included the story of Allard's relationship with the victim; the child he'd supported because she told him it was his; and her cruel taunts on the day of her death right after she'd shot him up with heroin. "I'm leaving you. My boyfriend's getting out of prison and I'm going with him. And the kid? It's his. You don't think I'd have your chink kid, do you?"

So Connolly got the whole story to the jury without having his client tell it on the witness stand where he'd then have to withstand Eric Wright's typically sarcastic cross-examination.

Some police officers remembered Connolly as the lawyer who'd defended a cop killer. There had been times during that trial when Tom Connolly found .45 caliber bullets on his car with threatening notes.

But almost everyone, at least in the Portland area, recognized Connolly as the lanky lawyer with the long-billed fishing cap, a cap he wore everywhere he went, except in the courtroom. He'd been wearing it ever since his undergraduate days at Bates College where he'd won the New England Debating Tournament once and qualified for the National Debate Tournament four times. He was his class valedictorian, too, but he hastens to correct anyone's misconception: at Bates College, valedictorians are not the student with the highest grades. They're elected by the students. Actually, Connolly says his class standing was "only thirty-ninth." And how many in his class? "Well, four hundred."

Connolly had just finished two back-to-back murder trials and he believed Dechaine guilty for no other reason than his standard practice of beginning every defense with that notion. Most people charged with crimes are guilty. He takes their cases because our system of law provides that every accused deserves representation and, without that protection, none of us can expect justice. Despite the request by the mentor he revered, Connolly remained less than eager to take on a high-profile case of a man accused in such a despicable crime. When Dechaine's family called, Connolly quoted a fee he thought would discourage them—$30,000.

But the family agreed to his fee. "Dennis didn't do it."

Lawyer Carlton had been asking for $50,000.

George M. Carlton, Jr., was a very different kind of lawyer. Chosen initially on the simple recommendation of Nancy Dechaine's employer, Carlton was up in years. One lawyer described him as "good in the courtroom, but erratic." He revealed his early take on this case in his letter to a South Carolina physician, one day after his brief initial meeting with Dechaine, asking the doctor to conduct an examination regarding "the death of a child which apparently was at the hands of my client."

Connolly didn't know Carlton that well but he consented to keeping him on as co-counsel in the hope that an older hand might exert a steadying influence on Connolly's own more passionate personality. Then, too, he hoped that Carlton's friendly relationship with the judge in this case "might help to keep Bradford off my back" when crucial decisions lay within the judge's discretion.

Tom Connolly says that the rare instances when he discovers his client to be innocent are pure delight. He met with Dechaine, and he'd recall a dozen years later that he "felt an instant affinity." Both were thirty years old, similar in life outlook, alike in their personal values. He sensed Dennis's sincerity, and he'd recall that his opinion regarding guilt changed then and there. A bond was formed.

That's how Connolly remembers it now. But memories of yesterday are often colored by our knowledge of today. Connolly's contemporaneous notes shed a less rosy light on their first meetings

At the prison in Thomaston, one guard greeted the lawyer by name in the front lobby, then kept him waiting for slightly over an hour before taking him to another room where he signed a pat-down authorization and had his personal items—sunglasses and the trademark long-billed cap—taken and placed in a locker. Another guard gave him a most intimate feel down before leading him, "*sans* hat," Connolly noted, "despite my objection and despite the fact that he was wearing a hat," outside the prison to a garage area where they passed through a series of locked doors to a hallway where he waited a while longer before his client was brought to him—blue sweatpants, sandals, no shirt, well-groomed. A small desk, the kind Connolly recalled from parochial school, was provided for the inmate to face his attorney in that hallway.

Dechaine was glad to see his new lawyer. Carlton hadn't been around when the client needed him and he'd given Dechaine information that proved utterly false.

Connolly informed him of the charges against him—something Carlton had never done—and there was some superficial discussion of the date of the murder, July 6th. Dechaine told of using amphetamines and, after that, Connolly's notes report, "he was totally unsure of anything that happened. He has sporadic recollections of bits and pieces but for the most part he has no recollection of the events whatsoever."

It wasn't the sort of story that inspires an attorney's confidence.

The good news was the volume of letters from friends who'd give character testimony. Connolly said he'd like a $20,000 retainer and another $5,000 to hire experts. Dechaine described his and Nancy's assets: the greenhouse business, $60,000 equity in their home, and Nancy's father had offered to front him whatever money was needed. Connolly's overall impression was that Dennis Dechaine was intelligent, frightened, and unsure, but straightforward in his answers and relieved that someone else was on his side.

Much of Dechaine's confidence in Connolly was based on discussions with friends who were acquainted with the attorney's law school mentor, Orlando Delogu.

At the conclusion of the interview—at the very instant the lawyer told Dechaine, "Well, that's it."—a guard popped around the corner to take the prisoner back to his cell.

Letter from Nancy, August 1, 1988:

Today was especially hard for me. I feel more love and longing for you than ever since this case began. I can't get your sweet face out of my mind. I wish I could. I wish I could just push a button and turn off the love. It would make things so much easier. I'm missing you next to me. I want to say, "OK, this is long enough. I'm ready for you to come back now." I know you. I know how tender and gentle you are. I just blink and gulp in disbelief that you could have done what you're accused of. I feel so alone. My baby, you are *so much* a part of me, I have a hard time coping. I feel a prisoner of my emotions....

The pain of loving and missing you consumes me, Dennis. The legal and business responsibilities are beginning to overwhelm me. You said you needed to know—& my intention is not to upset you, but I feel so alone now, like there's no one to help.... I love you my soul mate & kindred spirit. Don't give up faith.

The next day, Dechaine was arraigned at the Lincoln County Courthouse. Connolly met with him in the basement lockup call. They conversed through the bars. Carlton arrived a short time later, talked with them for a few minutes, then left.

Dechaine was still in a fog about July 6th. Connolly's contemporaneous notes document his unease:

> At several points during our conversation he became teary-eyed at the thought of what he may have done to this girl. The sex charges in particular strike him as very brutal and difficult to deal with. He indicated that he and his wife have a normal sexual relationship and that he has never, in recent times at least (I did not press him on anything else) had any affairs or any such things.

On August 10th, Debra Cherry Crosman, acting as executor for Sarah, lodged a wrongful death lawsuit against Dechaine in the amount of one million dollars. Nancy divorced the husband she loved in order to retain her share of their property. Later, the AG's people and others would point to the divorce as an indication that Nancy thought her husband guilty. The civil suit went unopposed, since trial strategy was to focus on the crucial criminal trial but, as intended, it stripped Dechaine of funds to finance a truly formidable defense—investigators, forensic experts, and the fee an attorney would earn for this kind of trial.

Professionals in Maine's legal community doubt that this victim's family, untutored in bare-knuckle trial tactics, would ever have come up with this strategy on their own.

Letter from Nancy, August 15th:

Hi Dennis,
I apologize for the upset yesterday. I feel much better today. I had been missing you so and needing to resume normally with you. I was trying to be so strong and when this issue of a suit came up....

Dennis, I love you so much. My dreams are filled with us loving and playing. Waking up to an empty side of the bed is increasingly difficult. But you're right. I do have you next to me. I love you and miss you. See you Sunday.

Letter from Nancy, August 18th:

Hello Dennis, my love,
Did you know that I love you immensely?? I do. I miss you. Life isn't the same without you to keep me happy and make me smile and laugh. You certainly had a magic with me....

Listen, Hendsbee is *bad news*. His daughter was sexually abused and he's *hell bent* on seeing suspects of child abuse *hang*. About my future plans. I really don't know what I'll do.... Dennis, please realize, I love you as I've never loved anyone—you are my soulmate. Parting from you will be beyond difficult; but may be inevitable.

Please prepare for it, as I am doing....

I know your incarceration is difficult and I'm amazed at your strength. You possess a characteristic which I have internalized from you—integrity....

I love you, Dennis.

In preparation for the trial, Connolly sat in his office poring over the "discovery" material—reports furnished him by the state to meet their legal obligation of disclosing anything that incriminates a defendant along with any information known to the state that might suggest his innocence.

Tom Connolly's office is a small room on the fourth story of an ancient row building in Portland's chic Old Port section. On the same floor, there's a bathroom and kitchen and space for table and chair because, when he first started his practice in 1982, he was single and he lived here. What's now his office was his bedroom back then. Now its walls are lined with bookshelves, souvenirs of past cases, and filing cabinets. Behind him stands a full-sized skeleton—an exhibit from another trial—its hollow eye sockets staring across his shoulder at visitors who sit in the plain, wooden captain's chairs before his desk.

In those early days, a tiny room down a narrow staircase on the third floor served as his office. Now this space is occupied by his secretary, Ida Bilodeau—tall and slender with red hair and a cheery personality that keeps her and Connolly's minds on an even keel amidst the misfortunes that clients trundle up those twenty-eight steps from the sidewalk entrance. Ida's cramped space allows for her desk and chair, two filing cabinets, a small photocopier, one bookcase bristling with texts and yellow legal pads, and a large window looking down on busy Fore Street. Visitors squeezing by on their way upstairs to Connolly's office see the photos of Ida's husband, boatbuilder Steven, and their daughter, Stephanie, born three years after they took on the Dechaine case.

❖

Tom Connolly needed to know his client's background. Following a conference with Judge Carl Bradford where both sides agreed to psychological evaluations, the judge ordered prosecutor Wright to afford Connolly access to Dechaine "without any guards being present." Connolly dictated notes into his own file:

> We need to forward to him as soon as possible medical releases and financial releases and academic releases for as many purposes as are possible for the time being. In particular, what we are looking for are any prior psychological issues which may have arisen in his past.... Those records are imperative to get. In addition in both 1974 and 1975, the Def. attended an "upward bound" program at Bowdoin College....
>
> Apparently, there is a wealth of psychological profiles and other psychological type information that can be obtained and should be obtained as soon as possible.

Ida transcribed Tom's notes, listed those sources, obtained appropriate releases from Dechaine, prepared the requisite letters and sent them off.

Ida Bilodeau will also tell anyone who asks that she likes working for Tom Connolly. Ida began her legal career in 1984 as a clerk at the district court in Portland. When she took over handling the court's juvenile caseload, she came into frequent contact with Connolly because he took on numerous court appointments in those days. One morning in October 1988, chatting on the phone with Connolly's then-secretary, Sandy, she learned that Sandy was leaving to have her second child. Ida said, "Tell Tom I want the job."

Ida recalls, "I was thirty-three and ready for a change, and this seemed perfect. Everybody around the courthouse liked Tom."

Sandy made an appointment for her and she recalls Tom explaining all there was to do and asking, "You really want this job?"

"Yes!"

Already familiar with Ida's work for the court, Tom said, "You're hired."

When she gave her notice at the district court, Ida says, "the other clerks were miffed because they hadn't known Tom was hiring."

She's been happy ever since, and it shows in her sunny personality. "I just can't stay depressed about anything," she says. "One joke ends any discouragement for me."

❖

Bowdoin College was concerned about the situation. Their attorney told Connolly they'd regarded Dechaine as their "prized student"—the best model of achievement that their Upward Bound Program for high school students had produced to date. "The fact that he's been charged with such a grisly crime has really flipped them out." But Upward Bound's reports were interesting — especially those from his second year in the program. One of his instructors referred to Dechaine by his high school nickname:

> Mouse went on The Apprentice Shop trip, and worked fairly well although he also complained a fair amount. While working, though, he opened up and talked a lot about himself, his home, and school, and showed himself to be very bright and aware of himself and his situation.

His French teacher stated, "Dennis is able to produce good work, often after some slight encouragements. He has a nice and open personality, sensitive to the others, and often willing to help."

The Director of the program wrote,

> I, for one, saw an immense improvement in Dennis's general maturity. Over and over again, in a whole variety of situations, I saw Dennis's honesty and good judgment replacing the rather immature, self-centered, sometimes whining attitude that he seemed to have on occasion last summer.

The staff psychologist who'd administered the IQ test routinely given to all rising seniors reported:

> Dennis presented himself as an affable, friendly young man who was generally quiet, but he definitely came across as a "nice kid." He worked consistently under the

direction of the examiner and showed very logical problem solving skills in most of the tasks which he undertook. He obtained a full scale score which places him in the 80th percentile, the Bright Normal range of intelligence.

State Police Detective J. P. Madore's efforts in Madawaska yielded no past actions presaging the crime Dechaine was accused of. He reported that Dechaine's mother died when he was ten; his father, Madore stated erroneously, when Dechaine was fifteen. Older brother Phillip had raised him through his high school years. Teachers termed him quiet although he'd been involved in the high school newspaper and yearbook, the winter carnival, and the Upward Bound Program. His IQ was reported as average but he was usually among the top group of students, academically. Local police said Dechaine was never involved in any of the incidents they'd responded to over the years but he was "always in the picture." After his father's death, one policeman said, Dechaine seemed to find trouble more often—incidents like rock throwing. One former classmate described him as "a quiet kind of guy." An underclassman said he "hung out with druggies." Overall, the consensus was that Dennis Dechaine was a quiet, mind-my-own-business kind of guy.

Portland Press Herald reporter Tom Bradley talked to Bowdoinham neighbors who knew Dechaine as generous and thoughtful, sharing a happy life with his wife, raising sheep and goats and hens and ducks and geese, growing vegetables, and making Christmas wreaths. He and Nancy loved cats, and they frequently went bicycling together along country roads.

Melinda Lake of the *Brunswick Times Record* quoted Russell Cox of the Rotary Foundation Committee describing Dechaine as "a typical all-American young man, happy working on his family farm."

While the attorney general's people labored to clad their case in cast-iron, and Connolly planned his trial strategy, and Dechaine languished in the terrifying environment of real killers, the average Mainer—anyone with eyes to watch TV or ears to hear a radio—accepted the case as solved, the danger past. New developments reported by the media made an interesting diversion but most folks' lives went on as usual.

5

Gearing Up

On August 23rd, Prosecutor Wright telephoned Connolly to find out the status of the proposed psychological evaluation. Connolly told him, in no uncertain terms, that he didn't like the fact that impounded documents had been released to the lawyer filing that civil suit against Dechaine. Wright agreed, yes, it was totally inappropriate and he'd try to work the situation out with Detective Hendsbee. He also proposed that Connolly would get at least half of the blood sample taken from the defendant for comparison purposes.

Among the discovery documents furnished Connolly, one report by Detective Hendsbee told of a woman named Wendy who phoned to say that if Dechaine was the same man she'd dated, years ago, she knew some things that might interest the police.

Hendsbee visited her, showed her the mugshot of the suspect. Wendy was "99 percent sure" it was the same man she'd met about ten years ago when she was taking a summer course at the University of Maine. She'd introduced herself to him at a keg party one night and, after that, they'd gone out daily for the few weeks until the course ended.

Hendsbee's report of the interview relates Wendy's account of meeting Dechaine and having sex with him afterwards on several occasions. Hendsbee asked her specifically whether Dechaine had ever used bondage on her. She said no, he hadn't. She also said she'd try to find any papers Dechaine had mailed to her, but Hendsbee never reported hearing back from her.

When Connolly showed this sheet to Dechaine, his client worried—would the state use her in court? The things she claimed were "extremely slanderous and filled with lies," Dechaine said. "She did introduce herself to me at a keg party and asked me point blank if I'd have sex with her except, well, she wasn't that reserved about her choice of words. I never dated her, never confided in her, never led her to believe I loved her, never told her I'd see her again, never wrote her a single word. She was a willing floozy."

"I slept with Wendy twice," and that was all there was to that.

The state never brought Wendy to the courtroom. Her allegations, irrelevant to the case as they were, sowed uneasiness and diverted the defense from important issues. But prosecutors had no choice. Discovery rules absolutely required them to give everything that might possibly bear upon guilt or innocence to Connolly. It's unfortunate that, with respect to more crucial pieces of evidence, the state's zeal to satisfy the discovery requirement fell short of compliance.

❖

On October 13th, the state's psychologists conducted their examination. Dechaine was subdued but candid about his drug use—marijuana, cocaine, and LSD once in high school. Asked why he used drugs on the day in question, he said simply that he'd enjoyed his and Nancy's four-day Fourth of July vacation with family in Madawaska, and didn't feel like getting back to work. He wanted to extend the holiday weekend, and he was alone. Nancy had gone to her job at the surveying firm. When the doctor asked how the drug he'd taken that day affected him, Dechaine described feeling "very alive, more vibrant. Everything was more alive—leaves shimmering, grass quaking, changes in hues." He was still feeling high when the Buttricks picked him up and fearful he wouldn't be able to hide it. Yes, he'd lied to them about where he lived and worked; he didn't want people knowing who he was.

At one point during the seventy-minute session, Dechaine told the psychologists, "I really believe that evening, during the interrogations, that I was made to believe I was responsible for this. I wondered if I had done something crazy that day. I guess what really shocked me was when I saw that girl's picture in the newspaper and I had never seen that girl before, and that made me feel it wasn't possible that I could be involved in this. At least I would have remembered what the girl looked like."

This version of Dechaine's reaction to seeing Sarah's picture can't be disputed. This interview, unlike his interchange with Detective Westrum, was videotaped.

The state psychologists' report to the Court would conclude that Dechaine understood the issues relating to trial competence; that he was not mentally ill nor suffering from mental defect at the time of the alleged offenses and, that at that time, his mental state did not preclude his ability to distinguish right from wrong.

Letter from Nancy to Attorney Connolly, November 30, 1988:

Dear Tom,
I need to share with you some feelings I have after my last visit with Dennis. Prison life in a 6' x 8' space with another man is changing him. The dehumanizing, dignity-stripping treatment is changing him. My feeling is that you will not have a testimony in trial from the man that Dennis is. You will have testimony from a decent being with a broken spirit.... The Dennis I see is neither the Dennis I know nor the man you represent. I wish something could be done. He's an innocent man 'til he's proven guilty....

Tom, I know you've seen for the most part how I've dealt with this ordeal. I am not an alarmist. I am, however, alarmed at the change in my mate. His broken spirit is not because of his conscience, but because of the dehumanizing humiliation that he is undergoing....

Also, I want you to feel comfortable with asking whatever you need to concerning our more intimate & private affairs—issues concerning our sexuality, drug use, etc. I have nothing monumental to offer, offhand, but I don't know what kind of things the state will be looking into....

In a mid-December phone conversation with Wright,

Connolly said he wanted additional testing of the blood found under Sarah's fingernails. Wright said that would be okay with him. When they talked again, two weeks later, Wright indicated once more that he'd be amenable to having the DNA tests performed.

Christmas and New Year's Day passed. On January 22, 1989, Dechaine was transferred from the Detention Corridor back to Southside in the "admin seg" unit. His cellmate had a record of arson, aggravated assault, and terrorizing along with a psychological profile which, Dechaine said, "would make [serial killer] Ted Bundy look like the Pope."

A week later, two months before the scheduled trial date, Connolly appeared before Judge Bradford with a motion to have the blood beneath Sarah's fingernails subjected to DNA testing. The only test conducted by the state lab had identified the blood type as Type A. Dechaine's was Type O. Sarah's blood was type A. The state was contending that the blood beneath her fingernails was her own, deposited when she'd clawed at her wounds.

But Connolly preferred a scientific test to the state's assumption.

One lab, in California, was capable of testing the miniscule traces left after most of the sample had been consumed in the state's limited test. The California lab's process allowed them to reproduce a small sample, then reproduce the results of that procedure and repeat this action until they had enough for a test. The FBI wasn't utilizing this technique yet but Connolly offered articles from scientific journals and material showing that Scotland Yard had used the process, which was already accepted in the British courts, to nail a serial killer.

Prosecutor Wright, so agreeable about DNA tests in his earlier phone conversations with Connolly, now called State Forensic Chemist Judith Brinkman to the stand. She'd telephoned the California lab and, according to Brinkman, they regarded the process as experimental. Brinkman didn't think enough blood was left to do this test. She'd used up eight of Sarah's fingernails in performing her simple test. Brinkman quoted the California lab person as telling her that, "what I described to her didn't sound like the possibility of getting good results."

The California person, never named by Brinkman, "also kind of concurred with my opinion that if there was a mixture [of different bloods] involved here, you would expect to find something along those lines—tissue, some indication that would lead you to believe there was a mixture." Brinkman said she'd been told that it might be three months before the California lab could begin testing, and the process would take a few weeks. Results may not come, Brinkman said, for "four months, possibly five or six."

Since there remained two months before the scheduled trial date, such a delay could postpone the trial for another month or two—possibly, per Brinkman, even longer.

Connolly's cross-examination demonstrated the lawyer's impressive knowledge of blood types, testing, and the procedures employed by the FBI and other laboratories. "In fact," he asked Brinkman, "even Jennifer Mahavolin [of the California lab] has been able to do this kind of testing under circumstances where it was considered all but hopeless in other cases. For example, that ABO testing came back inconclusive and enzyme tests came back inconclusive, but the DNA testing was able to determine some identification. Is that right?"

"I don't know," the state chemist replied. "I didn't ask her that."

Connolly argued to the judge that, "Even if the court ultimately determines there may be only a 10 percent chance that the tests would be exculpatory, then...given the fact that there are no eyewitnesses in the case, that there's circumstantial evidence which is persuasive but at the same time not ultimately conclusive as to the defendant doing the deed, I think the evidence should be allowed to go forward, and that's my argument."

Eric Wright acknowledged that one might ask why the state didn't want to nail down this blood evidence since—despite the chemist's conclusion that the blood was type A like Sarah's—he said that the H antigen allowed some remote possibility that the blood could be type O, the same as Dechaine's. But the fingernails showed no evidence of skin tissue. In addition, Wright argued, "While Mr. Dechaine's body had some small scratches on them, they were not of such significance as to have caused him to have bled. The likelihood, therefore, that there is blood from him is so remote, I think, as to be really nil."

Perhaps the experienced Wright missed Connolly's thrust: that there might be scratches on the *real* killer which *were* "of such significance as to have caused him to have bled." Perhaps not.

Wright mentioned the tiny sample remaining, the

uncertainty of obtaining definite results and, "what we are doing here is doing nothing more than delaying a case which is, as the court knows, very troubling to the community emotionally. They want it over with...I guess what I'm saying here is the short delay isn't worth the gamble. I concede that there is a theoretical possibility of a successful result that may be helpful to one side or the other but the theoretical possibility is not very great...."

Connolly cited rape cases where the procedure had been successful and the results admitted as evidence.

Judge Bradford's ruling concluded, "Weighing everything in the balance here...in the light most favorable to the defendant is the possibility that the blood under the two remaining thumbnails was the blood of someone other than Sarah Cherry and other than Mr. Dechaine, and the possibility of that happening is so remote that I cannot grant the motion to continue this case...."

It's difficult to fathom how Judge Bradford could see suppressing potential proof of Dechaine's innocence as viewing the situation "in the light most favorable to the defendant."

Dechaine wrote Connolly a long letter filled with anguished questions:

> It seems the entire state knows more about what's going on than I do—no doubt the whole prison does. In our last meeting, you said you felt you weren't going to be ready for March—let me tell you, that has me worried. Has all this been for nothing? How many other commitments have you made in anticipation of a continu-

ance? What are we going to do without the DNA analysis of the blood samples? Why didn't they see clearly enough to realize the importance of that test? What are you going to do about the investigation of the stepfather [Senecal]? What about the witness who described the blond man? When will jury selection begin? What questions will you ask? Will I be part of this selection process? Did you ask for a change of venue to a less hostile location? Just how am I going to get prepared in one month when I've barely seen the state's evidence? What about our witnesses? Will they all be available then? Will bringing in an expert on the value of DNA evaluation benefit the case? What about the slander that's already occurred concerning the Green River Murders? What good is that? You'd spoken of that as reason for a mistrial along with the possibility of showing subjectivity on the part of the investigators—will any of this surface? What about the lead in NH? What's become of that? What about similar crimes in N. N.E.? Was the state within the law when it supplied the girl's mother with information to attach my property? Can you show that they intended to cripple me financially making a fair defense virtually impossible? What about Hendsbee's statement saying he'd see me indigent before trial...?

His questions went on and on.

An innocent man is expected to offer an alibi. Dechaine didn't. It's impossible to exaggerate the negative effect of "I can't remember" on the police, on Connolly, even on Nancy, even upon Dechaine himself. His utterances shifted between "I couldn't have" and "I must have." Whether he was lying or he really couldn't remember, his vague vacillations combined with the evidence of those papers, the ropes and his proximity to the body to create an inference of guilt that seemed unassailable.

With only three weeks before trial, Connolly visited Nancy at the Dechaine farmhouse. He was dismayed when she showed him a scarf quite similar to the one used to strangle Sarah Cherry, and troubled that she knew of that similarity until she explained the source of her knowledge: the search warrant executed at the house had described the scarf used in the crime. Connolly was disappointed and concerned again when Nancy showed him various knots tied by Dechaine in the barn: three of those four knots were tied in yellow polypropylene rope like that used to bind the victim. Connolly realized that he was no expert in knots but, as he entered in his notes, "it does appear on its face that the knot does match and if it does, in my opinion, that means that it is virtually certain that Dennis Dechaine did the crime."

As it turned out, these knots, and all the knots previously confiscated by the police, bore no resemblance to those which bound Sarah.

Dechaine received mixed signals from fellow inmates [names used here are aliases]. One sent him this note:

> The state pigs came to see me, Dave, plus Frank. I don't know what went on. But with me the cops ask me how

you and I get along. I told them great, plus they ask me do you ever talk about the case.

They ask me if I know Dunn. And I told then yes. And that Dunn told me that he was going to lie in court by saying that you told him you kill her. And that Dunn told me that you never told him that he was just going to lie in court so he could get out on his own case. They ask me if I thought you kill her I told them No, and that I don't belive [sic] you could ever do anything like that.

Plus I told them if they need me in court on your behalf, please bring me down. Cause I really belive your inocent [sic], and I want to help in any way I can.

Your friend,
Bob Stan Becker

Then there was this note:

Dennis you dont have anything to worrie about Because I am not going to court to testifi [sic]. I dont know any thing about your case you never told me any thing. As I see it we have always been good friends and I want to keep it that way. I hope we are still good friends Dennis.

Frank Dunn

But, whether or not he intended (or was asked) to testify, Mr. Dunn had, indeed, had a chat with the police.

Detective Al Hendsbee recorded an interview with inmate Frank Dunn, twenty-eight, serving time for manslaughter. "Primarily," Hendsbee told him, "what I want to talk to you about is what Dennis Dechaine had made conversation to you back—"

An eager Dunn cut the detective off: "See, to start it off is, there's a bunch of guys...were picking on him and giving him a real hard time so they used to let him out [for exercise] by himself. I used to get out before he did. So me and him got to knowing each other, you know. Started talking to him and everything...so then me and him become closer and closer like friends, and so then I said why did you do that for? He goes, well my lawyer says he can get me out of it, and I said I really don't mind telling you, you're in for the same thing, so I'm sure you're not going to say nothing."

Hendsbee said, "Slow down a little bit, okay? When you talk."

"I said okay. I said, ah, he goes well, he goes I took, he goes, I figure if I left the truck there, where he left it—he didn't say where he left it there—he goes I could report it stolen and then they wouldn't...they wouldn't, the police might [think?] you left it there so report it stolen so they wouldn't think that somebody had stole his truck and killed this girl, and he showed me, I think it was the right side of his face with fingernail marks on his face where he got scratched, and ah, he said he stabbed her with a little knife, I guess that's what they call it, little diddling knives, and ah, I said to him what's you do that, what's you do that for? He said I really don't want to go into it. I said no, you don't have to. You don't have to tell me nothing. I said, ah, why did you, why did you go up to this girl's house anyway? He goes because I was damned depressed, him and his wife was having some problems I guess and she was talking about leaving which I don't know if she left or not...."

After some questions about whether Dechaine was using drugs in the prison (nothing useful there), Hendsbee asked, "What kind of a guy does he appear to be like?"

"Calm, cool, and collective [sic]."

"Calm, cool, and collective?"

"Yup."

"He doesn't get upset too easy?"

"No. I mean them guys on the north side [of the segregation unit] they put him through pretty hell, but he never blew up at them or anything."

Hendsbee began winding down the interview, putting on the record the fact that he hadn't promised Dunn anything. And Dunn assured Hendsbee that he rarely bothered reading the newspapers, so his "knowledge" of the crime hadn't come from those sources. He was giving this information because, when Dechaine discussed the murder, "he'd start laughing about it and that's all funny. I don't like to see people like that."

"Okay, he didn't tell you anything else he might have done with the girl?"

"Not that I, oh wait a minute, something about a rape. While he was raping her, that's when he killed her. I think he's, that's what he said now that I remember right. While he was raping her afterwards then he killed her."

"Did he tell you that or did you hear that in the news?"

"Yup, no, no, I didn't hear that on the news. I'm not a news watcher either."

Nor was Mr. Dunn alone in his desire to "cooperate" with the police.

Joel Shyer, age twenty-two, serving his first prison sentence for "criminal mischief"—a category that covers a multitude of crimes—told Detective Steven Drake he'd been having a smoke outside the cell occupied by Dechaine and Dechaine's cellmate, Blakely. Blakely, according to Shyer, was bragging about how he'd entered a trailer owned by a man named Bailey, shot Bailey in the head with a .25 caliber pistol, then tossed the pistol into a pond. Shyer had more to relate of this killer's admissions but Drake interrupted, "O.K., so let's go back to Dennis Dechaine first. Take it one at a time."

The young inmate said, "All he was saying was how he needed sex because his wife wouldn't give it to him. And he was saying he went out and this thirteen-year-old girl, he wanted to have sex with her. She wouldn't give it to him and he, ah, she kept saying I'm gonna call the police, I'm gonna call the police. This is the way I heard him saying it. And then he said he didn't want no police involved and he didn't say how he did it but he said he did."

On February 18th, three weeks before trial, Connolly visited the prison again. According to his notes, "Dennis, quite frankly, was a mess. I am quite concerned about his status right now, given the fact that he has lost track of his personal appearance and hygiene as well, and his mental state is terrible. He was snappy and argumentative as well as bitter and plain old exhausted."

There were two basic causes. First, his and Nancy's relationship had deteriorated dramatically. The foundation which had sustained him was failing. The second influence was his confinement with Blakely—according to the official record, the murderer of five who'd been declared insane by a New Hampshire court and spent a dozen years in an asylum before being released, whereupon he killed again. Now, locked with Dechaine in this six-by-eight-foot cell—more cramped than the nine-by-twelve "reclusion" dungeons afforded prisoners as special punishment on Devil's Island, the infamous penal colony regarded as barbaric and closed by France a half-century earlier—Blakely babbled incessantly. He threatened inmates at random, including Dechaine, with no provocation. On at least one occasion, he'd assaulted Dechaine physically, and the man's sexual aggression kept Dechaine in a constant state of fear that he'd be sexually assaulted. There were, as time passed, other cellmates: the arsonist, the inmate who'd just come off suicide watch, the hyperactive burglar with Attention Deficit Disorder, and another burglar who couldn't stand light. Added to all that, the authorities now denied Dechaine access to any programs and even the hour-a-day respite from his cell for exercise, a privilege afforded everyone else in the Seg Unit.

Connolly noted, "Dennis continues to insist that it is his belief that the body was placed around his truck after the truck had been identified as his. It is Dennis's belief that, since no dogs sniffed out the body of the girl and since the search party did not find her until the next day, that somebody could have placed it there after his truck was labeled as involved with the crime. He indicated that the notebook in the driveway could have either come from himself stopping there, or more to the point, of him being set up. He honestly didn't know what happened and was trying to find some answers to the obviously very difficult questions facing him."

Dechaine's repeated insistence that he'd been "set up" seemed paranoid. It wasn't the wind that snatched his papers out of his truck and blew them miles through the air to land, side by side, at a crime scene. And who'd want to frame a gentle farmer with no known enemies?

From now through March, the media reported any and every act or comment about the case statewide. There were interviews with, or information released by the state police or the prosecutors, and there were citizen reactions to those statements. Television stories were accompanied by a replay of the file footage—a harried Dechaine being hustled in handcuffs from his arraignment.

Mark Twain once expressed, better than most, what most lawyers know: "We have a criminal jury system which is superior to any in the world; and its efficiency is only marred by the difficulty of finding twelve men every day who don't know anything and can't read."

6

The Prosecutor's Case

TRADITIONALLY, COURTS ARE BUILT to resemble churches—imposing structures with clock towers like steeples. The judge is robed in black, like a priest. The high bench where the judge presides is not unlike an altar.

The effect is premeditated.

Sometimes—God knows how often—in order to preserve the law's sacred image, its high priests reach back to ancient rites and sacrifice an innocent human before that altar.

The trial began on March 6, 1989, in Rockland, fifty miles up the coast from Bowdoin, because it was close to the state prison where Dechaine was being held and because, presumably, jurors could be found there who'd formed no opinion despite an intense nine months of sensational publicity. The state reported anonymous death threats aimed at the alleged child-killer. Security was tight. Spectators passed through metal detectors. Purses and jackets were checked by one of the seven security guards. Whether or not these precautions were necessary, they were certainly dramatic. And newsworthy.

The ninety-three-member jury pool filled the small

courtroom. There was no room for the press. By the end of the first afternoon, it was clear that these were not enough to find twelve jurors and two alternates untainted by publicity and otherwise acceptable. Another fifty subpoenas were sent out that night. Thirty of those called showed up the next morning.

We see juries as the backbone of fairness in our American judicial system. Chosen at random and summoned to the court, they are supposed to be men and women with nothing to win or lose by the outcome, no axe to grind. Ideally they can view the evidence objectively because they are strangers to everyone involved in the case and they're not contaminated by rumors, gossip, or any information that's irrelevant to the question they must decide.

This jury didn't quite fit that mold. Every man, woman and child in the State of Maine who read a newspaper, heard a radio or watched television knew all about the crime—all that the media had quoted from its official sources. The authorities, determined to satisfy the public's right to know, or to calm the citizenry, or coppering their courtroom bets, had armed future jurors with details, comments, and predictions, all of which implied Dechaine's guilt.

One man admitted during the *voir dire* questioning that he'd read about the case and had felt at the time, based on what he read and saw on TV, that the police arrested the right man. Connolly had exhausted his peremptory challenges. A challenge for cause failed because Judge Bradford accepted the man's assurance that he would be objective, set aside his pre-trial conclusions, and consider only that evidence presented at trial.

The twelve jurors and two alternates who were finally selected included a sail-maker, two teachers, a registered nurse, a former bookkeeper, a nursing control technician, a bank teller, a nautilus director, a manager, a cashier, a homemaker, a nursing home attendant, and a biology professor.

With a jury finally seated, reporters crammed the spectator section. The grand old brick and granite building hadn't seen so many cameras since Hollywood filmed scenes for *Peyton Place* here, thirty years before. The trial would continue until March 18th.

Assistant Attorney General Eric Wright—thin, angular, dressed in a gray suit—was well-experienced. He had graduated from Johns Hopkins University in Baltimore and Catholic University Law School in Washington. A prosecutor for ten years—the last five with the attorney general's office—he had a reputation for a quick mind, an unqualified grasp of the rules of evidence, and meticulous preparation. The son of librarians, he catalogued his evidence methodically. He'd drill his witnesses thoroughly before each trial. He'd have them say and repeat for the jury even the least significant facts. Eric Wright was a man who planned for every contingency.

Wright opened with a request that jurors focus on two questions: what happened, and who did it. "Perhaps it will be useful for you to understand that Sarah Cherry had just turned twelve years old last summer when, under circumstances that you shall hear about in painful detail, this defendant, Dennis Dechaine, took her life. Nobody else saw him do it. How then will we prove his guilt? We'll do it through the combined effect of physical evidence, the defendant's own words, and we'll conduct a relentless pursuit for the truth.

"Sarah Cherry would have been in the seventh grade this past fall. She had been in a gifted students program at her school and was active in scouting and church activities."

Wright took jurors through Sarah's acceptance of the babysitting job, her disappearance, the search and discovery of her body. He outlined her injuries, the disarray of her clothing, the appallingly brutal and dehumanizing indignities perpetrated upon her. He described Dechaine's conduct: his proximity to the place where Sarah was murdered; the lies he told to the Buttricks about where he lived and worked; his lie to the police about the car keys. Wright previewed evidence that the rope binding Sarah's wrists was the same kind as that found in his truck and in his barn. "But more than that, upon painstaking examination later at the state police crime laboratory, this last piece of rope found in the woods between Sarah's body and the truck was found to have been cut from the rope found in the defendant's truck. Those two pieces of rope were once one."

Wright told the men and women of the jury "that with respect to count one of the indictment, the state must prove to you that a death occurred intentionally or knowingly." He paused for a moment. "The word 'intentionally' means that one had a specific purpose in mind at the time he acted. The word 'knowingly' means that he was practically certain that a result would be accomplished by his actions...."

"Count two charges the crime of depraved indifference murder." Wright explained the legal elements of that crime. He did the same regarding the charge of kidnapping and the two charges of gross sexual misconduct.

"Now, the state's job is to have you understand this case just as clearly as you possibly can. Your focus should be on what the evidence is, and not what it is not...."

Wright also told the jury that, "Dechaine admitted to deputies that he had killed Sarah Cherry." Wright got away with distorting the officers' actual allegations of Dechaine's words because some judges let lawyers get away with practically anything in their opening and closing statements. It's pointless for opposing counsel to object.

Defense lawyer Tom Connolly began by reminding jurors that they'd taken an oath to be impartial. Then he said, "This will be a difficult case because what was done to that little girl was abominable. You will see no justification for that little girl's murder, for the killing of that little girl. She was blameless.... She was an innocent. She has been subjected to terrible crimes. We'll not defend the crimes themselves. What we'll do is point out during the course of this trial what the evidence shows, what it doesn't show, and bring forward our own evidence as to what was going on in Bowdoin, Maine, on July 6, 1988.

"As a preliminary matter, I want to give you an idea that has been with me since first getting involved in this case. It's a quotation from Albert Einstein. Einstein once wrote in a letter to Harry S. Truman, that every problem has a solution that is simple, and easy, and wrong. The state will have you believe that throughout an incredible series of possibilities and possibilities, that the defendant, Dennis Dechaine, who had never had any contact with either the Henkels or with Sarah Cherry, randomly happened upon her driveway where she was babysitting, randomly went into the house, seized her and committed the acts which are complained of. The possibility of that occurring is an enormous number. But that alone does not prove, of course, that the defendant did not do it.

"The state has referred to you a number of different pieces of evidence.... What they rely on primarily is as follows. First, a notebook found in the driveway. Secondly, the little girl is missing. Thirdly, the defendant appears from the woods and he couldn't find his truck. Fourthly, when they finally recover the body her hands are bound with a rope that came from the truck....That is the essence of the state's case as to physical evidence....

"And here is the dark secret of this case. Here is the part that causes defense attorneys and defendants to have numerous difficulties. I will be blunt. The explanation for the defendant's behavior on July 6, 1988, in response to the questioning of police officers as to the explanation of why he was in the woods is not favorable. It is not something that we are proud of.... What he did is, he went into the woods in the morning of July 6, 1988, and he used drugs. He went into the woods and got high. Now that is out. That does not mean he committed this murder. What it does mean is that he's in the woods at the time in the general area on the date in question. He's an easy set-up. That's what it means.

"Mr. Wright tells you that when the notebook is found in the driveway at approximately 3:30 that the police focus on Dennis Dechaine, and that will tell you an enormous amount about where the defense is going to go. From 3:30 until today they have focused exclusively on Dennis

Dechaine as the person who committed this offense. They have looked virtually nowhere else and they have ignored enormous evidence....

"There are no fingerprints in the truck. The prosecution tells you that is not to be concerned with because sometimes you aren't going to have fingerprints in a truck. That may very well be true. There is no hair in the truck. There is no blood in the truck. There is no indication in the truck that the little girl was ever there. At the house, the Henkel residence where she was abducted between 12:00 and 3:30 there is not a hint of a struggle inside of the house. There is not a hint that Dennis Dechaine was there physically. There is not a fingerprint, not a hair, not a fiber, not a footprint, no witness that will place him there. What is there is a notebook with a receipt in it that was found there. The State will tell you that they didn't bother to fingerprint the notebook because it was handled by too many people. I submit to you based upon your own experience you know that items can be taken from a vehicle and placed elsewhere. If that is the situation, then the notebook is not only not conclusive of the defendant's involvement in this crime, but the contrary. It can be used to show that he was in fact set up....

"During the course of the struggle which occurred between Sarah Cherry and her captor, the State would have you believe that no transference occurred, no fibers, no hairs, no blood ever transferred.... She has blood under her fingernails. Type A blood. What type is Dennis Dechaine? Type O blood....

"The state would have you believe, if you remember, that he parked his truck on the opposite side of the roadway from where her body is found and brought her across the roadway in plain view of anyone passing by in order to do his fiendishness. That is the theory that the state has. Then the state will have you believe that continuing until now, Dennis Dechaine will lie about his involvement in this crime...."

Prosecutor Wright called Sarah's mother, Debra Crosman, to the stand. She told of Sarah's excellent school performance, her enjoyment of baseball, basketball, soccer and cross-country skiing, her involvement in Brownies and Girl Scouts, the YWCA summer camp, and the Youth Fellowship at church.

Wright asked, "What happened when you last saw Sarah before leaving that day?"

"She was still in bed," Debra replied, struggling to maintain her composure. "I went up and kissed her goodbye and told her don't worry. If anything happens don't be afraid to call either me or her grandmother or Mrs. Henkel at work."

"Had you given her any other instruction about how she should perform her duties as a baby-sitter?"

"Not that morning, but the night before I had."

"Tell us about that."

"It was the same thing. We always told the kids when we leave don't let anybody in the house; if anybody calls don't tell them that they are alone; don't be afraid to call somebody if you need help."

"If you can say, what was her kind of feelings or attitude about the job she was about to undertake?"

"She was excited and a little nervous because it was

the first time she baby-sat a baby."

"An infant child?"

"Yes."

"Had she done any baby-sitting outside of your family?"

"Just one other time."

"Sarah was an athletic child?"

"Yes."

"She was a good athlete?"

"Yes."

"What position did she play in baseball?"

"About every position there was."

"She did basketball and cross-country skiing?"

"Yes."

"She was no wimp?"

"No."

"She was a little on the tomboy side?"

"Yes."

John Henkel took the stand to tell about receiving a phone call at work from his wife, telling him Sarah was missing. Upon arriving at his home, he saw unfamiliar tire tracks in the gravel driveway, so he placed a series of stones around the tracks to keep them from being obliterated. (Later, a state police technician would testify that these tire tracks were "consistent with" the front tires on Dechaine's Toyota.) Mr. Henkel identified the notebook and receipt his wife found in the driveway, and told of driving about with a neighbor searching for the truck described on the receipt. They'd driven up the Hallowell Road from Dead River Road to Litchfield Corners and back, twice passing the side-spur where Dechaine's truck would be found, later that night, without seeing it.

Wright asked, "This all was being done while it was still daytime?"

"Yes."

Henkel described his television set inside a cabinet in his living room with windows to either side of the cabinet.

Wright asked, "If the TV set was being viewed, merely by standing up one could look out into the driveway?"

"Yes."

"And it's fair to say that upon the approach of a vehicle or even if a vehicle is going by slowly, the dogs get sometimes agitated and excited?"

"Yes."

"They are two hundred pounds of dog, so they make a good bark together?"

"Yes."

Connolly saw no reason to cross-examine. The court recessed for lunch.

Under questioning by Eric Wright, Rose Knodt, Henkel's employer, testified, "We weren't eating lunch so I don't know if he went out for lunch or—I'm not sure about that. But throughout the whole day he was there."

"Except if he went out for lunch?"

"Yes."

"Had he done that, if he had, how long would he have gone out for lunch?"

"The most would have been an hour."

"Do you have any independent recollection that indeed

he went out for an hour that day?"

"No."

She'd been to the Henkel house and the travel time was between thirty and forty-five minutes from her business.

"And aside from the time when he may have been gone for lunch, he was with you for the entire day?"

"Yes."

"Let me here understand. Is it your testimony that he could have been with you all day but he might have been out for that time period you described."

"Yes."

Jennifer Henkel recounted her instructions to Sarah that morning and, "It was a very hot day also. So I thought she might, for a little break in the middle of the day, want to take the baby outside. So we went downstairs and I took the stroller out and unfolded it and showed her how that worked. She seemed to think she might want to have a break in the middle of the day. So we did that and went back inside and I kind of made sure she was comfortable...."

"Did it seem to you that Sarah was up to the task of taking care of Monica?"

"Yes. She seemed to be excited. She really loved babies and children and I had seen her with the children for a long time and had really admired how she was with them. She was very kind and understanding and gentle and self-possessed...."

"Upon leaving did you lock the doors to your house, or leave them unlocked?"

"I did not lock them."

"Why not?"

"As I left I stood there thinking...she might want to go outside and play or sit in the shade and get some fresh air while the baby is sleeping. I didn't want her to get locked out of the house. So I left the door unlocked. I didn't want her to accidentally have the door slam and not be able to get back in."

Downstairs and upstairs doors were both shut, but unlocked. Around noon, Mrs. Henkel called her home. "I spoke with her and found out that everything was indeed under control. She was feeding the baby and about to fix herself some lunch." They talked for about two minutes and Mrs. Henkel could hear her baby making the gurgling and banging noises babies make when they eat.

Mrs. Henkel told of coming home at about 3:20 P.M. and finding the papers in her driveway. Wright asked, "How far apart were these two items, the notebook and the piece of paper?"

"Only a couple of inches. It was six inches. They were quite close together." The only other thing she noticed as she walked to the house was the stroller. It was where she had left it, parked in the same position. When she reached the house, the door was ajar about an inch-and-a-half.

"Did that strike you as odd?"

"It did strike me as odd, yes."

"Tell us what happened next."

"I went upstairs. And when I got to the top of the stairs, the upper door was open. And I thought that was pretty odd, too."

"How far was that door open?"

"The same. An inch-and-a-half. Just slightly."

"What struck you as odd about the fact the doors were slightly ajar?"

"It was summertime and we don't have screens on the doors. We live in the woods. You usually don't leave the doors open. It struck me as strange. You try to keep as many mosquitoes outside as we can."

She described going inside, seeing that baby Monica was sleeping peacefully, and looking for Sarah. She called out, she searched her home, she went outside and looked around the yard, called out some more. No Sarah. She called a neighbor, but the neighbor hadn't seen anything unusual. She phoned her husband and he came home. She called the police and Sarah's mother. A short time later, sheriff's deputies arrived.

A resident along Dead River Road testified to seeing a man in a blue shirt come out of the woods and pass behind his house at about 8:30 on the evening in question. He couldn't identify the man—"I never saw him face-on."

Mrs. Buttrick told of her and her husband's encounter with Dechaine at 8:45 P.M. She recounted his lies about where he lived and worked. She also said he acted like a gentleman.

Deputy Sheriff Leo Scopino told jurors how he'd responded to Mrs. Henkel's call and begun the search for the Toyota described on the auto repair estimate found in the driveway. He and Deputy Reed had gone down the road to check a similar truck but that was a red and white Dodge Ram. No, he hadn't photographed it. No, he didn't recall the driver's name. "He was in the woods. He was a soil tester. He was out there with his whatever they do, screw something in the ground and pull the plugs up. That's what he was doing."

Scopino told of questioning Dechaine and seeing fresh scratch marks on him.

On cross-examination, Connolly asked, "Is it true that a person with little experience with police officers, in your experience, gets frightened when they are in custody and getting searched?"

"Objection."

"Overruled."

Connolly continued, "Sometimes it's terrifying; is that not true? You've had people under your custody that wet themselves?"

The judge said, "There are two questions pending."

Connolly repeated, "People get terrified when they are in custody, isn't that true sometimes?"

"Not all the times, no."

"Sometimes, sir?"

"It's a possibility."

"Especially if you are being accused of something very serious, isn't that true?"

"It could be."

"If he was being accused of kidnapping a girl he would be right to be terrified, wouldn't he?"

Wright said, "I would object."

"Sustained."

Connolly asked, "His eyes were wide open?"

"Yes."

"Is that an indication of somebody being terrified?"

"Objection!"

"Overruled."

Scopino allowed, "It exists."

"He was cooperative, wasn't he?"

"He was okay for me."

"How would you describe his trembling?"

Scopino demonstrated how Dechaine had shook.

"Is that consistent with a person that is frightened?"

"Could be."

"You don't know?"

"No, I don't." Scopino said he searched the suspect and found nothing of value.

"You were trained, a police officer that would have noticed anything else that was on a person of consequence."

"Yes, I guess."

"We are not asking you to guess. We are asking you to be sure."

"Yes."

"When Mr. Dechaine was asked to empty out his pockets, was he cooperative with you?"

"I had no problems with him."

The worst was yet to come.

But so was the best.

7

The Hidden Key

THE NEXT MORNING BEGAN with prosecutor and defense lawyer in the judge's chambers. Connolly wanted to cross-examine officers regarding Dechaine's mental state during the interrogations by different officers. "In essence," Connolly told Judge Bradford, "he's attempting to be cooperative but he's very concerned because he's getting leaned on pretty heavily at the time."

Wright—worried that Connolly would object to statements Dechaine made to officers after being advised of his Miranda rights and asking for an attorney—told the judge, "He's waived that by not filing a motion to suppress. It's a matter of constitutional right. He's chosen not to exercise it."

The judge told Connolly, "I don't question your right to bring out testimony that will explain the circumstances, but you can't use the tactic of cross-examination to attack any statements that otherwise would have been subject to a motion to suppress under Rule 41A."

Judge Bradford acknowledged that Connolly had been on solid ground "in attacking Scopino yesterday because that was almost like the gang that couldn't shoot straight; the manner in which the left hand didn't know what the right hand was doing." He allowed that the lawyer had "an absolute right to bring out the circumstances such as mental condition, physical condition, emotional condition of Mr. Dechaine at the time these statements are made. But it's one thing to bring that line of inquiry out from an arresting officer and quite another to attack the officer as somehow having done something wrong."

Connolly agreed to proceed with the utmost caution.

Eric Wright wound up his direct examination of Deputy Daniel Reed with the question, "Had you, Deputy Reed, to that point that evening, or any other officer to your knowledge, ever told Dennis Dechaine that Sarah Cherry had been abducted, kidnapped, taken, whatever the phrase might be?"

"No sir, I did not. I informed him that we were investigating a missing twelve-year-old girl."

"His response was that the girl had been grabbed?"

"Yes."

Deputy James Clancy told of finding Dechaine's Toyota on the night of July 6th as he drove down the Hallowell Road with his car's "alley light" shining off to the side. He estimated the pickup was parked down an old trail, about seventy-five feet from the road. Some foliage had sprung up behind the Toyota after being driven over, but Clancy was able to see it from Hallowell Road.

Trooper Bureau recounted his and Detective Hendsbee's walk from Dechaine's truck through the woods behind the tracking dog. He told of hearing deer in the woods off to one side. He described the dog's finding a piece of rope the next day—between the trail his dog had apparently lost, and the spot where the body was found—a length of rope which lab experts certified as having been cut from a piece of identical rope in Dechaine's pickup.

Detective Hendsbee related the events of his investigation, his interrogation of the defendant, and the goose bumps he'd observed when he predicted how this girl's killer would feel goose bumps every time he remembered the girl.

Tom Connolly's cross-examination focused on Dechaine's behavior throughout the interrogations by different officers.

Prosecutor Wright objected. "There has been no—that's a misleading question entirely."

Connolly turned to the judge, "Your honor—"

Wright said, "He wasn't with him for six-and-a-half hours."

"If you gentlemen are through," the judge said, "my ruling is that the objection is sustained based upon the limited knowledge of this police officer testifying or answering that question based upon his own knowledge. The objection is sustained."

Connolly turned back to Detective Hendsbee. "Based upon your knowledge, what time did the defendant first appear in the gracious custody of the police?"

"Between 9:30 and ten o'clock."

"He was finally released at what time?"

"4:10 in the morning."

"How many hours is that?"

"Six hours."

"Was that voluntary or not?"

"Yes."

"He voluntarily consented, did he not, to a search of his truck?"

"Yes."

"He voluntarily consented to a search of his pockets?"

"I don't know that."

"He voluntarily consented to have his picture taken?"

"Yes."

"And his body parts examined?"

"Yes."

"The only odd behavior you saw was goose bumps, is that correct?"

"Yes. It was strange."

"You saw no blood on his clothing?"

"That's correct."

"You saw no unexplained hairs or fibers on his clothing?"

"I didn't examine him for that."

"He was in your gracious custody for how long?"

"Two hours."

"You are an eighteen-and-a-half-year detective or trained officer; is that correct?"

"Yes."

"You have been through multiple training courses on examining physical evidence; is that correct?"

"Yes."

"And it's true that you understand the importance of fiber evidence in the prosecution of a serious crime?"

"Yes."

"The same with hair evidence; you've used it yourself in many cases?"

"Yes."

But Hendsbee said he hadn't looked closely at Dechaine's clothing. "As a matter of fact, I wanted his shirt and pants."

"Did you ask him?"

"I didn't push the issue." Nor was Hendsbee surprised at Dechaine's cooperative conduct. "Most people I talk to are cooperative."

"Do you find that people, the fact that people are cooperative has anything to do with whether in fact they are involved with what you are talking to them about?"

"No."

Sergeant Allen of the Warden's Service told how he'd been summoned to where the body was found, touching Sarah's forehead and finding it cold. He'd called out but there was no response.

Sailor James McGee related how he and fellow volunteers from the Brunswick Naval Air Station had searched for and found the body. He's also found footprints in the mud of a stream bed a few feet away, and more footprints further upstream. They were unlike the boots worn by the Navy volunteers. They'd been made by a street shoe.

Connolly had no questions for the sailor. Court recessed for lunch.

❖

The parade continued throughout the afternoon. State police lab man Joseph Gallant showed photos of footprints found near the body along with a five-minute video of the entire scene, and described various items he'd found in searching the area: a red fiber stuck to a tree; a hair from a branch a few feet from the ground; and a cigarette butt found beside Dechaine's truck.

Next came Dr. Ronald Roy from the state's office of the medical examiner—tall with glasses, his hair just beginning to gray, wearing a gray tweed sport jacket over a white shirt and red bow tie, and slacks. An important witness, his testimony fills fifty-six pages of the official transcript.

Called to the scene when the body was found, he described what he saw: Sarah's corpse covered with five or six inches of foliage and sticks, enough to fill two large garbage bags. The amount of blood on the ground beneath her head suggested to him that she'd been actively bleeding there.

Dr. Roy said she'd been stabbed with "a small knife," although some might wonder how he knew that, since any pointed blade, even a stiletto, can be wielded to make small, shallow wounds. Dr. Roy didn't explain. Perhaps it's unfair to assume that his conclusion was based solely on the state's evidence that Dechaine had once carried a tiny pen-knife on his keychain.

Wright asked, "What was the condition of rigor mortis in this case upon the removal of debris from the body and further examination?"

"Rigor mortis was still present," Dr. Roy said, "but it was broken relatively easily. In my opinion, it was passing off."

"Given the body that you found, could you reach any conclusion as to the time of death?"

"The passing off of rigor mortis suggested that we are talking probably thirty hours or more. And I do know when she disappeared and the changes are consistent with that time, consistent with having occurred two days prior."

He went on to explain for the jury how the process known as rigor mortis—this stiffening of the muscles after death and its subsequent passing off—is affected by environment. "Temperature will hasten the processes. An elevated temperature will speed it up and make its onset quicker and its disappearance quicker....Strenuous physical exertion may hasten the onset of rigor mortis...."

Wright asked whether anything in this case was "inconsistent with what you've already suggested to have been the passage of time between death and discovery of the body?"

"Well, somebody found in the woods in August [sic] who had been dead for two days, I would expect to find more fly activity. But her body was covered with debris which accounts for why it is not as advanced as I would have expected it."

"Fly activity meaning what?"

"Flies who land on the body and lay [eggs] on the body at sites of injury and the eyes."

Dr. Roy described the position of the body when he first saw it. "She was lying on her back with most of her torso turned to the left. Her face was turned towards the left. Her legs were flexed up towards her stomach and were laying on their left side. Her hands were in front of her and they were tied together by plastic rope...moderately tight. It could have been tighter. It would be difficult to remove your hands."

He described her clothing. "She had on a light purple-colored shirt, a short-sleeve shirt, and there were blue jeans which were pulled down to around her knee level so they were pulled down beyond the feet. There was no underwear.

No lower underwear. And at the autopsy I also found she was wearing a brassiere." The bra was pushed up above the small breasts. The top half of Sarah's shirt was bloodied but there were no holes in it. The gag in her mouth was a blue bandanna held in place by a woolen scarf—a scarf that was also wound very tightly and knotted twice around Sarah's throat. That ligature had constricted Sarah's neck to a diameter of two-and-a-half or three inches.

"There were birch sticks," Dr. Roy went on to say, "one stuck in the vagina and one in the rectum, protruding from these orifices." Each of the inch-wide sticks had penetrated to a depth of nearly four inches. He certified that Sarah had been a virgin and, from the bleeding, that the injuries were inflicted while Sarah was alive.

At one point, Dr. Roy held the clothes Sarah had worn that day, pointed out her bloodstains. He showed jurors the scarf that had strangled the life out of the little girl. He showed them the ropes...and the sticks.

Some jurors were seen wiping tears away.

The body was transported to Augusta. During the autopsy, Dr. Roy catalogued a knife wound under Sarah's chin; marks of a sharp instrument run across her neck; eight stab wounds on her head, neck, and several clustered around Sarah's left breast. But the incisions were superficial, just breaking the surface of the skin. And they were done while Sarah was alive.

Wright asked, "Did that suggest anything to you as to the manner of what was going on when those were being inflicted?"

"That sounds like torture to me. I can't think of any

other reason for doing it."

He described abrasions and bruises on the girl's lips.

Wright referred to evidence that Sarah had eaten hotdogs around noon on Wednesday and asked, considering the state of digestion revealed by the autopsy, "does it suggest to you that the hotdogs appeared to be eaten for lunch?"

"Yes. This is consistent with her last known meal. And that death occurred within a few hours of eating her last meal."

Tom Connolly was at something of a disadvantage, since none of Dr. Roy's reports which had been furnished to him with the discovery material had mentioned any opinion regarding time of death. In the autopsy form's block for Time of Injury, Dr. Roy had written simply, "Found 7/8/88."

Connolly began his cross-examination with a few general questions.

Then, "In reference to the time of death, Dr. Roy, it would be fair to say that it was reasonably elastic in the sense you cannot be precise as to the time of death?"

"That's correct."

"The variable would be at a minimum a six-hour period, perhaps even longer?"

"I wouldn't accept six hours, no. Not at all." After a few more questions, Dr. Roy summarized, "The parameters of rigor mortis suggests probably a minimum of thirty to thirty-six hours and it could well be longer. The presence of food in the stomach indicates it happened most likely a short time after she ate, so I know she is missing two days. All of these findings are compatible with the fact when I saw her she had been dead two days." He wouldn't say she'd been dead as early as three or four or five o'clock on that Wednesday afternoon.

"So it is fair to say that the time of death is July 6th and nothing more. Is that a fair statement?"

"That's a fair statement."

"So it could be as late as ten or eleven o'clock on July 6th, it's possible?"

"Yes."

"It's possible it could be as late as midnight?"

"I don't see why not."

Connolly brought out the absence of any bruising caused by the rope binding Sarah's wrists, but he was certain that the strangulation occurred after the infliction of the stab wounds.

Connolly asked about Sarah's feet.

Dr. Roy hadn't noticed Sarah's feet.

On redirect examination, Prosecutor Wright asked how likely it was that Sarah was still alive as late as eleven o'clock that Wednesday night "if she was last heard of at noon and given the information you know about the remnants of lunch or what you found in the digestion of the hot dog?"

"I couldn't rule it out."

"What is the likelihood?"

"I don't know."

Wright went on to bring out Dr. Roy's opinion that the defendant could easily have inflicted these small wounds on Sarah without being spattered with any of her blood. Nor did he believe that the blood under Sarah's fingernails came from her assailant.

Fingerprint examiner Ronald Richards told of finding four latent prints on the Toyota. Three were Dechaine's; one, found on the truck's hood, couldn't be identified. Another lab technician introduced impressions of the Toyota's front tires, plus two unidentified fingerprints lifted from the door of the Henkel house.

Forensic Chemist Judith Brinkman testified to her examination of the Toyota's contents, then described hairs clinging to the scarf that had strangled Sarah—her own hairs—and blood found beneath the girl's fingernails. The blood was Type A, the same type as Sarah's. Dechaine's blood was type O. Brinkman's conclusion: the blood had gotten there when Sarah clawed at her wounds. Brinkman also certified the rope binding Sarah's wrists as consistent with rope found in the Toyota.

Detective Hendsbee returned to tell about Dechaine's statements when Hendsbee and Lieutenant McCarthy came to serve the search warrant on his house. "When I pulled in, Dennis came down off the porch toward my car, and at a rapid pace. His wife was following him. Dennis stated that I know what you are here for. I can't believe I could do such a thing. It's not—"

The prosecutor interrupted, "If you don't remember, please refer to your notes."

Hendsbee opened his notes. "He stated: 'I don't believe that I could do such a thing. The real me is not like that. I know me. I couldn't do anything like that. It must be somebody else inside of me.' At that time, I hadn't even gotten out of my car."

"It must have been somebody else inside me...?"

"Who is doing this."

"You hadn't said that. It must be somebody else inside me doing this?"

"Yes. At the time, I hadn't even gotten out of my car. I asked Dennis to step away from the door so I could get out of the car, at which time he did. But he kept saying 'there has got to be somebody else inside of me doing this. I couldn't have done such a thing.'"

Hendsbee told of the difficulties in searching such a large house and keeping an eye on the residents to make sure they didn't change anything during the search. He'd taken the recently laundered shirt and trousers from the clothesline, and Dechaine had given him the Nike sneakers he'd been wearing on Wednesday. Prosecutor Wright asked how Dechaine was behaving during the search.

"He was real nervous. He was sad at times. Basically real nervous."

A short time later, Hendsbee said, "I arrested him."

"Tell us what his reaction was to being placed under arrest."

"He was upset."

Sheriff's Detective Westrum was recalled to the stand, where he assured the court that there had been no interrogation of the suspect: Westrum had posed no question to him. But at one point, in the men's room, Westrum said, ". . . he started to wash his hands and he said: 'I don't know whatever made me do that.' I didn't answer him. Then he said, 'I can't believe it happened.'"

"During that time did his demeanor change at all?"

"He started to cry somewhat."

Back in the booking room, Westrum testified, Dechaine had said, "Oh my God, it should never have happened.... Why did I do this?...I went home and told my wife that I did something bad and she just laughed at me."

Westrum now referred to his notes but the rest of Dechaine's statements were just repetitions of what he'd already been quoted as saying.

Wright objected to a number of Connolly's questions to Westrum. Following one of these objections, Connolly requested a sidebar conference with the judge.

"Your Honor," Connolly said, "he has given a conclusion as to professionalism, which requires an opinion based upon his experience which is, that he thought Officer Reed was acting professional." Connolly felt that he had a right to ask whether certain conduct constituted professional behavior.

The judge asked, "Assuming what you say is true, how is this relevant?"

"To establish that he was inconsistent with professional behavior."

"You've established that *ad nauseam*," the judge said. "Not only through Deputy Reed but up to this point with this witness. So, under Rule 403, I'm going to exclude it."

Later on, when he caught Westrum embroidering onto his earlier statements with new allegations, Connolly asked bluntly, "What else have you left out?"

"That's it," Westrum said.

"Are you sure?"

"To the best of my recollection."

"If I ask you in ten more minutes are you going to add something in?"

Wright objected.

The judge sustained Wright's objection.

Court was adjourned. Jurors would have the night to mull over Westrum's account of Dechaine's statements.

When testimony resumed in the morning, jailers told of hearing Dechaine tell them he ought to be locked "in isolation" because, "I'm the guy that killed that little girl."

For all the good it would do him, Dechaine would always claim he'd told the jailers that he was the man "accused of" killing the girl. And use of the term "in isolation," as opposed to the more common civilian use of "solitary," by a farmer with no previous jail experience would suggest that someone—probably an officer accompanying him to the jail—had suggested he make this request for a private cell. But no juror would consider that a defendant's word outweighed the testimony of two jail guards.

With the jailer's statements, Prosecutor Wright said, "The state rests, your honor."

Now, all Tom Connolly had to do was dim the horrifying pictures of Sarah's last hours; explain his client's papers at the scene, his ropes, and the "confessions." And overcome every juror's innate assumption that no man would be on trial if he wasn't guilty.

8

Dechaine's Defense

Tom Connolly paraded witness after witness before the jury to tell how long and how well they'd known this man whom they swore was a shy, friendly farmer, a man who simply didn't possess the personality that could commit such a ghastly crime.

Kent Womack told about one night in India. "Dennis and I were walking around the streets of the neighborhood where we were staying. This was in Delhi. We had stopped to admire a stand of fruit and flowers that the street vendors had, despite the poverty and unsanitary conditions. It was a beautiful display. Dennis was particularly interested since it was his line of work.

"As we were standing there, perhaps fifty yards up the road we heard an argument break out. As we turned, one of the men had a bottle which he hit the other man with and dropped the bottle and ran away. There was a large crowd of people there who immediately surrounded the injured man who was bleeding profusely and seemed trying to get themselves organized, trying to do something with him. This was early in the evening. Both Dennis and I, I think, had similar reactions. Dennis described it as—"

Wright stood up. "I would object to it."

Judge Bradford said, "Sustained."

Connolly explained to the witness, "You can't quote somebody else. How did he physically react? What was his attitude and demeanor and his response?"

"He felt physically repulsed. He felt like a hollow feeling in his stomach. And that evening neither of us felt like having dinner because it was just very upsetting to see that kind of behavior."

Asked whether he had ever seen any similar response to violence from Dechaine, Womack told of an incident after they'd returned home from India.

"Dennis was giving me a tour of the farm that he and Nancy had just bought where they keep goats. I asked Dennis what can you do with goats? He said—"

"Objection."

Wright objected again because Womack's answer would have constituted hearsay, i.e., "a statement, other than one made by the witness while testifying at a trial, offered in evidence to prove the truth of the matter asserted."

It is doubtful that anyone believed Womack's recollection of Dechaine's comment was being offered to prove the truth of what a person could do with goats, but the judge sustained Wright's objection anyway.

Away from the jury and spectators, the judge held a conference in chambers with prosecutor Wright, Joseph Field as lawyer for indicted child molester Douglas Senecal, an assistant attorney general named Marchese who was there to represent the Department of Human Services (DHS), Tom

Connolly, and the first lawyer Dechaine had consulted, George Carlton, still hanging in on Connolly's sufferance as co-counsel.

Connolly wanted to call Senecal to the stand. The man had already been indicted for having sexually abused Jackie Crosman, the natural daughter of Sarah's stepfather, Chris Crosman, a girl who'd been living with her natural mother and Senecal. But that case was dismissed because Jackie vanished. Chris Crosman told Sheriff Haggett he'd received a phone call from Jackie who'd told him she was living at the YWCA in San Diego because her mother, Maureen, Senecal's wife, had given her money to leave the state. Eventually, the case against Senecal was dismissed—coincidentally by Judge Bradford—because the state's witness, Jackie, was unavailable. But that dismissal didn't occur until after Sarah's murder.

DHS worker Bonnie Holiday had given all this information to Detective Hendsbee when she heard of Sarah's disappearance. She also stated that the family was very violent, and that Senecal "has been behaving real strange since [Sarah's] death. Not sad but strange. The whole family went to the funeral except for Doug Senecal."

On the day of Sarah's disappearance or the day after, a witness named Pam Babine took a bicycle to Senecal's home for Jackie's sister. She'd stated that Senecal was shaking so much he couldn't hold the bike.

Then Connolly summarized the meeting he'd had with Senecal, lawyer Field, and Eric Wright, where Senecal had offered four witnesses to account for his time on the day in question. But each of them had been interviewed by

Connolly's investigator at the time, Jim Pinette, "and not one of them can confirm his statement." His wife, Maureen Senecal, could account for his time between noon and 1:20 P.M., but that was all.

This was Connolly's position: Jackie's sister, Jessica, stayed at the Crosman home with Sarah during the days just before the crime; Sarah told Jessica where she'd be babysitting on July 6th; Jessica told Senecal. Connolly believed that Senecal wanted to make sure Sarah wouldn't testify against him in the sexual abuse case. Since he was under court order not to be near Jessica, and Jessica was staying with Sarah, the only way he could see Sarah was to catch her away from the Crosman home.

If Dechaine was innocent, Connolly told the judge, someone else did it. "The fact that Doug Senecal had a motive, perhaps arguable, that the jury could conclude the opportunity because he was driving his pickup truck which fit the description of the vehicle seen on Lewis Hill Road during the period in question, a jury could conclude, as the finder of fact, in the light most favorable to the defendant, that he knew her whereabouts."

The absence of evidence indicating a struggle would suggest that she knew her attacker and voluntarily entered his vehicle. For whatever reason, things got out of hand. Afterwards, Connolly believed, Senecal used items from Dechaine's truck to frame him.

Senecal's lawyer, Joseph Field, told the judge that he had no reason to believe Sarah would have been a witness in the case against Senecal. "The only information I got in response to my request for discovery was basically a very brief report from [Sheriff] David Haggett and a copy of the defendant's speeding record.... It could be inferred from the police report that Jackie Crosman and [DHS worker] Jennifer Dox and David Haggett would have been the witnesses in the case."

This paucity of information seemed odd to Connolly because, on the day he'd had that interview with Senecal, Joseph Field's file on his client was about two inches thick. Connolly couldn't inquire into that because Joseph Field, as Senecal's attorney, had a strict obligation to maintain his client's confidentiality. That vow of client confidentiality is so ingrained in the law, so vital to the functioning of a fair judicial system, that it's enshrined as one of the very, very few privileges which no court can violate.

Eric Wright argued that Senecal would probably take the Fifth Amendment if he were called to the stand; and the sister had already denied knowing where Sarah would be that day. "We don't have evidence in an admissible form. We don't have evidence that Doug Senecal can properly give before the jury, and we don't have any reasonable probability that any of this is going to pan out to anything." He called Connolly's efforts "silliness in the extreme."

"I have a right," Connolly said, "to put on evidence which would tend to exculpate this defendant. The defendant has pled not guilty. He's testified that he did not do this homicide. Therefore, there are facts that could lead a jury to believe that Doug Senecal was involved." He then prevailed upon Judge Bradford to read the confidential DHS file himself to see whether it contained any indication that Sarah had been a witness.

After a brief interval, the judge told the others that there was nothing in the file regarding Sarah. Therefore, "it is the judgment of this court that it would be inappropriate for defense counsel to call Mr. Senecal for the purposes outlined in the offer of proof."

Connolly moved on to the matter of the murder. Susan Norris lived in Bowdoinham, though she didn't know Dechaine. She was forty-one, a secretary at the local cable company. Her husband worked for the State Fire Marshal's Office. They had one child. She testified about informing Detective Hendsbee regarding the red pickup that pulled into her yard when she was expecting someone in answer to her ad, offering a tractor for sale. Its driver was an average-sized male wearing a ball cap. His companion, seated close to him, was a small girl with curly, light brown hair. After just a moment, the man had turned around and driven away quickly. Yes, she'd been shown a copy of the statement she'd made to the detective.

"Are there some irregularities in that statement?"

"A couple."

"What are those?"

"It referred to the truck as being a small truck. And I didn't say it was a small truck. I said it was a full-sized pickup truck."

Nor had it backed out. "If it had backed out, I couldn't have seen the tailgate." The tailgate was damaged. The next weekend she'd seen what she believed to be this same truck. It was parked in front of the house where, she was told, Dechaine lived. But Dechaine's Toyota was still at the state police lab in Augusta.

Yes, she'd reported this sighting to the police.

The prosecutor cross-examined Mrs. Norris. Yes, she was certain that the truck in the photo shown her by police—Dechaine's Toyota—was not the vehicle which had pulled into her yard.

"The driver of the vehicle that you saw on the sixth had glasses on?"

"Yes."

"The person who was with him may have been a woman?"

"Yes."

"Who was sitting close to the driver?"

"Yes."

"As if a boyfriend-girlfriend type of thing?"

"Possibly."

Justine Dennison, thirty-four, married, and living in Bowdoinham, knew Dechaine. She told of passing Dechaine, driving north in his Toyota, at about noon on July sixth. Her husband, Brian, took the stand to relate conversations he'd had with Dechaine in the past regarding fishing holes and a pond just off the Lewis Hill Road that looked like a good spot.

Gary Jasper testified about passing a red Toyota pickup on the Dead River Road the afternoon of July 6th. Its driver "had long, dark sandy-colored hair and he was wearing a dark shirt." He couldn't say, one way or another, whether that man was Dechaine, but he'd been at the home of a friend, Ralph Jones on the Dead River Road around 7:30 that evening, and Jones had seen a man getting into that same truck.

Connolly wanted to call a witness who could testify to a break-in and the killing of a cat at the fruit stand where Dechaine kept the notebook later found in the Henkel driveway. The prosecutor objected. Judge Bradford decided: there was no proof that this notebook had been taken in the break-in, nor that the killing of the cat had any relevance to this case. "It would be pure speculation that someone was trying to set Dennis Dechaine as a fall guy for a crime and would go beyond that to a point of killing Sarah Cherry and to lay the blame on him. Everything is so remote at this time that I can't let this kind of evidence in."

Dechaine's former wife, Nancy—she'd divorced him to preserve her half of their marital property from the Cherry family's lawsuit—testified to his inability to hurt the farm animals. Regarding their attempt to slaughter their own chickens, she said, "We decided at a dollar-fifty, it was worth trying it ourselves. I didn't want to be part of it. Dennis said he would try. He killed the chicken and said I can't do it. It's worth a dollar-fifty for someone else to do it."

"You raised rabbits?"

"Yes"

"The same situation?"

"Yes."

Connolly wanted to show photographs of the building of two greenhouses.

Prosecutor Wright objected, "because the photographs are designed to prey upon the jury...I think they suggest some sort of character traits about the defendant which are beyond that which the court has limited us to in this inquiry."

The judge selected one of the ten pictures Connolly offered, "one that shows the general outline of the site and what a greenhouse looks like under construction." He thought that would be sufficient.

Regarding the evening TV broadcast of Sarah Cherry's photograph, Nancy testified that Dennis' reaction was "non-recognition."

Connolly asked what he'd said.

Wright objected.

Connolly argued that Dechaine's statement qualified as "an 'excited utterance' exception to the hearsay rule." Wright's objection was overruled.

"What did Dennis say?"

"He said, 'My God, I've never seen that girl before.'" He'd also told Nancy he'd never kidnapped anyone.

Connolly produced photographs of ropes suspending the fluorescent lights in the Dechaine's greenhouse. "Did you see who tied the knots on those?"

"Yes."

"Who tied those knots?"

"Dennis did."

Connolly wanted the photos introduced as evidence. The knots were different from those that bound Sarah's wrists.

Prosecutor Wright said, "I'm not certain as to the relevance. I would object."

"Overruled."

Nancy testified, too, that, "I had a 1980 Chevrolet full-size pickup." It was red with a green door. Yes, the tailgate was damaged. The keys for that vehicle were usually kept in a side table in the Dechaine kitchen.

Next, Nancy told of waking up one night long ago, and hearing Dennis in the bathroom. When she got up to see whether he was all right, she heard him lock the door. She'd asked him what he was doing. He said he'd be right out. "So I kicked the door and found Dennis with a syringe and needle in his arm."

"What was your reaction?"

"Very upset."

"And this was a family issue? Did it suddenly become a marital issue?"

"It certainly did."

"And did you give him an ultimatum?"

"I did." She told her husband she'd leave him if she ever caught him using drugs again.

❖

Clinical psychologist Dr. Roger Ginn examined Dechaine before the trial. The drug use was already before the jury, and Connolly wanted to dispel the notion that the drug had converted this gentle farmer into the fiend who'd torture and murder a little girl.

Among Ginn's conclusions, stated in the report Connolly had given Wright as the defense obligation in the discovery process:

> There is nothing to suggest problems with anger, aggressiveness, or hostility. In general, he appears to be a very unhostile individual. He has no apparent history of aggressive or antisocial behavior. While he has used

drugs in the past there is nothing to suggest problems or issues with chemical dependency. He does, however, show some naiveté about the risks he was taking when using drugs. There is nothing to suggest problems with interpersonal relationships. There is no apparent history of relationship problems. He values his relationship with his wife and this appears to be a very important relationship to him. There is no data to point to any problems with sexuality or sexual expression. In summary, the overall picture of Dennis is one of a highly intelligent man who in spite of some negative experiences, particularly having to cope with the death of his parents while a teenager, has turned out to be a well-functioning individual who shows no signs of a significant mental illness or personality disorder....

With respect to Dechaine's behavior during his interrogations—reactions the officers described in a way that made them seem incriminating—Dr. Ginn reported:

Dennis stated that while he was with the police he was telling himself that he had to stay cool because he did not want the police to know he was high. He said his recollections of his interview with the police was one of being terrorized by one of the deputies who kept yelling at him. Dennis said he could not believe they were trying to accuse him of being involved with this girl's disappearance. He said that the experience left him rattled. Dennis stated that he did recall the incident with the keys, and does recall pushing them under the seat. He said the reason for that was because he felt terrorized by the police. He did not want to have to be confronted by them any more.

Dr. Ginn testified to these conclusions outside the presence of the jury.

Wright objected. Nor did Wright want the jury to hear anything from the psychologists appointed by the state to examine Dechaine.

Previous decisions by Maine's high court held that psychological testimony may be admitted to establish that a defendant did not possess a culpable state of mind. Judge Bradford referred to this and stated, "If the evidence offered by the defendant did not tend to negate the mental element of the crimes charged it would be properly excluded."

The judge concluded, "It is just as consistent [with Dr. Ginn's testimony] then to conclude that [Dechaine] was not in a drug-induced psychosis. Therefore, based upon the testimony of Dr. Ginn, I do not find that he fits within the guidelines set forth in *State versus Murphy*, and that his testimony, if received by the jury, would lead only to confusion of issues and confusion of the jury. Therefore, his testimony will be excluded."

Then the judge announced, "We'll take a five-minute recess."

❖

According to Judge Bradford's interpretation, psychiatric testimony can be used to show that a defendant is crazy, but a defendant can't use it to prove he's not crazy.

Jurors were given Dechaine's admitted use of drugs, then

left to imagine how it might have affected him. They were not informed of the conclusion acknowledged by Judge Bradford—that Dechaine had *not* been suffering from any sort of drug-induced psychosis.

❖

A friend named Mike Hite testified that Dechaine was, indeed, very squeamish and, further, that he never locked his truck when he parked it.

Dechaine took the witness stand. He told of his childhood, his education, his marriage and their work at the farm in Bowdoinham. He spoke of being introduced to marijuana in high school and using it occasionally in the years since then. He admitted drinking beer sometimes during his teen years. He'd used cocaine a few times. He admitted using amphetamines ("speed") from time to time. Some time in June, he'd seen a man selling speed in the lavatory of a Boston museum, and he'd purchased some.

He recounted the morning of July 6th. He recalled passing Justine Dennison near Topsham and waving as they passed one another on Route 24. Later on, he'd parked his truck down an overgrown skidder trail off the road, gone into the woods and injected himself with some of the drug he'd bought in Boston. Then he got back in his truck and drove around on dirt roads for a while, stopping here and there to wander through the forest. On one of these occasions, he became lost. He couldn't find his truck.

Shown a photo of where his truck was later found by police, he said, "I never completely determined where my truck was. I've never seen that location since, so the photographs I've seen don't seem familiar to me in terms of vegetation and so forth.... That may well have been where I left my truck."

He told the jury of his initial interrogation by Deputy Reed in the cruiser. He described the increasing intensity of the questioning and, when Reed returned to ask if he'd answer more questions, "I told him after the way you behaved I wouldn't." Given a Miranda waiver form, he checked NO and signed it. When asked where the truck keys were, he said he'd really believed they were in the truck. Then, finding them in his pocket, "I panicked.... I did not want to have another go-around with Officer Reed."

So he hid the keys under the front seat of the police car. Already afraid they'd discover his drug use, he was even more frightened by accusations of responsibility for the disappearance of a young girl.

Dechaine recounted the rest of the night: the photographs, Hendsbee's questions, explaining the scratches and the handprints on his shirt.

At this point, court was adjourned for the night.

Dechaine was led away, the spectators were leaving, the judge had departed. Connolly sat at the counsel table, feeling good about how things had gone.

Wright walked over to him. "I can't believe you did that."

Thinking that Wright was amazed at Connolly's excellent performance, he smiled. "What?"

"I can't believe you put him on the stand."

Now Connolly thought that Wright believed Wright's own performance had been good. Connolly smiled again and stretched his lanky frame back in his chair, fingers interlaced behind his head.

But Wright said, "That's the most unethical thing I've ever heard about."

This made Connolly figure that Wright was alluding to the old rule that says, "Never let a defendant testify."

Like many old rules, that one survives because of its solid foundation in trial logic. Without a defendant's testimony, the focus of the case is on the state's evidence and their burden of proving guilt beyond a reasonable doubt. When a defendant testifies, the jury's focus shifts, from that abstraction of the state's burden to the actuality of how the defendant testifies, how he looks and acts. Jurors ask themselves, "Do we believe him?" Focus moves from the abstract and becomes personalized. If a defendant seems to lie about anything, jurors will believe he's lying about everything.

When a defendant doesn't testify, jurors may wonder. But the judge's instructions will forbid them from considering that fact because defendants in our system have an absolute right to remain mute and let the state meet its burden of proving guilt. If jurors can't consider it, they can't talk about it among themselves, and that unspoken question of why he didn't testify tends to get lost in the jury-room discussion of the state's evidence.

Connolly knew that old rule, and he knew that Wright knew it. He asked the prosecutor, "What are you talking about?"

"Your guy confessed."

"Those statements to Hendsbee and Westrum? They're not confessions. That's bullshit."

"No. He confessed to you!"

Connolly's mind flashed to rumors about Carlton babbling some kind of bullshit to the AG's people. If Carlton had actually said anything indicating Dechaine's guilt, the AG's people would believe it was based on the defendant having confessed to Carlton. If they believed that, they'd also believe he'd confessed to Connolly. And if they'd told the judge what Carlton had said, Connolly thought, "That's why Bradford's been on my ass."

The next morning, March 16th, a livid Connolly cornered Carlton near the holding cells in the basement of the courthouse. He accused the older lawyer of telling prosecutors that Dechaine had admitted the crime.

Carlton asserted, "I never told them that. That's not true."

❖

Dechaine's testimony resumed with his inability to sleep after the police had brought him home, and his visit to the lawyer, George Carlton.

Connolly asked, "Had you ever been to a lawyer before?"

"Objection."

"Overruled."

Dechaine answered, "No."

On Friday, when Hendsbee had come with a search warrant, Dechaine had already heard on the radio that Sarah's body had been found. Believing himself to be the only suspect, he'd waited at the house with his wife.

Yes, he'd once had a small knife on his keyring but he'd removed it months before the crime to break open some bales of Pro-mix in his greenhouse, and he'd left the knife there. He viewed the knots in the ropes that had bound

Sarah and told the jury that he didn't use that kind of knot.

He had been distraught over his predicament and even more so when they arrested him.

"What was your level of anxiety and worry and concern during this period of discussion [with Detective Westrum.]"

"Probably as high as it had ever been in my life."

He didn't remember making any of the incriminating statements attributed to him by Hendsbee or Westrum. With respect to the statement quoted by jail guards Maxey and Dermody, Dechaine's version was, "I'm the man *accused of* the murder of Sarah Cherry."

He believed that the repair estimate found in the Henkel driveway had been in his truck but he wasn't certain where the notebook had been before.

Connolly asked Dechaine for his reaction to Dr. Roy's testimony detailing what had been done to Sarah.

"Objection."

"Sustained."

Connolly went at it from another angle. "Did anything that Dr. Roy said in reference to that body and what was done strike a chord or memory or experience in you?"

"Oh no. What he described is entirely out of—"

"Objection!"

The judge said, "The question has been asked and answered. There will be no voluntary statements especially as to any reaction from Dr. Roy's testimony."

"Did you ever go to the Henkel residence and abduct Sarah Cherry?"

"No, I did not."

"Did you ever tie her up?"

"No, sir, I did not."

"Did you ever bury her?"

"No."

"No further questions."

Eric Wright unwound his bony frame from his chair and walked around the prosecutor's counsel table to face Dechaine.

"Did the real you kill Sarah Cherry, or did somebody else do it?"

"No part of me did."

"You told Detective Hendsbee that the real you couldn't have done it."

"I said I couldn't have done it."

Channel 13 television reporter Linda Holstein would tell viewers that Wright's cross-examination proclaimed his "disgust and disdain" for Dechaine's answers.

"You said the real you couldn't have done it."

Connolly objected, "Asked and answered."

"Overruled."

Dechaine said, "I told him I couldn't have done it."

Wright allowed a pregnant pause to lengthen. Lawyers do that in the hope the witness will fill the silence with something he shouldn't say. When Dechaine didn't take the bait, Wright asked, "You told Detective Westrum that there was something inside of you that made you do it?"

"No."

Wright peered over his glasses with an expression of disbelief. "You deny that?"

"Yes, I do."

"You originally denied to Detective Hendsbee before the

discovery of Sarah Cherry's body anything to do with her being missing, didn't you?"

Wright hammered away, confronting the defendant with every incriminating admission attributed to him by the detectives. Dechaine denied them all.

Wright accused Dechaine of making no effort to produce the knife that his wife had said once was on his keychain.

Connolly objected and moved for a mistrial.

"Motion is denied. I will instruct the jury." The judge reminded the jurors that the presumption of innocence remains; that the prosecution must prove its case; and that "the law never requires a defendant to produce any evidence or witnesses whatsoever. So therefore, you will disregard that last question by Mr. Wright."

Tom Connolly summed up as best he could, considering the evidence laid before the jury. He emphasized the importance of witnesses who "know Dennis Dechaine. They have worked with him. They have socialized with him. They have seen him under various circumstances. The character evidence as to his reputation for peacefulness and non-violence is not an insignificant factor in this case, especially when you juxtapose it with the enormous gravity of this crime.... Mr. Buttrick, who'd talked with Dechaine minutes after he'd emerged from that woods, stated that 'the defendant behaved like a gentleman.' Neither of the Buttricks noticed any wetness on his clothing. They noticed no blood. They noticed no aberrant behavior. They said he was a gentleman."

Connolly reminded jurors that Dechaine cooperated with the police. He answered questions; he gave them permission to tow his truck away for a thorough search; he let them take pictures of his body. The truck had yielded no sign of Sarah's presence.

Connolly reminded the jury that there was no sign of a struggle at the Henkel home and suggested that the evidence—the situation where no one could approach the house without the dogs alerting anyone inside—this fact suggested that Sarah had seen and recognized the visitor and gone downstairs, leaving the door ajar so she could hear the baby if she cried, to talk with that person. He pointed to what he termed an absence of evidence pointing to the defendant: no witness. Dechaine's wife testified it had been months since she'd seen that little knife on the Toyota keychain; a friend who'd borrowed the pickup had testified there was no knife on the keychain. And despite an intensive search of the woods and roadside by police using a metal detector, no knife was ever recovered. Nor were Sarah's underpants ever found.

Connolly acknowledged that items from the truck were used in the offense—the ropes; the papers found in the driveway. But there was no indication the truck itself was used. There were items discovered near the body—a red polyester fiber on a tree and a shred of pink insulation in no way connected to the defendant.

And he asked the jurors to ponder how Dechaine could have taken Sarah from his truck, then locked the vehicle which required one to press the button down and hold the outside button in while closing the door; then how 135-pound Dechaine could have carried 98-pound Sarah, with a scarf and bandanna, across the road. None of it is consistent with logic, he said. As for the dog evidence, Trooper Bureau's testimony proves nothing. The knots in the rope binding Sarah were not like any Dechaine was known to tie. The tire tracks in the Henkel driveway weren't matched to Dechaine's truck. They were merely similar, that's all.

Connolly's final words to the jury were, "I think you know what is in front of you. That you understand that this defendant has not been proven guilty beyond a reasonable doubt. During the course of your deliberations I ask you to hold to that thought. That two plus two makes four...."

Wright rose to give the State's summation. To counter the absence of clues in Dechaine's truck. ". . . whether it be fingerprints or fibers or hairs or what have you, sometimes you have it and sometimes you don't. I can give you no better answer than to say that's the way God made it."

". . . nor would this responsible young lady have left voluntarily leaving behind the infant child with whom she was caring for that day. Like it or not, her selection was random. All the evidence leaves you with is that she did not know her killer. She did not know Dennis Dechaine. Obviously, someone abducted and tortured and sexually abused and murdered Sarah Cherry. The only question is who."

Wright acknowledged that the police had focused on Dechaine as a suspect, but "for one very good reason. That is precisely to whom the evidence led them. It never led anywhere else nor would it ever have done so. What clues led elsewhere? None at all." He warned against being misled simply because the evidence is circumstantial.

"You have in this case quite astounding evidence of the

defendant's guilt. His papers and his alone were found at the Henkels'. They were in his truck on July 6th. There was a tire impression left at the Henkels' residence consistent with the truck tire of his truck...a neighbor across the road heard a vehicle slow down at the Henkels and not go by. She heard the dogs barking as they will when people turn into the driveway. And then she saw, fifteen or so minutes later, a dirty or old Toyota pickup truck heading northbound exactly in the direction in which later Sarah Cherry's body was found. All this between 1:00 and 1:15 in the afternoon of July 6th, perfectly consistent with, as you now know, Sarah Cherry had to have been abducted.

"The defendant had been absent from everybody, everyone, during precisely the time when Sarah Cherry was killed. This defendant and this defendant alone later emerged from the very woods where Sarah Cherry's body in the meantime had been killed and later was to be found.

"No one knew where the defendant was that day but he alone. So nobody else could have gotten to his truck. He himself said he saw nobody else in the woods. The defendant's truck and no one else in this entire world was found within just a few hundred yards of Sarah's body. The truck was locked. You know there was no spare Toyota key in it. So the truck had not been moved.... Indeed, the defendant himself acknowledged to Detective Hendsbee early on the morning of the 7th, and to you in testimony, that no one else could have driven the truck as far as he could tell."

It was Dechaine, Wright said, who'd tried to hide the truck keys and—despite his "slick denials"—he did that because he had to distance himself from that truck. The prosecutor reminded jurors that the rope on the ground between truck and corpse had been cut from a piece of rope in the Toyota. "The other piece of rope in the woods appeared to match the rope on Sarah's wrists, but Ms. Brinkman is conservative and wouldn't call it a match unless it was a match because this rope frayed apart...."

Wright told the jury that the evidence failed to "show you any realistic alternative killer. The defense seems to suggest in the evidence that all this is only an unfortunate set of coincidences. You have a stark choice: either the defendant is guilty, or you believe the defendant's claims that he was set up and you find him not guilty." Wright ridiculed the logic that anyone else could have committed the crime and framed Dechaine. Then he led the jurors through a graphic reprise of every despicable injury inflicted on Sarah.

Among prosecutor Eric Wright's final words to the jury: "There is no evidence, ladies and gentlemen of the jury, in this case of an alternative perpetrator. There is only the sheerest of speculation...."

The jury retired to consider its verdict.

9

Elation

IT WAS FRIDAY. THE JURY DELIBERATED into the night. The jurors slept on what they'd seen and heard and what their fellow jurors had said the previous evening. On Saturday morning, they got up and dressed and had breakfast and resumed their deliberations. At noon, after ten hours of considering and discussing the evidence, they returned their verdict: Guilty on all five counts.

Dechaine hung his head and wagged it back and forth. Then he looked up, expressionless.

Sarah's family cried and hugged one another.

Reporter Melinda Lake of the *Brunswick Times Record* quoted one member of the family as saying, "There is justice. There is a God." The family's lawyer explained that it had been important for them all to sit in the courtroom throughout the trial, even though the testimony reminded them "time and again of the savagery, brutality and depravity of the crime. They feel in some sense they can rest for Sarah, that justice has been done."

An aunt told reporters, "It will never be over, but that piece of it is over."

Detective Westrum, the *Times Record* reported, "says his

own office feels elated that Dechaine was convicted.... I had a problem with the defense tactic that made us out to be liars. Why four police officers would lie is beyond me."

Lawyer Tom Connolly vowed an appeal but praised the jury for doing a good job with the evidence they were given. Dechaine, he said, "expressed deep sorrow for the family of the victim and for his own family."

Prosecutor Eric Wright said he was "relieved and elated for Sarah's family," and he'd never doubted Dechaine's guilt. "Not from day one."

No trace of doubt colored his comments to the press. When Dechaine testified, Wright told reporters, "He was cool. Too cool. His denials of guilt were too cool. It was implausible, incredible." Wright would like to ask the court to impose one punishment, "but it's not authorized by law."

A few days later, he'd tell *Brunswick Times Record* reporter Bernie Monegain, "I distrust anyone who has the answers for almost everything. Dechaine struck me as that way—contrived, an answer for everything. You look at those stories and they're lies within lies." It had been his personal opinion, "and I have no proof of this," that Dechaine was casing houses for burglary to feed his drug habit when he came across Sarah Cherry at the Henkel home. "But that is speculative," he told the reporter. "I'm not one to advance speculative theory to a jury."

Sarah's grandmother, Margaret Cherry, wrote to the judge:

> Even after eight and a half months, Sarah's death and manner of dying still causes me deep pain. I've tried to

return to my normal life.... I worked as a dental assistant.... Grief spasms would overwhelm me at inopportune moments.... My God and my church are very important to me. It's the faith and belief I have that Sarah is whole and safe in loving care that enables me to continue on....

A hand-printed letter to the judge said:

The loss of Sarah from our lives is certainly bad enough but the method she lost her life is what is really causing so much pain in our lives. She was a very bubbly person full of energy and love and someone that loved life. She touched many, many lives during her short life through her love of the outdoors, sports, school and church.

Our family is a very close family that spends a lot of time together. But these get togethers aren't the same any more. Every one has the fact in the back of our minds that she isn't here with us. Many members of the family are being counseled because we don't understand how anyone could do to Sarah what Dennis Dechaine did to her. I don't understand how any one could torture a beautiful young person like Sarah. That is what is so hard to understand. I spend a lot of time thinking about this and it really upsets me. I do not believe he should ever be given the opportunity to go out in the public again to do this crime again. He should be given the maximum sentence so he can suffer some pain that he has caused all of us. After sitting through the trial I believe you are a just judge and will give him what he deserves.

Sincerely yours,
Lloyd R. Cherry, Jr.
Sarah's Pop Pop

Sarah's mother, Debra, wrote of her difficulty in expressing what she'd been through: the nightmare, when a daughter is missing, of not knowing what is happening to her. "I imagined the worst, being raped, tortured, sexually abused, and being killed. But I also thought God wouldn't let it happen to my girl. And my worst nightmare has come true." She told the judge how she and Sarah had been friends and companions, sharing her plans for the future and what Debra planned for her.

I don't feel right wishing a person to suffer, but I want him to die a slow death for the rest of his life. He has caused a lot of people to suffer, especially me, my [stepdaughter] Hilary and my family. I believe he should get the maximum sentence spending the rest of his life in prison. I'd feel a little better knowing he'll never torture or kill another little girl again. Maybe someday he'll realize there is no reason why he can't say why he did what he did to Sarah. I need to know. Besides, why does he deserve to get a second chance in life? Sarah never had a second chance.

When the time came, Wright spoke of his disbelief that Dechaine had been using drugs that day but, if he had, "such use served only to lower his inhibitions and so permit him in combination with already existing deep-seated problems, to do what otherwise he might not have done." The atrocities perpetrated on Sarah "demonstrate that the defendant is truly a forceful and violent person."

Wright described those acts in appalling detail, "and during those last five minutes or so of her life we know from the petechial hemorrhages on her eyelids and from her blood and from thread from the scarf on her hands, that Sarah fought and struggled even then against death."

In the legal absence of a death penalty, Wright demanded life imprisonment.

Tom Connolly focused his final plea on Dechaine's good works and reputation for gentleness but he had to know this battle was lost when the jury convicted his client. The perpetrator of this crime fully deserved the worst a court could hand down.

Judge Bradford agreed.

In Maine, where there is no parole, a life sentence means "until you're dead."

Most Mainers don't approve of the death penalty. But many of us who'd followed this case in the newspapers and on television thought Dechaine got off easy. There is no "appropriate" punishment for the creature who killed little Sarah Cherry, not in any civilized society. But the death penalty wasn't possible under Maine law. The law had been followed. Case closed.

But it wasn't closed.

The people who'd known Dennis Dechaine—in the Bowdoinham–Brunswick area and from Madawaska where he'd grown up—were devastated by the jury's verdict.

Friends grew into a movement. The movement took a name: Trial & Error. Their stated purpose: "To raise awareness of the inadequacies of the judicial system."

On May 4t, 1989, they held their first meeting. Carol Waltman, the group's organizer, heart, and backbone, said, "We had eighteen members show up. Most of them didn't know Dennis but they're interested because of the outcome of the trial. We received many phone calls from people who wanted to be part of our support group but just weren't able to attend this meeting because of their work schedules."

Meanwhile, letters came to Connolly's office from the length and breadth of the state—from people who'd never known Dechaine, but they'd followed the case in the press—letters expressing criticism of the police performance and doubts regarding Dechaine's guilt.

Trial & Error scheduled another meeting for June, and Carol Waltman began work on a benefit dance in July to raise money. "It's a lot of work," she acknowledged, "but every bit of it is worth a lifetime to our best friend, Dennis."

Carol Waltman came from a proud French family of ten boys and nine girls, so close to Dechaine that she considered him an eleventh brother—"as if," she'd write to Judge Bradford, "we needed more in the family. He's one of us in so many ways. In his letters, he asks for prayers so that 'the person who did this will confess.'

"We grew up together, he was my husband's best friend and next-door neighbor. He was the type of person everyone wanted to be around. Never would he put anyone down or talk bad about anyone. Never would he laugh at anyone because they were less fortunate than another. He always made things seem good when good was not around. When someone would try to cause problems, as teenagers, Denis [Mrs. Waltman used the French spelling of his name] would always find something good about this person. He'd never judge anyone or hurt them in any way."

Carol, herself, had survived three major operations to deal with an embolism in her lungs—doctors at one point gave her two days to live—but her towering religious faith and the prayers of her friends, Dechaine included, had brought her through that crisis. Her letter to Bradford continued:

> As a third-grade religion teacher, I believe in God, Love, and I believe in justice.... I believe & pray that this nightmare will soon be over. For a lot of people, this is going to be over and forgotten soon. As for Denis, his family, and friends, it goes on in our life every day.
>
> I know when this is all over, if an appeal is granted and they get the right man who did this, I know Denis will find it in his heart to forgive everyone who has convicted him. That's the kind of man he is. We pray daily that there will be peace, love, and courage in the days ahead for Denis and for the Cherry family. The poor child is at peace and may God bless the children that have to go through all this cruelty in the world.
>
> Dear Sir, Please, please find a way to help to get the right man, he's out there on the prowl and God only knows whose life he will end next. May God send His spirit upon you and all the men who work for justice in the world. God Bless.

This was the character that generated the strength and fervor which allowed Carol Waltman to juggle her organizational efforts, care for husband and children, and operate her own business, Carol's Country Crafts, with implacable tenacity and an absolute determination to see her friend freed from his false imprisonment.

Trial & Error members wrote to the editors of every newspaper in the state. They gave talks at grange halls, community centers, and churches. Within months, their ranks neared four hundred members and cash contributors.

These people asked one another, and anyone else who would listen, how that jury could have believed Dennis Dechaine capable of such a horrendously violent crime.

And they provided an answer: jurors hadn't heard the whole truth.

They pointed to the court's refusal to let Tom Connolly offer evidence of an alternative perpetrator—specific facts naming that person and revealing the motive for Sarah's murder. Aside from that, they saw no real evidence proving that Dennis had ever had anything to do with Sarah Cherry or the ghastly acts which were totally beyond the capabilities of this gentle man.

The man Dechaine's friends believed guilty was Doug Senecal.

When Chris and Maureen Crosman divorced, ten years earlier, the court granted joint custody of their daughters, Jackie and Jessica, to both parents. Chris later married Debra Cherry and they lived together with the three young girls—Jackie, Jessica, and Debra's daughter, Sarah Cherry. Late in 1987, Jackie moved back to live with her mother, Maureen, and the man Maureen had married—Doug Senecal.

Two months before Sarah vanished, the Sagadahoc County Grand Jury charged:

> COUNT I: That on or about August 1, 1983, in the Town of Phippsburg, Sagadahoc County, Maine, the above-named Douglas E. Senecal did intentionally subject a person not his spouse, namely: Jackie Crosman, to sexual contact, the said Jackie Crosman not having in fact attained her fourteenth birthday; the said Douglas E. Senecal being at least three years older than the said Jackie Crosman.
>
> COUNT II: That on or about June 1, 1983, in the Town of Phippsburg, Sagadahoc County, Maine, the above-named Douglas E. Senecal did intentionally subject a person not his spouse, namely: Jackie Crosman, to sexual contact, the said Jackie Crosman not having in fact attained her fourteenth birthday; the said Douglas E. Senecal being at least three years older than the said Jackie Crosman.

Some believed that Senecal had killed Sarah to prevent her from somehow corroborating Jackie's accusations. Ten days after the murder, the state asked for a continuance in the Senecal case because, "Jackie Crosman, the victim and essential witness, is absent from this area and unavailable for hearing." The district attorney had information that Senecal and his family had spirited Jackie out of the state.

This information came from Caseworker Jennifer Dox of the state's Department of Human Services. She'd visited the

Senecal family the day before Sarah vanished. Doug Senecal acknowledged that Jackie had been in contact with her mother (he was prohibited by a court order from having any contact with the girl) but added, "I'm not going to get involved with you about this."

Dox talked to Senecal's nine-year-old daughter, Erin, who informed her that Jackie was in California, "where it's safer."

Dox was about to leave when Senecal told her, "When all this is over, you'll see how wrong you were in trying to do this to me. When it's all over, Jackie is going to come back here and live with her mother and me and finish school.... You'll see, no matter what you've tried to do to me, I'll be able to hold my head up in this community. You were wrong to involve the courts and the police without first talking to me...because you don't know that this family takes cares of its problems in its own way."

On the day Sarah disappeared from the Henkel house, Sheriff David Haggett was told by Chris Crosman that he'd had a phone call from Jackie a week earlier. She was "staying at a San Diego Y.M.C.A. [sic] close to the bus station. She told Chris that her mother, Maureen, had paid her way to California."

On August 12th, the judge granted a continuance in the Senecal case. On January 25, 1989, the case against Senecal was dismissed by Superior Court Justice Carl Bradford—the same judge who'd convene the Dechaine trial seven weeks later.

Retired state police homicide investigator Jim Pinette operated a private investigation agency called The Sherlock Group. Retained by Tom Connolly with funds from Trial & Error, he interviewed Senecal in the presence of wife Maureen. Senecal said he'd been framing and pouring a concrete floor for a small addition he'd constructed on a customer's home in Cape Popham from the Fourth of July through the eighth. He asked why he was wanted to testify at the Dechaine trial.

Pinette explained that it was because he'd been reported as having abused his child two years ago.

Senecal and his wife seemed disturbed by the situation, a reaction Pinette attributed to their relationship with Sarah. They asked Pinette to phone the customer right then. When he did, the woman confirmed that Senecal worked for her on July 8th because she remembered hearing on the radio that Sarah's body had been found and relaying the news to Senecal, but she'd have to consult her calendar and call back about July 6th.

Jim Pinette considered the Senecals cooperative and eager to provide facts that would account for his whereabouts on the day in question. They gave no sign of having prepared for questions about their activities on the day Sarah vanished, and only recalled July 8th because of receiving the news that Sarah was dead.

On the first of March, Pinette attended a meeting with Tom Connolly and Doug and Maureen Senecal at the Brunswick offices of Senecal's lawyer, Joseph Field. Assistant Attorney General Eric Wright, who would prosecute Dechaine, was also present. Based on lawyer Joseph Field's advice that Senecal exercise his Fifth Amendment rights regarding the pending indictment alleging sexual misconduct with stepdaughter Jackie, it was agreed that this topic would be off-limits. Connolly had little choice.

Field told the others that, "Mr. Wright is here at my request." Senecal wasn't a rich man and the lawyer didn't want his client put through this kind of ordeal twice. But Field had other pressing matters to attend to, so he wouldn't stay. "Have at it, have fun," he said. "When you get off where he was on the 5th or 6th of July, whatever it is, give me a shout."

Under Connolly's questioning, Senecal gave his name, address and occupation, his family situation, and his purchase of the truck he drove, a red and white 1986 Ford Ranger pickup truck with four-wheel drive.

While they spoke, Jim Pinette went outside and took photos of that truck.

Senecal recounted his activities on July 6th: at 10:00 A.M. he and his eight-year-old son had driven to Popham Beach to discuss the job he'd do for the customer there. He'd given the lady an estimate, brought some materials out of her shed and found he needed a saw blade, so at about 11:30 he'd driven ten miles to Bath to buy one. He produced a copy of a receipt documenting the purchase. Then he'd gassed up at the Pine Tree station in Phippsburg and stopped to chat with Charlie Holbrook at Holbrook's Auto Sales because his wife was having clutch problems with her Dodge station wagon. "I can't even remember, I know it was that day, I can't remember if it was going down or coming back."

He also produced a receipt from the Pine Tree gas station, although he couldn't be certain it was he who'd made the purchase. He had several people working for him and it may have been one of them who bought the gas and charged it to him.

The next night, July 7th, Senecal had driven his wife's car "because my truck, the wiring and everything just blew up in my truck." And he remembered July 8th because he was at the customer's house and she'd told him that they'd found Sarah's body.

Connolly asked whether Senecal wore glasses. He did.

Connolly asked whether he was right-handed or left-handed.

"Right."

"What size shoe do you have?"

"I wear all hand-me-downs so they're going to go between $9^{1/2}$ and eleven."

Yes, Senecal said, his stepdaughter Jessica and Sarah had been friends. Sarah had visited the Senecal home, but not often. He'd never met Dechaine, nor the Henkels. He smoked Merit cigarettes—Ultra Light. No, there'd never been any tension between him and the Crosman family. "We always got along."

"And you got along with Sarah fine?"

"Yeah."

Maureen added, "She was a good kid."

❖

The owner of the Pine Tree gas station couldn't tell Private Investigator Jim Pinette who had made that purchase charged to Senecal. Charlie Holbrook couldn't definitely remember talking to Senecal on July 6th.

Pinette interviewed Mrs. Norris, the Bowdoinham witness whom the police named as having seen "a small red pickup." But the red truck she'd seen was full-size. Moreover, upon being shown Dechaine's Toyota, she'd told them that wasn't the truck she'd seen on the day in question. It was another little tidbit missing from the discovery material furnished to Tom Connolly.

The Phippsburg Police Chief told Pinette that Senecal was caustic and abrasive, and capable of almost anything.

Jim Pinette reported all of this to Tom Connolly prior to the trial, but the court prohibited the introduction of evidence suggesting Senecal's involvement.

Nevertheless, Connolly went ahead with preparations to appeal the case.

❖

Ron Morin—the Madawaska private eye who'd telephoned Detective Hendsbee during the search for Sarah to relay a psychic's vision of a man saying, "It shouldn't have happened"—was now consulting another psychic, George Anderson in Long Island, New York. A CBS *48 Hours* program would describe Anderson as a former operator for the New York Telephone Co. who sees himself as some sort of spiritual switchboard for dead people. Anderson has written several successful books, and others have written books about him. Many people have implicit faith in his ability to talk with the dead and Morin hoped that—for Anderson's $1,000 fee—he could contact Sarah Cherry.

Morin asked, "Do you feel a female spirit around?"

"A female friend," Anderson replied. "If not a friend, a relative. Do you know her?"

"A victim."

"A child not related in any way, shape, or form? This is hard if she's not related. A missing person? A case you're working on? She's passed on. An investigation out of state. Do you know for a fact she's passed on?"

Morin assured him, "I definitely know she's passed on."

"Do you know her family? Out of your home town? Has the body been found? What do you want to know?"

"Is the right person in jail?"

"Somebody in her family? In her town? She says 'Home, home.' This person lives in her home town. A male. Is he a teenager? Very young or something. Maybe he seems younger than he appears to be. Maybe he's fifty and he has the mentality of a seventeen-year-old. Is he off his rocker or something? Maybe a little schizo. Was she sexually abused? She was definitely sexually...Does Jennifer mean something? I'll just have to leave it with you. I hear her say, she's calling for Jennifer."

"Is it Jackie?"

"No, it sounds like Jennifer. Was she cut up?"

As the hour passed, Anderson asked whether the person in jail had a record.

Dechaine had never been arrested for anything, but Morin answered, "Drugs only, nothing violent."

Anderson asked about sisters, then half-sisters.

Morin told him "Half-sisters, there's been a series of marriages."

Anderson: "I heard somebody over there say yes, stepfather, stepfather. I could be wrong."

Later on, Morin asked, "Could she tell you if it was a knife?"

"Well, cut up, I'd have to assume it was a knife."

Morin asked where Jackie might be.

"Western states. Looks like maybe deserts or a lot of open space."

There was more and, two years later, the leader of Trial & Error—grasping at any straw—would see significance in some of Anderson's questions and comments.

Attorney Tom Connolly, meanwhile, was working on the appeal. Seven months after the guilty verdict, on October 16, 1989, he filed a 123-page brief along with more than 200 pages of supporting exhibits.

Prosecutors, arguing against Connolly's grounds, cited the *Vanassche* court decision which had concluded:

> Even though it appear that the State may have failed to provide important discovery materials to the defendant in a timely manner, we find that the Superior court [*sic*] acted within its discretion when it chose not to sanction the State by dismissing the State's case or by suppressing evidence....

The *Vanassche* case, cited by the state to support their position that withholding discovery material didn't matter, had been a trial on a charge of drunk driving.

Nancy wrote to Connolly:

> I think often of Dennis. I place hope in his appeal. I truly believe Dennis does not belong incarcerated and should

be allowed a fair trial.

It is my hope that you realize I am still here for questions, consultation and, of course, witnessing.... I think often of you and your part in this ordeal and I continue to feel endeared and touched by your dedication. Thank you.

On December 12, 1989, Dechaine wrote to inform Connolly that he'd been transferred from the Seg unit.

I came into the population with lots of apprehension.... After one week, I can safely say I have no regrets. Though I've received my fair share of threats and verbal abuse, I've also made my connections. I run with the school, acting no differently than anyone else.... I've landed a job in the Braille office, enjoyed the library, walked under the moon and stars and I've seen beautiful sunsets. The way I feel is that each day here is worth a lot and if some psycho decides to take me out, it'll have been worth it.... I have a single cell now! What a relief! ...

I hate to torture myself with thoughts of freedom, but it seems I have every reason to believe that a fair trial would yield just that result. I'm anxious. I think a fair decision on the appeal will set the ball in motion.

The "job" Dechaine had volunteered to do—using a Braille typewriter to copy textbooks for a blind college student—was eventually curtailed. Security concerns sometimes made Braille production difficult. When a job came up in the upholstery shop, he took it.

In February of 1990, Dechaine wrote:

Dear Tom,
I wanted to write just to let you know that things here are going pretty well, even considering the anxiety, the wait for a decision....

I can't say how distressing it's been to run the worst scenario through my mind. For that matter, the best scenario, assuming it's a new trial, doesn't bring me any great relief. I know Eric Wright well enough to know that he'll be going for the jugular.... It worries me that he could conceivably destroy my credibility by preying on variations or discrepancies in the description of a day that had little significant occurrences to make it memorable....

The *Maine Times* ran an editorial comparing Dechaine to Boston's Charles Stuart, the man responsible for his wife's murder on a dark Boston street. Connolly fired off an angry letter to their editors:

...The point which is lost on [the writer] is not that Charles Stuart was a middle class killer but that another man, Willie Bennett, was wrongfully charged with the crime. [The writer] ignores how police agents established a web of circumstantial evidence which led to Bennett's indictment. She seems unaware that a so-called series of "admissions" were allegedly made that he had killed Carol Stuart. These statements have now been shown to have been manufactured out of whole cloth by the police to convict an innocent man. The police intimidated witnesses, lied and perjured themselves to make their facts fit the crime and thus get Bennett for the murder. The analogy should make her hair stand on end....

The Stuart case establishes that it is easier to believe circumstantial evidence than to do the work necessary to find the truth.... The answer to [the writer's] question "Dennis Dechaine, Maine's Charles Stuart?" is no. The real question is "Dennis Dechaine, Maine's Willie Bennett?" The answer to that is yes.

The state supreme court denied Dechaine's appeal. Prosecutors were right, they said. The trial had been properly conducted, they said. Case closed.

But it wasn't closed.

On March 15, 1990, Dechaine wrote:

Dear Tom,

I was hoping I wouldn't have to write you because of the failure of our appeal, but that's the way things went.... I've read the appeal and reply on more than one occasion and found it filled not only with sound points of law but of your heart and soul as well. I've never felt hopeless because of the comfort your devotion and concern gave me.... You went above and beyond.... A mere thanks can't ever properly compensate you for your efforts, but it's all I can offer.

I recognize the increasing futility.... I also understand the need of others...many of them need your help, too.... Don't despair, Tom. One abuse of judicial privilege doesn't make the entire system useless. It's guys like you that are needed to stop the flow of injustice.

     Your friend,
     Dennis

And, two days later:

...I'm really starting to feel guilty about not compensating you for your help. I know you feel it necessary to pursue the matter and I know also that this takes money.... But also I want you to realize that I have no intention of taxing friends or family by begging for donations. If they approach you independently, bear in mind that they're really not in a position to offer assistance.... I just haven't enough faith in the justice system to see my family deprive themselves.... This tragedy has spawned a sea of victims and now I can't help but feel you've made the list.... I only hope you won't feel embittered by the volume of work that awaits you. What you've already accomplished is far more valuable than you'll ever know.

On May 2nd, Dechaine wrote to Connolly wishing he could access his frozen assets to compensate Connolly. Then,

...I have been out in population five months and, by the grace of God, lots of luck and careful living, I've avoided the thumpings I was promised.... I was often called a 'skinner, ripper, or piece of shit,' etc., etc. Now I'm occasionally called "nerd." In this place, 'nerd' carries a certain respect—it suggests I read and write....

In June of 1990, Connolly appealed to the U.S. Supreme Court.

In September, Dechaine's spirits slumped:

> This place keeps getting smaller, the company keeps getting worse and the feelings of hopelessness and abandonment loom ever larger. I seem to be drifting through life rather than living it.... Sometimes I think I'll die in here, an ocean of frustration wells up in me at my total impotence to change my lot in life. Only one thing could frustrate me more—to have to fill your shoes and be savior to a bunch of hopeless wretches.....
>
> Take care of yourself, Tom, and give my regards to Ida.

The United States Supreme Court declined to hear the case.

In mid-November, Connolly's secretary, Ida, answered a call from private investigator Ron Morin of Madawaska. Her note to Connolly said:

> He is very anxious about starting the investigation on the Dechaine case. Apparently he has spoken with Phil Dechaine who he says mailed you some money to start the investigation. He said that Phil, in his letter to you, recommended Ron Morin for the job but obviously you could hire someone else if you wanted. I didn't know of any letter or money so I didn't say anything....

Morin joined the defense team and, in canvassing the residents of Dead River Road, he turned up a man named Ralph Jones with some fascinating things to say about the alternative suspect, Doug Senecal. Then he tracked down a witness named Pam Babine, who'd vanished after phoning Connolly's office with some intriguing information about Senecal. Along the way, Morin was harassed by Sheriff Haggett and threatened with the loss of his PI license, but he hung in and made a number of useful contributions.

Funds for investigators were difficult to come by. Dechaine's brother, Frank, sent Connolly $2,500 for this purpose, but Jim Pinette had already cost the defense close to $2,000 and Morin's travel expenses mounted daily.

Two and a half years after Dechaine's conviction, he—and even Sarah Cherry—had slipped or been consciously blocked from the minds of most Mainers. The first Persian Gulf War was waged and won. New Hampshire teacher Pam Smart was convicted of having her husband murdered by one of her students. In faraway South Africa, their government admitted error and released Nelson Mandela from twenty-seven years' imprisonment.

The authorities in Maine would admit nothing.

Tom Connolly filed a motion with the state for a new trial, based on newly acquired evidence—primarily, the witnesses produced by Morin.

In October, 1991, Carol Waltman wrote about the progress of Trial & Error:

> As of [October] we have over 390 members. All these people were never contacted by us...[they] came to us because of the way the trial was handled and all are angry to see that it was unjust and not fair. A lot of members, at least 70 percent we don't even know, are very concerned. They write to us to encourage us to keep fighting....

She went on to inform Connolly she was sending affidavits from witnesses who'd been at the Madawaska gathering. They had seen Dechaine and Nancy there at too late an hour for them to have made it back to Bowdoin at the time when a state's witness swore he saw Dechaine's Toyota in the Henkel neighborhood. And, Carol wrote to Connolly:

> I myself have had a few meetings with Ron Morin.... A lot of the things I found that Ron told me were a little far-fetched. For example: Doug Senecal has a brother-in-law named Maurice Theriault. Ron told me Maurice belonged to a cult, was possessed, etc,. and that an exorcism was done on him. I couldn't take Ron's word on this, but I read a book written by Maurice Theriault (*Satan's Harvest*). It came out this summer. Maurice talks about the Senecals, etc. I still couldn't believe it until I contacted my parish priest, and I had him check into this exorcism performed in Massachusetts. My priest contacted the Bishop in Mass. and in fact it was true and an exorcism was done on Maurice. All this leads to is the strange family life Doug Senecal has had....
>
> All of this is perhaps a waste but I feel Ron Morin is holding back on some things that you could use to help

the case... We also had a benefit concert in June for Trial & Error. We took in $1,200 and cleared $800. We want you to know we are serious about helping to prove that Dennis is innocent. We won't stop until a new trial is granted....

Dechaine wrote in January 1992 to express concern about the witness who claimed to have seen his Toyota near the Henkel home while the Dechaines were still more than a hundred miles away, and his worry that this may not be admissible to gain a new trial because these facts were not "new evidence":

> ...how could we possibly know that the state would present a witness in the form of young Mr. Knight, who would falsely state that I had shopped at his store [on the day before] when in fact I was nowhere near the area? If you recall, he admitted on the witness stand that I always paid by check for my supplies, yet the last check written to his store was dated Friday, July 1.

Lawyer Tom Connolly had a wife and children. He had a secretary and an office to maintain. He had to earn a living, but he wouldn't let go of the Dechaine case. Supreme Court Justice Robert H. Jackson once offered his idea of "the vanishing country lawyer." It's a favorite of Connolly's. It's become a standard he lives by. In part, Justice Jackson said,

> The county-seat lawyer, counselor to railroads and to Negroes, to bankers and to poor whites, who always gave

to each the best there was in him—and was willing to admit that his best was good. That lawyer has been an American institution.... He knows that in this country the administration of justice is based on law practice. Paper "rights" are worth, when they are threatened, just what some lawyer makes them worth. Civil liberties are those which some lawyer, respected by his neighbors, will stand up and defend....

He resolved problems by what he called "first principles." He did not specialize, nor did he pick and choose clients. He rarely declined service to worthy ones because of inability to pay. Once enlisted for a client, he took his obligation seriously. He insisted on complete control of the litigation—he was no mere hired hand. But he gave every power and resource to the cause. He identified himself with the client's cause fully. He would fight the adverse party and fight his counsel, fight every hostile witness, and fight the court. He never quit. He could think of motions for every purpose under the sun, and he made them all. He moved for new trials; he appealed; and if he lost out in the end, he joined the client at the tavern in damning the judge—which is the last rite in closing an unsuccessful case....

A free and self-governing Republic stands as a monument for the little known and unremembered as well as for the famous men of our profession.

By the Spring 1992, Tom Connolly was ready with several witnesses to support his bid for a new trial.

An affidavit by thirty-eight-year-old Ralph Jones told of

seeing a red and white truck near the mouth of his driveway on the fateful July 6th. Through the bushes, he heard the voices of two men and a young girl. One of the men told the girl, "Get out and go, then." Jones recognized one of those voices as that of a man with whom he'd gone to high school: Doug Senecal. He also recognized Senecal's truck. Jones stated he'd run toward those sounds but the truck took off. Around seven that evening, Jones and his son went to a movie in Lewiston. When they returned, the Dead River Road area was swarming with police.

Jones phoned the sheriff's office but they'd only told him someone was lost. The next morning, he went to the state police command center down the road from his house, where he spoke with a trooper he knew and two detectives. They showed him a photo of Dechaine's truck but Jones told them that wasn't the one he'd seen. He also told them that there were tire tracks in the mud from the truck he had seen. Two days later, a pair of detectives came to his house and took a statement regarding what he'd reported. The officers showed no interest in preserving the tire tracks.

Connolly also had a sworn affidavit from Pamela Babine, thirty-eight, who'd been a tenant in the house Senecal owned next door to his own home. She told of seeing Senecal driving a small red Toyota pickup on July 6, 1988—the day Sarah vanished—and, later, seeing the same truck on television identified as Dechaine's vehicle. Babine then said that on that same afternoon, she'd met Jessica Crosman at a local store and that Jessica had told her that she and Sarah "had switched babysitting jobs that day because Doug Senecal told her to do so." Following Sarah's murder, Babine continued, "I observed Doug Senecal acting in a particularly odd manner, and he was extremely agitated and nervous almost to the point of paranoia."

Kristen Comee had known Senecal for years. Her affidavit to Connolly said how she'd asked Jessica—who'd babysat for her before—to baby-sit on July 6. "I became aware at that time that she had other commitments with some people on that day and she made arrangements for someone else to swap with her so she could babysit for us." Mrs. Comee now believed that Jessica had swapped with Sarah. When news reports were aired about a missing girl, she said, Senecal stated, "I hope it's not Sarah or one of her friends." And, "Jessica's reaction was very emotional, and given my experience with Jessica, the reaction was disproportionate under the information then known."

Another affidavit in Connolly's arsenal, this one by Arthur Landry of St. Agatha, Maine, placed Dechaine in Landry's garden shop, about 300 of miles north of Bowdoin, until about one o'clock on July 5. Dechaine's brother and sister-in-law gave affidavits placing him in northern Maine from July 1 through July 5.

The affidavit by Dechaine's wife told of their trip to that area in their Tercel station wagon. They'd left both of their pickup trucks at home in Bowdoinham. She further stated that they'd left the northern Maine area shortly after noon and driven home via scenic Route One, "since we had no pressing reasons to hurry home." They'd arrived home well after dark on July 5, making it impossible for Dennis to have been the person whom one of the state's trial witnesses had testified was driving their Toyota pickup truck in Bowdoin that afternoon.

Connolly's own affidavit to the court declared that, although he'd filed a request for "discovery" material from the state, and filed a motion for extended discovery, he'd never been furnished any information about Ralph Jones's statements to police, or Jones's identification of Senecal as being in the area. Connolly also stated categorically that none of these witnesses or their information had been available to him prior to trial.

Trial & Error members in Freeport wrote to the new attorney general, Michael Carpenter, expressing their concern about the Dechaine case and the "overwhelming evidence which was never presented to the jury." They criticized the absence of forensic evidence to incriminate Dechaine, the un-recorded "confessions," and "We find it a chilling concept that [the Ralph Jones and Pamela Babine] accounts could be so blatantly ignored at such an early stage of the investigation. We also find it of grave concern that the defense was never offered this information." They expressed dismay that, although the state had willingly used DNA testing in other cases, "it seems that once the blood type of the scrapings was determined not to be [Dechaine's] there was little interest" in conducting any DNA test. Their letter ended with an offer to pay the costs of DNA tests in this case.

Another Trial & Error letter—this one to anyone who'd read it—asked:

If you believe in the work we are doing, please help.

Members volunteer services and supplies whenever possible, but there are many other costs such as postage, printing, legal fees, traveling expenses. After four long years of hard work gathering new evidence, many hours of phone calls finding new information, the truth is finally coming to light. We are not done yet in proving the innocence of Dennis Dechaine. We have many more steps to take to get through this ordeal. If you wish to support us....

On June 5t, 1992, Trial & Error issued a challenge to the state to come out from behind the "veil of technicality" and allow a jury to hear all pertinent evidence. Again they offered to pay for DNA testing of the blood from Sarah's fingernails, and this bulletin was accompanied by a three-page list of deficiencies they saw in Dechaine's trial.

❖

The bid for a new trial was based in part on Connolly's contention that valid evidence had been improperly excluded by the trial judge. By tradition, the judge who'd hear this motion was the same judge who'd presided over the trial, Carl O. Bradford.

The state asked the court to dismiss Connolly's motion, claiming it was too late.

Connolly came back arguing that the period while the case was before the U.S. Supreme Court didn't count because he couldn't do anything in state court while the case remained under consideration by the highest court in the land.

Meanwhile, Trial & Error had sent packets of information to all the trial jurors. Leatrice Gamage, who hadn't been able to vote on the verdict because she'd been impaneled as an alternate juror, wrote back (and to local newspapers) saying she'd felt after the trial that the state's evidence was inadequate.

> ...I felt then that Dennis was at the wrong place at the wrong time, and was railroaded.... I am a mother of a daughter and I have six granddaughters. I feel that whoever committed this heinous crime should be punished to the fullest extent of the law. But I feel that this person is still at large....

Trial juror George Rossbach told Trial & Error:

> ... As I recall, I was aware at the time of the trial, the evidence was not absolute to support conviction or release from it, but evidence was strongly circumstantial for guilt, yet there was a possibility Dechaine was framed. In my mind, the greatest liabilities against Dechaine were:
> 1. Dechaine's alleged statements of guilt according to police officers.
> 2. Dechaine's admitted experimentation with drug(s) at the time of the murder, and his admitted confusion. Extreme influence of drug(s) could, I assume, have worked both ways for Dechaine, regarding guilt or innocence—guilt, by changing his personality to fiendishness; innocence of guilt by confusing his memory; and innocent by possibly aiding a (theoretical) other (guilty)

person to set up Dechaine as a patsy for framing....
I have worried, and support a new trial.

Clarence W. Goselin, an inmate at Maine's other prison, penned a poem that reflects the despondency of most first-time prisoners:

> Inside these walls there is no peace.
> At least not for the mind.
> You sit and search the depths of it,
> Afraid of what you'll find.

10

A Cynical Volunteer

It was late in June 1992 when I happened to spot a small article in the paper announcing a meeting at one of our local churches where friends of Dechaine would "prove" that he'd been wrongfully convicted. I remembered well the news accounts four years earlier. The state's case seemed pretty tight. To me, this looked like another one of those episodes where a bunch of ill-informed birdbrains get together to trash law enforcement. I was annoyed, but curious. Considering the evidence I'd read about in the papers, how could these people possibly think Dechaine was innocent?

About a dozen townsfolk sat on folding metal chairs in the basement of that church as the panel of four made presentations.

The most distinguished panelist was the elderly Episcopal Bishop Roger Blanchard. Two other men in their thirties—blond fisherman Bill MacDonald and brown-haired Steve Sandau, a friend and neighbor of Dechaine—spoke, too. But when Carol Waltman stood up, there was no doubt that she was their driving force.

She looked to be in her late twenties with something of the tomboy about her—a wiry body and tendrils of wiry, black hair drooping over her forehead; attractive despite her apparent indifference to clothes or coiffure—and she spoke with the French accent so common to those who live in the northern reaches of Maine. Her speech was articulate and her manner revealed that arresting combination of honesty and anger that suggests brains and strength, the kind of strength that shows itself in courage and determination.

The thrust of their arguments centered on claims that the police had refused to follow hot leads and had destroyed evidence. The prosecution also declined to make the DNA tests that might disprove the state's theory of Dechaine's guilt. During the trial, they said, the prosecutor had fought to suppress evidence pointing to some other suspect. Was he afraid of the jury's intelligence?

Their arguments didn't seem very persuasive but, by the time they'd finished their presentation, I was convinced of their sincerity. The state police in Maine enjoy a reputation for fairness, toughness, for assisting citizens in all manner of situations from disabled vehicles to serious injury—in short, they're considered the epitome of professional law enforcement. Seven years earlier, I'd retired from the U.S. Treasury's Bureau of Alcohol, Tobacco, and Firearms. My own contacts with these troopers and detectives over the years I'd headed ATF's office in Maine had been uniformly positive. Like other Mainers, I'd come to know the Maine State Police as a first-rate organization.

As weary as I'd become of hearing civilians trash law enforcement, I sympathized with these people. They weren't idiots. They were sincere, but naïve. They'd latched onto facts they didn't quite understand and inflated them into an unreal significance. It's pitiful, I thought, how earnest citizens can delude themselves to maintain their faith in a friend. So I stayed behind after the meeting, introduced myself, and offered to look into the case.

My offer had two conditions. First, that Dechaine would sign a release authorizing anyone—including doctors, lawyers, and public officials—to tell me anything I wanted to know. And second, that his lawyer officially request my services.

If my conditions were met, I told them, I'd investigate to find the truth. "Not to get your friend off. I made a career putting bad guys in. I don't get bad guys out."

In order to preserve my objectivity, I'd work the investigation *gratis*.

It was my intention and expectation that I'd find enough to clarify the case, to answer their questions and assuage their doubts, to convince Trial & Error's members that police and prosecutors had performed their duties and justice was done. It might take a month or two but I was still a cop at heart, still sensitive to the public's perception of my profession.

A week later, Tom Connolly telephoned. I met with him and gave him the same pitch. And, I added, if I uncovered more evidence of Dechaine's guilt, I'd give it to the police.

Connolly smiled, "Fine. Where do you want to begin?" He seemed like a nice guy, but that doesn't mean anything. Most lawyers, male or female, are nice guys. Hell, Dechaine's friends said *he* was a nice guy.

At the state prison in Thomaston, I had my first encounter with the convicted child-killer. The man struck me as the quintessential wimp—an observation reinforced later when I discovered that his childhood nickname had been "Mouse." My most charitable assessment: he was not a man I'd care to have a drink with. Or coffee. Or anything else. Just not my kind of guy. But Dechaine listened to my conditions and agreed. He was innocent, he said. He had nothing to fear from an objective investigation.

Big deal. He was doing life. He had nothing to lose.

❖

Everyone else involved in this case wanted it to remain closed.

For Sarah's family, the trial and conviction and life sentence was the most that society could contribute toward closure. Their sweet young girl was dead, buried, gone forever. All they could hope for now was an eventual diminishing of anguish that time might provide.

Police and prosecutors, of course, had moved onward with a brisk "case closed" and a sigh of relief that the public hue and cry for safety and justice was satisfied.

Dechaine's friends, still convinced of his innocence, focused their attention upon each tenuous fragment of the case so cunningly constructed by Prosecutor Wright. They kept adding the same numbers calculated by Wright for the jury and coming up with different sums.

Connolly had exposed some critical weaknesses in the state's case. There were no direct proofs. The circumstantial evidence was subject to conflicting interpretations. But the papers in the driveway, Dechaine's drug use and those "confessions" were damning.

On the other hand, I had to wonder whether the heartless fiend who'd kidnapped and tortured and sexually abused a sweet innocent little girl, then strangled the life out of her—would a creature like that ever be moved by any trace of a normal human conscience into admitting what he'd done?

First step: study the trial transcript and the discovery material the state had turned over to Tom Connolly. But even before that, I read Trial & Error's collection of newspaper articles and videotaped TV news programs. Reporters often pick up something everyone else missed.

❖

Melinda Lake's piece in the *Brunswick Times Record* included a disappointing quote from prosecutor Eric Wright, telling media people before the trial, "I'm satisfied that when all of you hear the case, the evidence is sufficient to show Dechaine caused the murder of Sarah Cherry."

Federal prosecutors see such pre-trial statements as unprofessional attempts to influence potential jurors. Rules promulgated by the Maine Bar Association forbid it. Wright reportedly confirmed for reporters that Dechaine's notebook and a receipt were found in the Henkel driveway along with "other documents" he wouldn't specify.

But I went through all of the police reports. There were no "other documents."

Lawmen caught Dechaine in little lies that ruined his credibility in the eyes of the state. I saw Wright's lies as worse. The "good guys" are paid to be honest.

Wright did decline to tell reporters what evidence had been found in Dechaine's truck but that was another kind of lie. This discreet refusal, following his earlier candor in confirming the discovery of those papers in the driveway, implied that incriminating evidence had been found in the truck. But police reports revealed that this was untrue.

❖

Professor Richard A. Leo, Professor of Criminology at the University of California at Irvine, wrote in 1996 that, "The 'gap problem'—the gap between how the law is written and how it is actually practiced by legal actors in the social world—has been an ongoing concern to legal scholars at least since the advent of Legal Realism in the 1930s."

Eric Wright's conduct was starting to irritate me. Nevertheless, a few sleazy comments to the media don't mean the state's position is wrong.

❖

Ordinarily, when a body is dumped in a remote wood, as it was here, research suggests that the killer is likely to be an outdoorsman familiar with the area. The schizophrenic kills first and abuses the body afterwards. He may cut off the breasts or place a stick in the vagina—some psychologists interpret these acts as an attempt to change a woman into a man. But the schizophrenic isn't likely to torture his victim.

Torture is the work of the psychopath.

Psychopaths fall into the category called "organized killers." He plans the crime, even if the "plan" is formed quickly when opportunity knocks. His victim is a stranger. He likes to restrain the woman—chains, ropes, gags—and he intensifies her fear by inflicting pain. Organized killers usually take the body away from the scene of the abuse and hide it. They also take, and keep, souvenirs of their experience.

Sarah's killer had taken her panties.

FBI profilers suggest that the man who'd commit a crime like this would be white, male, twenty-five to thirty-five years old, driving a pickup or van with high mileage. He'd also have a history of violence and a record of arrests for robbery and assault.

❖

The trial transcript of the lawyers' summations to the jury show that Prosecutor Wright marshaled his evidence effectively: witnesses saw the red truck on the Lewis Hill Road; there were the papers from Dechaine's truck in the driveway; ropes from the truck were used to tie the girl's hands; and the body was found in close proximity to the truck.

There was Dechaine's proximity to those woods. There were his lies to the Buttricks about where he lived and worked, and his lie to the police about the truck keys. Everybody said he was a gentle guy, but what did drugs do to a man? No memory of that afternoon, he said. Add his confessions to four separate officers. Dechaine claimed they were lying but Wright asked the jury, "Why, if these officers wished to make up confessions, would they not make up more direct confessions with more details?"

Wright's logic was sound. Unfortunately, however, Wright's fact was correct, too: those "confessions" contained no details.

Turning to the defense summation, Connolly's arguments were good. This *was* a surprisingly atrocious crime for a man with no criminal record. And the drug issue could cut both ways, as the juror Rossbach had already said—make Dechaine crazy, or cloud his memory. Besides, he'd cooperated. He allowed them to take the truck for a thorough search at their lab. He let them take his pictures. He answered questions. The evidence of the tracking dog seemed irrelevant. Police reports showed that the dog led no one anywhere meaningful. Knots Dechaine habitually tied were different from those used to bind the victim. How significant were these facts?

Yes, an innocent man would be nervous, even terrified to find himself accused of a crime like this. But the cooperation angle might not mean much. I've seen guilty men cooperate—act innocent—hoping to allay an investigator's suspicions.

Nobody saw Dechaine do it, but that meant nothing. Killers take steps to avoid witnesses. No knife was found. So? It was a big woods. It could be anywhere.

Connolly pointed out that lots of clues that could have been left were not present. So what?

My mind kept shifting back and forth. I had to struggle to maintain the discipline of objectivity because everything in my experience and my dedication to my profession urged me to believe the prosecution. And all of us have this tendency to believe what we want to believe.

The case came down to papers in the driveway, the confessions, and the truck.

Nor could there be any doubt that Dechaine's Toyota figured in—papers in the driveway, the tire track, ropes from the truck, and finding the truck so close to the body. Maine is a huge state but Dechaine, and his truck, were right there.

And yet, I was struck by Connolly's point regarding the mysterious absence of any evidence indicating that Sarah had ever been in that truck: no blood, no fingerprints, no hairs, nothing! No forensic evidence on the girl's body or in his truck. People don't always leave fingerprints in a vehicle, and there may have been no wounds to bleed until Sarah was taken into the woods. But after they'd vacuumed the entire cab of that truck and subjected what they'd gathered to microscopic examination, the state's experts should have found *something* to suggest the kidnapped girl had been there.

Hendsbee had promised Dechaine that permitting a search of the truck would, "help us clear you, or we'll find evidence that you took that girl. It'll either tie you in with her, or clear you from the case." And State Police Lt. Arnold had informed the press that, "in some cases microscopic evidence can point the finger at one person, in others it can prove that a prime suspect couldn't have committed the crime."

If Dechaine was guilty, they should have found something. But they didn't.

Prosecutor Wright explained this to the jury: "That's how God made it."

11

Comes the Dawn

Prosecutor Wright had said there was no other suspect.

But if one listened to the Trial & Error people, that wasn't quite true.

Wright hadn't actually committed an outright lie. Since he'd successfully prevented the jury from hearing any mention of Douglas Senecal, he was technically correct when he said, "There is no evidence, ladies and gentlemen of the jury, *in this case*, of an alternative perpetrator...."

In the larger sense, however—in the realm of truth, versus precise accuracy—Wright was wrong. Still, rigorous training and hard experience as a Treasury agent taught me the danger of reaching a conclusion before I'd seen all the evidence.

I re-read the trial transcript: 1,482 pages, not counting the judge's instructions to the jury and their announcement of the verdict.

Something didn't fit.

It didn't really matter that someone claimed they'd seen Dechaine's truck on the road near the Henkel house, or that Nancy Dechaine did her laundry before the police asked for the clothes Dennis had worn. It was interesting, but the very same facts would apply to hundreds of Mainers. Most of the state's evidence was fluff.

The case stood on three legs: the papers found in the Henkel driveway; Dechaine's truck which (like himself) was near the spot where the body would be found; and the confessions. The papers, the truck, and the confessions—these were the foundations of the state's case. If they stood, he was guilty.

❖

The confessions seemed damning.

Confessions documented by professionals typically include something more than a simple, "I did it." A real confession reveals some detail no innocent person could know. That's how we know that the confessor isn't an attention-seeker or a crackpot. In this case, though, the officers couldn't try to elicit corroborative proof. Once Dechaine requested an attorney, they were prohibited from asking questions. And yet, somewhere among all the reports of Dechaine's words to officers—much of which they wouldn't document for the record since the detectives were only writing down what they saw as useful—you'd think that amidst these virtually endless babblings, a killer would have dropped at least one reference to some incriminating fact: how he'd abducted Sarah, something he'd done to her or how she reacted.

One fact was clear: any man who commits such heinous atrocities, especially against a helpless little girl, has to be a sociopath. The sociopath doesn't see men and women as he and she. The sociopath sees another person as "it." And they never admit guilt unless they see confession as the path to personal advantage, like a reduced sentence in exchange for a plea of guilty. But Dechaine wasn't asking for a deal. The guy just seemed to be floundering—one minute "I couldn't have done it;" the next "I must have done it."

Professor Richard A. Leo of the University of California at Irvine has published numerous studies reflecting decades of research regarding confessions. One bit of false "common knowledge" Professor Leo points to is the naïve belief that nothing short of dire threats or torture would make anyone confess to a crime he hadn't committed.

Professor Leo describes the reactions of an innocent person, suddenly accused of a crime he hasn't committed:

> An innocent person is likely to experience considerable shock and disorientation during the interrogation because he is wholly unprepared for the confrontation and accusation that are the core of the process, an will not understand how an investigator could possibly suspect him. A innocent individual may become progressively more distressed, confused and desperate as he is told of evidence that incriminates him. He will express doubt and dismay when the investigator claims to possess lengthening list of damning evidence. When an investigator assures an innocent that the evidence does in fact exist, the suspect will likely insist that someone has made an error or is trying to frame him.

Dechaine's reactions fit this pattern.

"Persuaded confessions," as described by Professor Leo, are those given after a suspect has become convinced, despite having no memory of the act, that he committed the crime. Indeed, a Clearwater, Florida man told police, "I still can't believe I did it. I guess all the proof's in." But this man was later proved innocent. And a Manchester, Connecticut man signed a statement for police which said, "If the evidence shows I was there and that I killed her, then I killed her, but I don't remember being there." He was proved innocent, too. There are numerous such cases.

Professor Leo offers the "hallmark of the persuaded confession"—whether it was generated by interrogators or the suspect's own mental cogitation—as "the suspect's uncertainty in his conclusions. The persuaded false confessor typically alternates between expressing minimal certainty in his guilt and minimal confidence in his innocence."

Something else began to bother me. Despite the prosecution's persistence in referring to Dechaine's "confessions," technically the statements he made were not confessions. His worst words were "Someone inside me must have made me do it." In legal terminology, this would qualify as an "admission." It's a small point, but Eric Wright's semantic manipulation—like his assertion that "there was no other suspect"—struck me more like the artifice of a sleazy mouthpiece than the conduct I'd expect from the attorney representing the people in the cause of justice.

The Psychology of Interrogations, Confessions and Testimony was written by a clinical psychologist from the London Institute of Psychiatry named Gisli Gudjonsson. I probably saw his book as more compelling than tomes penned by pure academics because Gudjonnson had also served as a state police detective in Iceland. His findings, based on ten years examining the psychological aspects of England's most notorious cases, included the crime featured in a film, *In the Name of The Father*, where a young Irishman confessed to a bombing he hadn't committed. Gudjonnson's book details his own research and that of others.

One of the cases treated in the book involved young Peter Reilly, brought to trial in Canaan, Connecticut after confessing to the brutal slaying of his own mother. Gudjonnson wrote:

> The prosecution argued that the evidence against Reilly was "overwhelming." In reality, the only evidence . . .except for some circumstantial evidence, was the self-incriminating confession. No forensic evidence was ever found to link him with the murder, and the prosecution tried hard to explain how Reilly could have changed his bloodstained clothes after the murder in order to avoid detection. It was emphasized by the prosecuting counsel that Reilly had been informed of his legal rights four times. Furthermore, Reilly was an intelligent, articulate, calm and alert individual and his alleged off-the-record comment, "I killed her," surely indicated his guilt. Reilly repeated his confession to two police officers after the interrogation was terminated, which was used by the prosecution to further indicate his guilt.

After Reilly's conviction, evidence was unearthed which

the prosecutor and police had concealed—proof that the boy couldn't possibly be guilty. Those cops were like the pragmatic cabinetmaker, hired to build a walnut table but lacking quite enough walnut stock to complete the job. He simply used a piece of maple and treated it with walnut stain. To those Connecticut detectives, Peter Reilly was no more than a stick of wood.

Gudjonnson reports several circumstances common to cases where innocent men admitted to crimes they didn't commit. Every one of these criteria fits Dechaine.

> 1. An inability—due to drugs or alcohol—to remember what had happened during the hours when the crime was committed;
> 2. Facts which he can't explain, shown him by confident officers as "absolute proof" of his guilt;
> 3. A combination of the subject's character traits:
>   a. low self-esteem;
>   b. great respect for authority; and
>   c. a compliant personality that makes him vulnerable to suggestibility.

A study quoted by Professor Leo involving sixty-five men proved innocent after confessing to homicides, found that:

> In a considerable number, the zealousness of the police...or the gross negligence of the police in overlooking, or even suppressing evidence, or the prosecution's over-zealousness, was an operative factor in causing the

erroneous conviction.

Professor Leo also points out in *The Decision to Confess Falsely*, that:

> Once police elicit a confession—even if it is obtained by questionable or prohibited means, is internally inconsistent, is contradicted by the case facts, and does not lead to corroboration—they will almost always arrest the confessor and consider the case solved. Criminal justice officials typically will not believe a defendant's retraction and may see it as further evidence of deceitfulness.... At trial, the jury is likely to treat the confession as more probative of the defendant's guilt than any other evidence and, if convicted, the defendant is likely to be sentenced more harshly because he failed to show remorse....

The factual similarities between the Reilly and Dechaine cases were striking: a terrible crime; circumstantial evidence; no forensic proofs; both men's intelligence; their personalities; and repeated confessions after being advised of their rights. But how important were these similarities? I've had bright but *guilty* men admit horrendous crimes after being advised of their rights and confronted with incriminating evidence. Fortunately, however, the cases I'd investigated as a U.S. Treasury agent benefited from corroborating evidence.

As a former lawman, I was irritated by certain portions of Gudjonnson's book. He made repeated references to the case portrayed by the film, *In the Name of the Father*, where

British prosecutors concealed a file containing facts that proved the defendants innocent—a file they'd labeled, "Not To Be Shown To The Defense." I know such things happen. No profession is free from unworthy members—not medicine or the law, not politics or the media, not even the clergy. Renegades always attract so much attention that their crimes seem like more than the rare occurrences they truly are.

As it turned out, though, I'd discover later that prosecutors in the Dechaine case had concealed information. And my first such discovery wouldn't be the last.

I believed the officers' reports of Dechaine's statements, but this research offset their significance. Nothing he said was corroborated. Nothing he said indicated any knowledge of what was done to the girl. The value of Dennis Dechaine's babblings shrunk to the level of those truck sightings on the road near the Henkel house. Not useless, but not very useful, either. Not without some verifiable link between him and the victim.

Even without the "confessions," there was still that truck. It didn't say much that tire tracks in the Henkels' driveway were "consistent with" Dechaine's tires. All that meant was that the state's expert hadn't noted any great difference and he hadn't found any unique similarity. An expert I consulted looked at the state's exhibits and told me that tens of thousands of vehicles in the State of Maine wore tires that were consistent with those tracks. But the rope binding Sarah's hands, and another piece of rope found in the woods, had come from Dechaine's truck. And papers found in the driveway outside the Henkel house came from that truck.

And yet, Tom Connolly had made another point in his summation to the jury. It was assumed that those papers in the driveway had fallen from the truck during the abduction. The police inventory of items found in the Toyota by the state's lab technicians listed everything from empty cigarette packs, candy wrappers and Styrofoam cups to loose change. Connolly counted each separate item and wondered aloud, what were the chances that, of these 180 items, the only two to "fall out" onto that driveway identified Dennis Dechaine.

The odds against that were high. But it was possible. Stranger things have happened. Coincidence can't survive in a good fiction novel but it happens in real life.

Connolly's theory that someone framed this quiet, gentle farmer seemed ludicrous. According to the defense, everybody liked the guy. Nobody even hinted at an enemy. Crooks always claim they've been framed. Even if someone despised Dechaine, nobody murders a little girl to set anybody up.

None of the evidence produced by the state really proved anything, but its cumulative effect might justify a guilty verdict. And yet, my mind kept whispering that something didn't fit. But try as I might, I couldn't put my finger on it.

They say the human brain resembles a computer, filled with facts and capable of finding connections between them. One method of seeking that vital clue is to quit trying. Get your mind off the case. Let your brain do the sifting.

So I put the transcript and the state's reports aside, and went for a ride.

It's easy to relax cruising Maine's countryside along two-lane blacktop through deep forests, here and there open areas of tall grass or an apple orchard. Thousands of yesteryear's farms are overgrown with trees—oak and beech, birch and maple, aspen and the ubiquitous evergreens. Once-cultivated fields, given over to pin-cherry and raspberry bushes, are still bounded by stone walls, mossy barriers constructed by the long-ago farmers who'd cleared the land by rolling huge rocks, or dragging them with a team of horses, to the edges of the fields they'd cleared. It's easy to let the mind wander into memories and thoughts of family and friends. It's easy just to hum along with a familiar tune on the radio, but I couldn't prevent my conscious thought from asking its questions. What the hell am I doing? Those Trial & Error people have a point.

The state's case is a collection of mismatched patches sewn onto those few hard facts. There's not a single scrap of direct proof—no eyewitness to anything important, no scientific finding of value. Maybe he did it. But "maybe" is no damned justification for giving a guy life in prison. And what if he didn't do it? Suppose he was innocent. How in hell could I prove that? The gold badge of the U.S. Treasury I'd carried for twenty-five years opened doors, opened files, opened mouths. Doors and files and mouths don't open for an old P.I. fighting the official law enforcement community. Besides, those guys were my colleagues. Life was going to be a lot easier for me if Dennis Dechaine was guilty.

That was the conscious level of my brain. My subconscious must have kept on with its scanning, sorting and sifting of the police reports and trial transcript I'd read. An enormous white barn with a clock set into the cupola on its roof caught my eye, and something clicked. At the next crossroads, I screeched a U-turn and sped home. Clouds grayed the sky and a slow drizzle began. By the time I'd settled into my soft chair with coffee and the trial transcript, a heavy summer rain drummed against my windows. It was there, in the easy comfort of a summer afternoon, that I found what I never wanted to find.

❖

There are benefits to being in a courtroom, seeing the witnesses and hearing how they testify. On the other hand, everyone from the victim's family to the defendant's camp carries the baggage of conflicting emotions and despair. They're all too involved to fully appreciate everything they see and hear. Some day after you've watched a movie, watch it again—the same film. You'll see and hear things that are new to you, things you don't remember from the first viewing because some act or some line of dialog diverted your mind into another thought and you missed the next few seconds, or perhaps an entire scene. The same thing happens during a trial, but more frequently due to pauses for lawyers to look at their notes, and the waits for dawdling witnesses to shuffle toward the stand and take the oath. If it can happen with a movie, produced by hundreds of professional artists and craftsmen at the cost of millions of dollars, with a tight story and performances designed to hold your interest, it's eminently more common in a real-life trial with its lugubrious procedure interrupted by lackluster debates citing arcane rules.

Despite the gravity and reality, the dreary delays and

imperative consequences of it all, criminal trials *are* plays. Scripts are based on material provided by criminals and cops. The witnesses become actors who've rehearsed their lines in their own minds, and often auditioned before officials. The director, the man or woman who edits the script and directs the drama, is the prosecutor.

In this trial, director Eric Wright decided the sequence of witnesses, the display of exhibits, the timing and pace of presentation—when to pause, what to repeat, when to dazzle with deft disclosures or plod with drear technical details, when and how to hasten along to something new.

The audience—family, friends, spectators and the jury—saw and heard what was shown them.

On the other hand, as cold case investigators know, there are advantages to examining the documents and evidence that remain beyond the trial—a trial transcript, lab reports and detectives' statements—in unhurried comfort without the emotion and immediacy of a trial. And this is the advantage I had over everyone else involved in this case. It doesn't require brilliance to be objective when you're not concerned with ambition or career, or answering the public's frightened demands for a solution to some horrendous crime, or defending your client against an array of despicable charges. It's easy to be detached when you're not related to the victim, or a friend of the defendant. It's easier to see the trees, rather than just the forest, when you're not being bashed by the state and your memory isn't cluttered by having observed the trial at a pace set by the prosecutor. This advantage of mine was about to bear fruit.

❖

Experience has given me a healthy skepticism toward the testimony of witnesses. Our memories are less than perfect. What any person says, even what we truly believe, is inevitably shaped by our desire to be helpful, to do "the right thing," or to be important—not to mention the possibility of less noble motives. When the police come around looking for clues, people try to help. They'll tell an officer anything that might possibly aid in the cause of justice. They don't have to be absolutely positive at this point because any piece of information, however tentative, might become the key to catching a crook. By the time a witness gets to court, though, it's plain that what he or she said is important, or the prosecution wouldn't have issued a subpoena to testify. The witness isn't about to change what he told the officer. Besides, since what he said at the time of the crime was then fresher in his mind, the witness is convinced that what he said is true. In most cases, it is. But not always. We're all human. We all want to help, to be right, to be seen as honest and intelligent.

There is one class of evidence I always trust: scientific proofs. Science has no axe to grind, no career to advance, no wrong to be avenged, no profit to be made, no personal advantage to be gained, no incentive to favor one side or the other. The laws of nature don't give a damn who did what, or who wins. Science is like the rain. It respects no one. It disrespects no one. The rain doesn't give a damn who gets wet.

The autopsy, performed at about 3:40 that Friday afternoon, detailed the injuries. Dr. Roy found a few fly larvae in

Sarah's eyes. He didn't save them or identify them. The species of fly can suggest how long a body has lain in the woods.

Nor did Dr. Roy examine the soles of her feet. Did she walk on the Henkels' gravel driveway? Across that dusty road between Dechaine's truck and the woods? On the dusty floor of some structure where her killer took her to inflict those injuries in private before bringing her to the forest? There might have been traces of soil.

ATF scientists pioneered the forensic use of neutron activation analysis. They've proved that several specimens of marijuana were grown in the same field; they've taken dirt from a truck's mudflaps in New York City and linked it to a specific farm in Georgia. What might science have done with soil samples from Sarah's feet?

Death isn't an event. It's a process.

Tissues and organs die at different rates. The first part of the process is a cooling of the body. Two facts important in determining time of death are the temperature of the body when found, and the ambient temperature. Unfortunately, State Medical Examiner Dr. Ronald Roy didn't record either of these elements. The weather bureau recorded temperatures at their station nearing ninety degrees throughout that week, but there is no record of the ambient temperature in the woods, twenty-five miles away where Sarah was found. No one can guess the body's temperature beyond the warden's comment on that sweltering July day that her forehead felt cold to his touch.

Rigor mortis is the result of the cessation of a complex

chemical reaction in the body's muscles. When respiration ceases and oxygen is no longer available, two kinds of fibers—actin and myosin—that normally link and unlink are no longer able to do so. They fuse and become a gel, resulting in the stiffness known as rigor mortis. It begins in the muscles of the head, face and neck, then progresses down through the body and into the arms and legs. It remains for a time, then dissipates in the same order until the stiffness has left the body altogether. Its onset is more rapid in infants, children, and old people. In the average adult under normal circumstances, rigor mortis disappears about thirty-six hours after death. The process is hastened (shortened) by heat, retarded (lengthened) by cold. Generally, however, if a body feels warm and it isn't stiff, the person has been dead for three hours or less. If it's warm and stiff, it's been dead between three and eight hours. Cold and stiff, somewhere between eight and thirty-six hours.

The autopsy report stated the cause of death as "asphyxiation due to strangulation by ligature with multiple stab wounds of the neck and chest." In the courtroom, Dr. Roy testified that she'd been dead for anywhere from thirty to thirty-six hours when he examined her body and, while the various wounds had been painful, Sarah was killed by the ligature. My only solace was the thought that the strangulation—one that constricted her throat to a diameter of two-and-a-half or three inches—didn't allow the girl more than a minute to realize she was about to die. After the terror and torture she'd suffered, and seeing no end to her agony, a girl with Sarah Cherry's spiritual faith may have welcomed death.

❖

Dr. Eben Osgood, a retired professor of entomology at the University of Maine—rather thin, with a face that suggested long experience—listened to the state pathologist's scant description of the fly larvae found on the body: "one-to-two centimeters in length." The temperature on the day in question hovered around the nineties. I asked Dr. Osgood what he could tell me about the significance of these larvae.

"The answer to that would depend on the type of larvae," he smiled, and shrugged. "I couldn't identify them without examining them under a microscope. Sometimes we have to dissect them to find out what they are."

But Medical Examiner Roy had discarded the larvae.

"Given what you've told me," Professor Osgood said, "they are most likely *calliphoridae* or *sarcophagidae*. Blow flies or flesh flies. Both species lay their eggs in warm places where they'll have something to feed on when they mature. Moist places, because drying is a hazard to survival. Where were these found?"

"In the victim's eyes."

"Yes, well that could be either species. Given the season and the temperature, the blow flies lay an egg that grow into larvae and attain the one-to-two centimeter size within a short time. The flesh flies lay larvae rather than eggs. Both species have extraordinarily sensitive olfactory senses but a human corpse might not reach a state of putrefaction that would attract them for a day or so. On the other hand, I've seen cases where a live person came into the hospital with an open wound that had larvae present. Flies aren't diggers. They lay their eggs in exposed places."

Thus far, I'd relegated Dechaine's so-called confessions to the realm of interesting-if-corroborated. His truck, and his papers in the driveway, didn't prove that he'd murdered Sarah Cherry, but they were strong clues.

And then, in an instant, my mind clicked. The state's own evidence proved that Dennis Dechaine couldn't possibly have murdered Sarah Cherry. He was innocent!

With the hearing on Tom Connolly's motion for a new trial about to begin, I took a break from my studies. I wanted to see the principals in action.

12

And In This Corner....

BY JULY 1992, MORE THAN THREE YEARS after Dechaine's conviction, most Mainers believed that he had murdered Sarah Cherry.

Sarah's family, convinced of his guilt, was tormented by this hearing's threat to the closure they longed for. Grandmother Margaret Cherry told the *Brunswick Times Record*, "I would have thought that by this time it would have eased up a bit—the hurt, the pain, the horror. But it hasn't. It's just as fresh as the day it happened."

Understandably unaware that lawyers instruct their clients to avoid impulsive, passionate behavior on the witness stand—after all, by the time a trial begins, no jury would believe that a defendant is shocked by the accusation—Mrs. Cherry said she'd known Dechaine was guilty because he showed no emotion in the courtroom. "An innocent person would have screamed bloody murder."

If the attractive, perfectly groomed grandmother's comprehension of trials and testimony was wanting, her feelings were deep and amply justified. "He took away something very precious, not only for us, but for the world." Little Sarah, active in her church's youth group, good at academics and athletics, wanted to be a teacher because she liked working with children. "She had a wonderful future."

And, Mrs. Cherry said, "I hope he lives a long time in prison, and when he finally does die and has to stand before God, then he'll start his second imprisonment."

Dechaine, interviewed in prison after the hearing, understood the family's feelings. "They lost a beautiful child. As much as I want them to know that I'm not the man responsible for that, I really understand their anger. There's probably nothing I can ever say." But he was angry with the state. "I think I have a right to be upset. Their investigation was a flop. They threw all this inconsistent evidence away, and it's essentially cost me my life." He blamed the press, which he termed merciless, for "parroting whatever the attorney general was giving them. I was convicted in the press long before my trial."

Indeed, Maine newspapers had publicized the state's side of the story long before the trial because the prosecution was the only side giving reporters anything to report. But the state's major newspapers were also guilty of occasionally exaggerating the truth. In the wake of Detective Westrum's testimony regarding the statements he claimed Dechaine had made to him—statements suggesting guilt to a degree that prosecutors termed them "confessions"—The Portland Press-Herald's front-page piece on March 14, 1989, shouted inaccurately:

DECHAINE SAID HE KILLED GIRL, OFFICER TESTIFIES

And the Lewiston *Daily Sun*, on that same day, headlined:

DECHAINE SAID HE KILLED GIRL

In the years after the trial, the minds of most Mainers replaced the facts of Westrum's actual allegations with the superficial, faulted shorthand of those headlines.

Now, with the hearing about to begin, one *Press Herald* article was headlined:

SUPPORTERS OF CHILD KILLER MAINTAIN HIS INNOCENCE

Well, he had been convicted. They were entitled.

Connolly filed a brief with the court stating that the discovery material turned over by the state contained no information about alternative suspect Douglas Senecal, nothing about Ralph Jones's identification of a red and white truck and Senecal's voice, and no report from Trooper Ron Jacques to whom Jones had given this information.

A few weeks before the hearing, Prosecutor Wright sent the defense a set of undated affidavits from witnesses supporting the alibi offered by Senecal.

Maine is best known for its rugged coastline with thousands of islands, the 10 percent of its land beneath 6,000 lakes and ponds and 5,100 rivers and streams abounding with landlocked salmon, trout, and other game fish. It's widely known that this is the most heavily forested state in America, where ancient herds of mastodons, mammoths, and even camels, lost in the Ice Age, have given way to a vast variety of moose and deer, bear and beaver, bald eagles and golden eagles, foxes and coyotes. The wolves were driven north by angry farmers a century ago, but now there's even a self-styled Maine Wolf Coalition striving to bring them back "to restore the balance of Nature." The state's industrial products range from toothpicks to the ultra-hi-tech Aegis destroyers, and everyone's heard of L.L. Bean. Everyone knows this Maine.

Less known is far northern Aroostook County, referred to by Mainers simply as "the county" because it covers more land area than the combined size of Connecticut and Rhode Island. Madawaska, on the Canadian border, is the most northeasterly town in the United States. Its largest employer is the Fraser Paper Mill, where Carol Waltman's husband works, but the town still remains a strong agricultural community producing potatoes, broccoli, hay, even flax. The number of farmers has diminished to about 10 percent of the number who tilled the soil there fifty years ago, reduced by competition from the Midwest and subsidized Canadians, and by intermittent hard times. They've progressed from the days when all they had was ox-power to the modern age of mechanization. But Nature still rules, and a year's work can be destroyed by rain or frost. Older farmers still remember 1950 when the "field price" for a barrel of potatoes fell from $5.50 in autumn to thirty-five cents by spring. Farmers are gamblers. They're also tough. And stubborn.

On a PBS documentary not long ago, Maine writer John Cole spoke of small towns where people trade with folks they know. "There's a relationship established," he said, "so that when you see them every day, it's like seeing a member of your family or a relative or a very close friend, and the human experience is nourished, and you feed on it, and it just makes you have a better day to have that back and forth exchange with people you've seen practically every day of every year of your life in that community." Madawaska, the town where Dechaine grew up, is one such community. Its residents are intellectually and economically like most other Americans and yet, there's something more that makes these people unique.

The predominantly French residents of Madawaska are honest, practical, very independent, very stubborn, very Catholic, and enormously proud of their heritage. Today, along with television and computers, fast food, modern schools, and soccer, they preserve their traditions of church, family, hard work, their music, and their language. Most are bi-lingual, and it's not uncommon for a conversation to fluctuate—sometimes even in mid-sentence—from French to English and back again to French.

Their ancestors originally migrated from the French province of Poitou to Nova Scotia. In 1755, however, in *le grande derangement,* they were evicted from the region they'd named "Acadie" and herded onto ships at gunpoint for refusing to swear allegiance to the King of England. Some were scattered as far away as Louisiana. Many settled in and farmed along the St. John River, naming their towns St. Agathe and St. David, Grand Isle and Presque Isle, Notre Dame and Frenchville. "Madawaska" derives from an Iroquois Indian word meaning "Land of the Porcupines"— appropriate, perhaps, since some officials in the office of Maine's attorney general came to regard Carol Waltman and Trial & Error as more prickly than any porcupine they'd ever met.

As the time neared for the hearing for a new trial, Trial

& Error member Steve Sandau was quoted as saying that, "We had some really good momentum for a while but it's tough to keep it up" after losing appeals (of the verdict) to the Maine Supreme Court and the U.S. Supreme Court. "When you start running into years rather than weeks and months and don't have much good news...."

Carol Waltman organized two score members, all wearing lime-green Trial & Error T-shirts and handing out two-inch lime-green buttons emblazoned with black "Trial & Error—Quest For Justice" to anyone who'd accept one. They chartered a bus. Some came in campers and cars and pickup trucks. They attended every session of the hearing. When an opportunity was presented, they allowed themselves to be photographed and interviewed by reporters.

❖

The morning of July 2, 1992, officially began with a conference in the judge's chambers where much of the argument revolved around Trial & Error's mailing of material to the jurors who'd convicted Dechaine, and the subsequent announcements by the only two jurors who responded that Trial & Error's evidence could have changed their verdict. Prosecutor Wright's first phony ploy was an attempt to suggest that the jurors' names had been acquired illegally. When that failed, he was ready with a list of prior court decisions which, he claimed, made such juror statements inadmissible.

Clearly annoyed by the Trial & Error activities, Wright told Judge Bradford, "Mr. Connolly once told me that he had nothing to do with Trial & Error, and wished they would stay clear of him because they were not being helpful in this case."

"That's not true!" Connolly said.

This was neither the first, nor the last time that lawyers from the attorney general's office would distort statements by Connolly—and others.

❖

Isn't it strange how certain dialog from books and films can stick in our minds?

The most cogent explanation for falsehood I've ever heard was in the 1962 movie, *Charade*. Cary Grant is playing the role of a U.S. Treasury agent stationed in Paris when Audrey Hepburn's character asks him, "Why do people have to lie?"

"Because they want something," Grant's character replies, "and the truth won't get it for them."

13

Bradford Rules

SARAH CHERRY'S FAMILY SAT to the right of the aisle in the spectator section of the courtroom, behind the prosecutor's table. The other side filled with men and women wearing the lime-green *Trial & error* T-shirts. When Dechaine was brought in—well-groomed and neatly attired in a sport shirt and slacks—they raised their hands in a thumbs-up salutation. He smiled and nodded his head. Connolly greeted him, then turned to check his papers one last time.

In order to win a new trial on the legally permissible basis of new evidence, Tom Connolly would have to show the court that this evidence was, indeed, newly discovered; that, even with due diligence, it couldn't have been obtained before the trial; and that this new evidence would have made a difference in the jury's verdict. He would meet these challenges by establishing the existence of an alternative suspect—the man named Douglas Senecal.

Once again, Connolly faced Wright. Once again—in keeping with the Maine tradition that trial judges also hear motions aimed at overturning their trials—Judge Carl O. Bradford mounted the bench and rapped his gavel for order.

The state moved to dismiss Connolly's action as filed too

late. Connolly argued that appeals to higher courts had extended that time limit. Judge Bradford said he'd rule on this matter later, but he ruled immediately that trial jurors who had already expressed reservations about the verdict could not testify. One was an alternate juror who lacked the advantage of participation in deliberations; the other couldn't really say what he might have decided without discussing *Trial & error*'s alleged evidence with his fellow jurors.

Connolly's first witness was seventy-three-year-old Margaret Steele, a short, plump woman in a brightly flowered blouse, her graying hair cut short with bangs across her forehead. She testified that Bobby Lapierre, who had lived with Senecal, told her one day while they sat at her kitchen table that Senecal had murdered Sarah Cherry.

She had given this information to State Police Detective Drake.

But the state never passed this on to Connolly.

And she recounted another conversation before Dechaine's arrest when Sheriff Haggett and Detective Westrum visited her. State and county officers often visited at her home for coffee and gossip and miscellaneous tips. Speaking of Senecal, Haggett had told her, "Oh yes, Margaret, [Senecal] did it. All signs point his way."

Then Mrs. Steele said, "And I looked from him and I looked right over to Mark Westrum and Mark looked me right in the eye and he never said a word."

As for Lapierre, she knew him well, too. He'd visit her often, and even after he'd moved to California he'd telephone her. And, "He writes all the time. I have letters in my pocketbook that he writes me."

And why had she kept Lapierre's statement to herself for so long?

She quoted Lapierre as saying something else that day. "But don't tell anyone, or he'd kill you and he'd kill me."

And she believed it, because she'd known Senecal for years and, "He's got a vicious, vicious temper. You better believe it!"

Eric Wright cross-examined. He had her repeat her age, seventy-three. He brought out that she'd lived alone since her husband died sixteen years earlier. He quoted from a letter she'd written to the editor of a newspaper stating, in the portions he read:

> I have a TV and I read two different newspapers daily.
> I have been one to praise the Sagadahoc County Sheriff's Department and all other police. But now I have to eat crow. I'm glad I did not have to sit on the jury for Dennis Dechaine. I'm also glad I was not the judge. Why? Because I will tell you, because I think the parties who did the investigation of it did a lot of screwing up on their job. I think others have to see it. Also I feel deeply so sorry for all; I really do. I think a lot of questions are unanswered.

Wright's rapid-fire attempt to nail down the date of her conversation with Lapierre prompted Mrs. Steele to reply, "I don't know if you are talking if—you went too fast for my hearing."

Minutes later, after another question phrased in an

uncharacteristically perplexing manner by the ever-precise Wright, Judge Bradford said, "Mr. Wright, I'm confused. So why don't you start over again and ask your question again."

Moments later, Wright told the witness, "And when he told you about that, I thought you said a few minutes ago that it was the summer of 1989."

"He was here," Mrs. Steele replied.

"No wait, I'm trying to ask it simply."

"Wait yourself. He was here in 1988 and he was here in 1989."

And yet again, moments later, Wright said, "All right, let's try it this way. Am I correct, are you confused about—"

"I'm not confused. I've got a damned good memory."

Wright questioned Mrs. Steele for about an hour, hopping from one topic to another and back again, without shaking her. He tried to paint her as a somewhat senile old lady. He failed.

On re-direct examination, Tom Connolly asked her whether she'd furnished valid information to the authorities regarding various crimes in the area.

Wright objected.

Connolly told the judge he was just trying to show that the police relied on her.

Bradford sustained Wright's objection.

Mark Westrum, who'd now been promoted to chief deputy and was currently running for the office of sheriff, acknowledged that Mrs. Steele had told him about Lapierre's statements. He'd notified Wright. Wright had dispatched State

Police Detective Drake to interview her.

Westrum acknowledged knowing Mrs. Steele for about three years, speaking to her often on the telephone, visiting her home from time to time. But when Connolly asked him about that conversation he'd witnessed between Mrs. Steele and Sheriff Haggett concerning Senecal, Westrum replied, "I'm not quite clear on that. There might have been some references to it a couple of years back, but it's nothing that stands out in my mind or a conversation that I participated in."

Connolly asked about instances where Mrs. Steele had provided valuable and accurate information to Westrum regarding various criminal matters.

Wright objected.

Bradford sustained Wright's objection again.

Connolly asked, "Chief Deputy Westrum, at the time of your first contact with Dennis Dechaine, how long had you been on the force?"

"Two days."

Connolly alluded to the envelope Westrum had, filled with his press clippings. "Who counted up the number of times that your name was mentioned?"

"I did."

"Who counted up the number of times you were on TV?"

"I did...."

Connolly led him through a series of questions to reveal that he hadn't counted the number of times Wright, Detective Hendsbee, or Judge Bradford was mentioned, and then he asked, "It's fair to say you have some ego involvement in counting the number of times you appear on TV and the number of times you appear in the newspaper?"

"Absolutely none."

Westrum also denied ever mentioning his key role in the Dechaine case during his stump speeches in his run for sheriff. He couldn't recall instances when Margaret Steele had provided information that resulted in criminal convictions. But Wright cut that line of questioning off with an objection.

Bradford said, "Sustained."

"Why do you bother going over to talk to her, then?"

"Because I feel she is a lonely, confused old lady that needs somebody to talk to off and on. She doesn't have family members. She doesn't have many friends. And I, quite frankly, feel sorry for her."

That answer seemed a trifle too saccharine. A busy man, practical and pragmatic, an ambitious man not noted for spending time on anything that didn't advance his effectiveness or his career, or both, Chief Deputy Westrum would have projected a more professionally impartial visage if he'd admitted that his visits with Mrs. Steele helped him do his job. But then he'd have to acknowledge that he relied on information she passed along, a fact that would imply that he considered her reliable.

State Police Detective Steven Drake—late thirties, neatly dressed although his belly lapped over his low-belted trousers—took the stand. He acknowledged having been sent by Eric Wright to interview Mrs. Steele. Later, Drake said, he'd received a phone call from a man claiming to be Bobby Lapierre. That person denied hearing Senecal admit killing Sarah Cherry. No, Drake didn't know where this man was calling from; the man refused to tell him. Nor would the caller supply his address or date of birth. Nevertheless, the caller's denial ended his investigation of Mrs. Steele's allegations.

❖

Connolly called Kristin Commee to the stand.

The thirty-eight-year-old mother of four, married to an architect, described her family's previously friendly relationship with the Senecal family and their daughter, Jessica, who often babysat the Commee children. But Wright's "hearsay" objections cut off her testimony about Jessica's conflict in babysitting jobs for the day Sarah was murdered. That and Jessica's shocked reaction when her mother Maureen had told her, before Sarah's body was found, that her half-sister was dead.

"Hearsay": any statement by someone other than the witness which is "offered in evidence to prove the truth of the matter asserted." But hearsay isn't objectionable if it's offered only to show the statement's effect on another person's actions. For example, in a bank robbery case, a car description transmitted from one policeman to the witness who was testifying was not objectionable hearsay because it was introduced only to show why the second policeman had stopped the defendant's car.

According to the rules of evidence as interpreted by Judge Bradford, however, even though Mrs. Commee witnessed Jessica's traumatized reaction after hearing Maureen tell her that Sarah was dead, this would constitute "hearsay" evidence. The only way it could come in, Judge Bradford told

Connolly, was for Jessica or Maureen Senecal to offer the testimony.

Mrs. Commee was able to testify about the series of phone calls she'd received threatening her and her children, calls from a man whose voice she recognized as Senecal's, calls that stopped abruptly in the summer of 1989 when Senecal moved from Maine to South Carolina.

Court was adjourned for the holiday weekend, to resume six days later.

❖

Ralph Jones's arrival at the Knox County Court House was rather bizarre. Garbed in brown coveralls and a slouch hat concealing his face, he rushed past the bank of TV and newspaper photographers, through the heavy glass door, and up the stairs. Inside the courtroom, his dark blue suit appeared freshly cleaned and neatly pressed. As the thirty-seven-year-old unemployed truck driver mounted the witness stand, however, spectators saw how the tail of his jacket spread wide in an inverted V. When he turned to take the oath, they saw how the unbuttoned collar of his white shirt flared, as if he hadn't had occasion to dress up for many years. But he was trying.

Jones's testimony boiled down to this: somewhere between 7:30 and 8:30 P.M. on the day Sarah vanished, he'd been outside his trailer home when a red and white pickup truck had stopped just past the mouth of his driveway on the Dead River Road. He hadn't been able to see its occupants through the bushes lining the road, but he'd heard two male voices—one he identified as that of a man who'd attended high school with him: Doug Senecal. Senecal, who was standing outside the pickup, said, "Get out and go!"

Wright objected. "Hearsay."

There was also the voice of a young girl. She was either laughing or crying; Jones couldn't be sure which. At this point, the man he identified as Senecal got back in the truck and it drove away.

Unaware of the police search, Jones went to a movie that night. When he returned, the Dead River Road was alive with police. Jones was glad to get home without being stopped because he didn't have a driver's license. But the next morning, he'd visited the state police command center just down the road from his home, discovered what was going on, and reported the incident of the night before to Detective Lehan.

Lehan, Jones said, showed him a photo of a Toyota pickup truck, but that wasn't the vehicle he'd observed the night before. He showed officers tire tracks left in the roadside mud by the pickup he'd seen, but they showed no interest.

Wright would later accuse Connolly of telling Jones to name Lehan, because Lehan had once before been caught lying under oath during a drug trial. For now, however, Wright began a lengthy cross-examination. At one point, Wright asked about the little girl's voice, "All right, but you said it was a happy voice?"

Connolly: "Your Honor, I object. It's a mischaracterization. He's trying to put words in the witness's mouth."

The judge told Wright to rephrase his question.

"All right. Did you not say on your first direct examination that the voice sounded happy?"

"No," Jones shook his head. "I did not say happy. I said

laughing or crying. That's what I said in the first statement when I gave it to the police, too."

"And okay, but you couldn't tell whether it was laughing or crying."

"No, because she was a real high voice. Young."

Soon afterward, in response to Wright's question regarding to whom the one man had spoken, Jones quoted "the other man" as having said "Let's go!"

"Excuse me, Mr. Jones," Wright said, "I didn't ask you what anybody said. Try to answer the questions for me."

Connolly rose from his chair, "Your Honor, he is trying to answer the question. The only way the question can be answered is by saying what was said. It's a trick question."

"Well," Wright said, "I don't mean to trick anybody."

"Not today," Connolly said.

Judge Bradford ruled, "The response as to what was said is ordered stricken."

Wright's next series of questions focused on Jones's ability to see on a dusty road as the sun was setting. Then he asked whether Jones was aware that his friend, who had also seen that departing pickup truck, had identified it in his testimony at Dechaine's trial as being a red Toyota.

Connolly again objected that Wright was mischaracterizing testimony. Transcripts were brought out. That friend's testimony was read, whereupon Wright stated, "Well, I don't want to get bogged down in the transcript . . . ."

Caught in one more untrue allegation, Wright moved right along, "Mr. Jasper, what was in the bed of that truck?"

"My name ain't Mr. Jasper."

"Mr. Jones."

Wright saved his attack for now. "Do you know who Gina Marie Graham is?"

"No, sir."

"Mr. Jones, it's true, is it not, that in the afternoon of September 27, 1990, you were arrested by Chief Brian Lemieux of the Sabbattus Police—"

Connolly was on his feet. "I will object. His arrest is irrelevant. Mr. Wright knows it. Impeachment may not be done by that kind of—"

Wright said, "I am not seeking to impeach him by means of the arrest at all."

"Then I move it be stricken on relevancy grounds, it's in 1990."

Court rules provide that one may "impeach" a witness with evidence of a conviction, but not a mere arrest. And Jones had never been convicted of anything.

"Well it's not the arrest," Wright said. "The facts of the arrest doesn't determine it. I just want to identify the date for him."

Wright's point was that Jones had been found in possession of various papers and cards bearing various names, one of which was the Gina Marie Graham, whom Jones denied knowing. Jones explained that he had purchased a variety of junk items which included a suitcase and, in the suitcase, there were numerous identity papers with various names. A policeman stopped Jones for a traffic offense, and found the suitcase in Jones's car. There was no indication that Jones intended to use these documents for any purpose, legal or otherwise. So Wright's claim that he wished only to "identify the date for him" was hypocritical.

That date was irrelevant. Wright never made any effort to connect it to anything. But he'd taken the only shot he could at Jones's past.

❖

Connolly's next witness, Pamela Babine, had lived with her husband in a house owned by Senecal and within sight of Senecal's residence on the road known locally as The Devil's Highway. She testified that on the day Sarah vanished, Senecal had driven a red Toyota pickup truck into her driveway and sat there for more than an hour. Later, when she'd seen that same vehicle on a TV news broadcast about the girl's disappearance, she'd screamed and told her husband, "We can't live here any more."

On July 8th, Mrs. Babine had had a conversation with Senecal which she'd reported to police, along with having seen him in the red Toyota. But Wright objected to any description of that conversation as hearsay and the judge sustained his objection.

The rules do, however, allow certain questions. Connolly asked, "What was his demeanor?"

"He was very paranoid.... He would get angry, he would blow up. It was—he was like a time bomb."

"And during this conversation...did he blow up with you?"

"Yes."

"Were you concerned for your physical safety?"

"Yes."

"Did you report that information to the Department of Human Services?"

"Yes."

❖215❖

"Did it relate to the death and homicide of Sarah Cherry?"

Wright objected. "I don't know—she reported it to DHS. I don't know beyond that what the details matter."

Bradford: "The objection is sustained."

Connolly asked whether, prior to that conversation, she had had an encounter with Jessica Crosman at a local store. "And did you have—at that time did you obtain knowledge about babysitting?"

"Object! It's clearly going to call for hearsay."

"Sustained."

Connolly tried another tack. "On July 6, 1988, did you know about Jessica switching babysitters?"

Wright objected.

"Sustained."

"Sir," Connolly said to the judge, "I am not asking for a statement."

Judge Bradford asked him, "What would be the source of her knowledge?"

"It would be hearsay."

"The objection is sustained."

Connolly brought out the fact that Mrs. Babine had left the state in fear of Senecal, because he knew that she'd made reports to the Department of Human Services regarding his alleged sexual abuse of his stepdaughter.

Wright began his cross-examination with questions aimed at revealing Mrs. Babine's negative feelings toward Senecal. Then he brought out the fact that, when she and her husband had first moved to the town of Phippsburg, they'd lived in a tent at a friend's house. "and [Senecal] gave you this house to live in, didn't he?"

"He gave it to us? No sir, he rented it to us."

"I didn't mean he gave it. Thank you."

Wright wanted to convey that Mrs. Babine's attitude toward Senecal derived from the fact that she'd had to move because he was trying to sell the house she was renting. He asked whether she'd told the DHS worker about Senecal being in the red Toyota.

She said, "Not that I know of."

"And you did not report that fact to any member of the police department at any time, did you?"

"I had told the Phippsburg Police that he was there."

"That he was?"

"At my house in a red Toyota. They dismissed it. They said it wasn't important."

"I am going to move to strike what she said they said to her as unresponsive to the question."

Judge Bradford said, "It will be disregarded."

And later, Wright asked, "As of the 6th of July, at that time you did not like Douglas Senecal at all—"

"I have—"

"—did you?"

"I have no feelings for Doug Senecal. Would you for the devil? That's what he is to me."

"All right, I take it you don't like the devil so you don't like Douglas Senecal; is that fair to say or not?"

"I don't like a man to watch me bathe. I don't like him to watch my house. I don't like him to watch my every move—so, no, I can't say I like being watched."

"Your Honor, I move that all that be stricken."

"Permission is granted."

Wright brought out that, after Mrs. Babine had vacated the house and received a check from Senecal returning her security deposit, she'd written, "Go to hell" and "Rapist of children" above her endorsement of that check.

❖

Connolly called Gerald Paradis to the stand, a stocky man with a ruddy face, red hair, and a full beard. Paradis testified that in July 1988 he'd bought the house owned by Senecal on the Devil's Highway—the house where Mrs. Babine had lived. In the month or so before that, he'd been negotiating for the purchase and working in the neighborhood, and their relationship had been friendly. Then, around the time of Sarah's murder, Senecal began drinking, became withdrawn and hostile. Paradis noticed scratches on Senecal's face; he'd asked about them.

Judge Bradford wouldn't let him repeat Senecal's answer. It was hearsay.

Connolly then brought out the fact that Mr. Paradis had grown up in Madawaska and he'd once known Dennis Dechaine.

Wright began his cross-examination with an attempt to convey that the name of the road where Senecal lived was not The Devil's Highway, but was actually named Stoney Brook Road. Paradis corrected him. Stoney Brook Road was another, nearby thoroughfare.

Then Wright asked, "Is your nickname Toad? Is that what they call you?"

"That's what Douglas Senecal baptized me as, yes."

"That's what I wanted to be sure," Wright said. "I

thought I'd heard the name Toad and I wanted to be sure it was you."

The thrust of Wright's questions sought to bring out the fact that Mr. Paradis had known these facts prior to Dechaine's trial. If this were true, it would not meet the standard as "new evidence," a requirement if one wanted to justify a new trial.

On re-direct examination, Connolly asked, "Mr. Paradis, in response to a question Mr. Wright asked about whether or not you had knowledge of what was happening to Dennis Dechaine and whether or not you chose to come forward, have you been waiting for a knock on the door for a while?"

"I object."

"Sustained."

Judge Bradford recessed court for the day.

The next morning, Connolly called Senecal's uncle Edward, to the stand. The short, sixty-six-year-old retired shipping clerk with a little white mustache had been close to Doug since his high school days and currently lived near him in South Carolina. Yes, he'd had conversations with Douglas's uncle, Patrick. No, he'd never talked to the police or Eric Wright about this case and no, no one had asked him anything about what he'd testify to today. Yes, he'd had about twenty telephone conversations with a private investigator from Madawaska named Morin. Yes, there was talk about his discussions with Doug Senecal regarding the murder of Sarah Cherry.

Connolly asked him, "Did you express concern to the private investigator at any time that if you provided testimony or a statement that you would be in physical fear of your own life?"

"Object!" Wright said. "Again, it's an out-of-court statement."

But Edward answered, "No, never, never."

This time, the judge said, "The answer may stand."

During Wright's cross-examination, Edward said, "I was drunk. I am an alcoholic. Most of the time he called I was drinking." But he was sure, now, that Douglas Senecal had never said anything about killing Sarah Cherry.

Senecal's uncle, Patrick, a distinguished looking, medium-built man of fifty, lived with his wife and their four children in Oxford, Maine. He was close to Uncle Edward; not close with Douglas. Douglas had threatened him over the phone.

Wright objected.

"Sustained."

The lawyers held a sidebar conference. Connolly told the judge that Senecal had told Patrick, "You better not testify against me. You have a daughter, too."

Judge Bradford took them back to the case charging Senecal with the sexual abuse of stepdaughter Jackie and the release of Senecal's name to the press. "Prior to that time," Bradford continued, "assuming for purposes of argument that Patrick Senecal had known or someone had told him that Doug Senecal had been fooling around with Patrick's youngest daughter, Brenda, okay, all of a sudden Douglas's name appears in the paper as someone who likes little girls for sexual purposes...." Bottom line, according to Judge Bradford: that phone call might have related to Douglas

Senecal's sexual abuse of Jackie or Brenda, but there was no proof that it related to the murder of Sarah Cherry. Hence, the judge ruled, Patrick's testimony about Doug Senecal's threat—a threat clearly related to Patrick testifying against Doug—would not be allowed.

Reading this colloquy, and the judge's assumption "for the sake of argument" that Patrick knew something, and guessing that the threat from Douglas "might have" been unrelated to the Sarah Cherry murder, leads to an examination of Bradford's rulings throughout the hearing. Whenever a decision rested within his discretion, it's difficult to see how the judge's rulings could be viewed as interpreting situations as the law required, i.e., in the light most favorable to the defendant.

Connolly tried another avenue, asking Patrick, "If Eddie Senecal had testified that no such conversations about Douglas occurred in reference to the death of Sarah Cherry, that would not be correct?"

"True."

"Were there specific times when you can recollect conversations occurred between yourself and Eddie about Douglas's involvement?"

"Yes."

"I object."

"Sustained."

Another sidebar. Eddie, Connolly said, had told Patrick that Douglas Senecal admitted killing Sarah Cherry. Eddie had told that to Patrick twice, under circumstances indicating the trustworthiness of his statements. Yes, that would be hearsay, but this was an exception to the hearsay rule because Connolly was offering this testimony to impeach Eddie, who'd claimed that Douglas never made such a statement.

But the judge held that that was against the rules, too. He didn't explain why.

Patrick Senecal was excused.

Forty-eight-year-old Bobby Lapierre identified himself as a writer living in California. He testified that he'd known Doug Senecal since their boyhood and he'd lived with the Senecals in the summers of 1987 and 1988. He was acquainted with Pam Babine and "Frenchy" Paradis—"he was stuck in the mud somewhere on Devil's Highway and I helped pull him out." But the alleged abuse of Jackie was never mentioned within his hearing. And, he said, he'd never told Margaret Steele that Senecal killed Sarah Cherry.

Eric Wright called retired Detective Corporal Alfred Hendsbee who testified that, had anyone advised him of Ralph Jones's allegations concerning Senecal and another man with a young girl, he'd have acted on that information. But throughout his testimony, Hendsbee was consistently reluctant, resistant, and vague about the evidence, claiming no memory of what had been found and what not found.

State Police Sergeant Ronald Jacque testified that he'd manned the command post on July 8; that many people had been in and out, but Ralph Jones was not among them. No, he'd filed no report whatsoever regarding his participation in the case.

Wright recalled Detective Drake and asked whether he

remembered Kristin Commee saying anything about Pam Babine.

Connolly objected, "That's clearly calling for hearsay."

He was overruled. Wright hadn't asked Drake what Mrs. Commee said, merely whether he remembered her saying anything.

But, minutes later, Wright asked Drake what Mrs. Commee had said.

Connolly objected.

Wright said his purpose was merely to impeach the testimony of Mrs. Commee.

Connolly's objection was overruled. Apparently, incomprehensible as it might be to the untutored masses, Wright's use of hearsay in an attempt to impeach Connolly's witness was somehow different from Connolly's request, just minutes earlier, to utilize hearsay to impeach Eddie Senecal.

Connolly's cross-examination centered on Drake's having told Mrs. Commee that she could legally ignore Connolly's request to appear in court because she hadn't been served with a subpoena. Drake quibbled on the witness stand but it became apparent that Drake was only trying to wriggle away from his attempt to sabotage Connolly's case.

State Police Detective Lehan testified he'd never spoken with Ralph Jones. He also acknowledged that he'd been caught testifying falsely under oath and falsifying official reports in a drug case, a practice he called common with respect to informers.

Wright called a storekeeper. Judge Bradford allowed this man to testify, over Connolly's "hearsay" objections, to statements Pam Babine had allegedly made about Senecal.

Then Wright called an employee of the hardware store where Senecal had said he'd bought a saw blade on the day Sarah vanished, a purchase which, based on the sequence of sales slips for that day, this employee guessed had occurred between 12:30 and 1:00 that afternoon.

Summing up, Eric Wright argued that no new trial was justified because Connolly had not met the burden required by law.

Connolly argued that he had produced new evidence, newly discovered evidence which couldn't have been obtained before the trial. And he argued that this evidence would have made a difference in the jury's verdict.

During Connolly's closing, Judge Bradford spent much of the time hunched over his bench leafing through first one, then another set of papers. When it was over, he promised to announce his decision following consideration of the evidence.

❖

Outside, when reporters asked Bobby Lapierre whether he believed Dechaine guilty, this was his only response: "I have confidence that the jury convicted him and sent him to jail for life."

Skeptical souls suspected that one of the AG's people had warned Lapierre that admitting that he'd accused Senecal during a conversation with Mrs. Steele would give Senecal all the grounds he'd need to sue for slander and win a healthy judgment.

Senecal's stepdaughter, Jackie, now twenty-one and married, told reporters she'd only fled the state because she didn't want to testify to statements she'd made to representatives of the Department of Human Services, statements she now said she'd made under pressure from officials.

Senecal granted an interview to television station WGME.

Trial & Error's next newsletter reprinted a newspaper report regarding that TV interview and then continued:

> Let us keep in mind that when Douglas Senecal made his appearance on T.V. he stated that he had to sell his house because of what Tom Connolly and Dennis had put him through. Therefore, why did he sell his house in July of 1988 when he had not been accused or his name never was publicized until the *Times Record* & the *Portland Press* asked the supreme court to release the alternate [suspect's] name in July of 19<u>89</u>. On January 5 of 1990, the alternates name was made public for the first time!

Why did Douglas Senecal say he had to sell his house in July of 1988 then?

14

Reverse The Clock

PIECES OF THE PUZZLE HAD FALLEN INTO PLACE for me while I took that drive along country roads after reading the transcript. A drizzle had begun. The "going home" segment of Dvorak's *New World Symphony* had flowed from my tape deck. I had spotted that clock on the cupola of a white barn, and something had clicked. I should have caught it before while reading the transcript, but I had been skip-scanning when I came to medical examiner Roy's testimony. Scientists know more about their field than I do, I thought, and their explanations are often tedious. Besides, why scrutinize a scientist's testimony? They're irrefutable. Science never lies.

When I finally figured it out, the clue that tugged at my consciousness was prosecutor Eric Wright's peculiar presentation of Dr. Roy's expert opinion. In every trial I'd ever seen or read, the prosecutor asks the medical examiner straight out, "Based on your examination, at what time did death occur?"

And the witness answers, "Between X and Y o'clock."

Prosecutors want to show the jury that the victim died at an hour when the defendant had an opportunity to commit the crime. Wright was experienced and methodical. He's a man who studies his evidence long before trial and preps every witness. But the way Eric Wright established the time of death in this case was odd.

This is from Wright's direct examination of Dr. Ronald Roy:

Q: What was the condition of rigor mortis in this case upon the removal of the debris from the body and further examination?
A: Rigor mortis was still present but it was broken relatively easily. In my opinion it was passing off.
Q: Given the body that you found, could you reach any conclusion as to the time of death?
A: The passing off of rigor mortis suggested that we are talking probably thirty hours or more. And I do know when she disappeared and the changes are consistent with that time, consistent with having occurred two days prior.

And later, Wright asked:

Q: Was there anything to suggest that in this case, given the location of the body under debris and so on, anything inconsistent with what you've already suggested to have been the passage of time between death and discovery of the body?
A: Well, somebody found in the woods in August [sic] who had been dead for two days I would expect to find more fly activity. But her body was covered with

debris which accounts for why it is not as advanced as I would have expected it.

Actually, witnesses who found the body said that Sarah's head was exposed.

When Connolly cross-examined, Dr. Roy stated:

A: The parameters of rigor mortis suggests [sic] probably a minimum of 30 to 36 hours and it could well be longer.... All of these findings are compatible with the fact when I saw her she had been dead two days."
Q: Would you be able to state she was dead as of three o'clock or four o'clock or five o'clock on July 6th?
A: No.
Q: So it is fair to say that the time of death is July 6th and nothing more; is that a fair statement?
A: That's a fair statement.
Q: So it could be as late as ten or eleven o'clock on July 6th, it's possible?
A: Yes.
Q: It's possible it could be as late as midnight?
A: I don't see why not.

Dr. Roy's autopsy report, consistent with his testimony, stated unequivocally: "Rigor mortis, on initial examination, is present in all the large joints and fingers and is broken with relative ease."

Wondering whether Dr. Roy could be fallible in his thirty-to-thirty-six-hour opinion, I turned to the leading texts on forensic pathology. *Investigation of Sudden*

Death—A Manual For Medical Examiners, a textbook by Robert C. Hendrix, M.D., a Michigan medical examiner and professor of pathology at the University of Michigan, states:

> The general rules indicate that rigor begins about four hours after death, progresses to maximum by eight to twelve hours, persists for about four hours, then gradually reduces over about the same span of time.

And *Forensic Medicine—A Guide to Principles* by pathologists Gordoin, Shapiro and Berson, states:

> ...in the adult, under average conditions rigor mortis commences within three to four hours after death, spreads throughout the skeletal muscles in 10-12 hours and disappears about 36 hours after death.

So Dr. Roy's testimony is supported by the textbooks on forensic pathology. And, since it was 2:00 P.M. on Friday when he first saw the body and noted the rigor mortis "passing off," his finding places the *earliest* time of Sarah Cherry's death at 2:00 A.M.; the latest at 8:00 A.M. on Thursday. Most probably it occurred even later, since the rigor hadn't yet completely passed off. But Dechaine's time is accounted for from 8:30 on the previous evening by state's witness Spaulding, who saw him emerge from the woods; then from 8:45 P.M. by state's witness Buttrick, who tried to help find Dechaine's truck and remained with him right up until they encountered sheriff's deputies. From that moment on, the police are Dechaine's alibi until they drove him home to his wife at 4:20 Thursday morning.

Dechaine *couldn't* have committed this murder! His innocence is proved by science and the sworn testimony of the prosecution's witnesses—*the state's evidence!*

Eric Wright had easy access to Dr. Roy and his complete autopsy report. He had months to ponder the evidence, months to prepare his trial presentation. An experienced homicide prosecutor like Wright would have to be a fool to miss the significance of these facts. Was Eric Wright a fool? Or did he calculate that no one at the trial would remember that Dr. Roy first noted the rigor mortis still present but passing off when he first viewed the body at two o'clock Friday afternoon, then count those hours backwards from that point, and realize that the state's forensic pathologist was certifying Dechaine's alibi. Can there be any other reason for Wright to deliberately present the time-of-death evidence in that odd and extraordinary fashion, without ever asking at what hour the medical examiner's findings placed the time of death? One fact is indisputable: specifying the time of death in the normal manner would destroy Wright's case.

Later in his examination of Dr. Roy, Wright tried this:

> Q: Dr. Roy, if you were to know that Sarah Cherry was last spoken to at noon on the 6th of July and that there were remnants of hot dogs at the house where she was baby-sitting, those were found at the homeowner's return at around 3:30, would you be able to reach any conclusion as to time of death in this case? Does it suggest to you that the hot dogs appeared to

be eaten for lunch?

A: Yes. This is consistent with her last known meal. And that death occurred within a fewer [sic] hours of eating her last meal.

The hypocrisy of this hotdog testimony is shown in Dr. Hendrix's text [ibid].

> The stomach usually empties itself in about three hours if it is not prevented from doing so. *Great excitement, marked fear, and actions of some drugs, severe injury, and death all delay or stop gastric activity.* [Emphasis added.]

Every treatise on this topic agrees with Dr. Hendrix's statement. Considering Sarah's certain terror from the moment she was abducted, there's little doubt that her digestive process halted long before she died. So the hotdog evidence which Wright took pains to draw from Dr. Roy was meaningless. The only purpose served by introducing meaningless testimony was to drive a spike into the concept that death occurred on the afternoon Sarah was abducted, and to hammer that nail deep before anyone took the trouble to make a mental calculation from Dr. Roy's primary conclusion.

On his re-direct examination, Eric Wright even renewed his effort to make the hotdog evidence seem relevant. But Dr. Roy's replies didn't help him:

Q: How likely is it Sarah was still alive 'till 11 on July 6th

if she was last heard of at noon and given the information you know about the remnants of lunch or what you found in the digestion of hot dog?
A: I couldn't rule it out.
Q: What is the likelihood?
A: I don't know.
Q: You don't?
A: No.

Eric Wright shifted swiftly to other matters.

❖

When I reported my analysis to Tom Connolly, he looked crestfallen.

It's easy to Monday-morning-quarterback anyone's actions. I didn't initially catch the clue, reading the transcript in the quiet comfort of my den. Perhaps there are readers who didn't appreciate the significance of this evidence when it was shown in the early chapters of this book. Noting every implication of every fact thrown on the table amidst the fast-moving battle of a courtroom is like trying to read those tiny-print conditions flashed for a split-second at the end of television commercials—the paragraph that explains why the ad doesn't offer quite what it seemed to promise.

Nor was Connolly pre-warned about this evidence. Reference to time of death on Roy's reports should have appeared in the blank which asks: "Time of Injury." But the only thing Roy wrote there was, "Found 7/8/88."

❖

Eleanor McQuillen, M.D., former chief medical examiner for the State of Vermont with a three-page *curriculum vitae*,

Time-of-Death Timeline

Sarah was abducted between 12:00 noon and 3:20 P.M. on Wednesday.

Dechaine was with Mr. and Mrs. Buttrick, and the police, from 8:30 P.M. Wednesday through 4:20 A.M. Thursday.

Sarah died between 2 A.M. and 8 A.M. Thursday, if Dr. Roy noted rigor mortis passing off when he first saw the body where it was found in the woods around 2 P.M.*

Sarah died between 3:40 A.M. and 9:40 A.M. on Thursday, if Dr. Roy noted rigor mortis passing off when he conducted the autopsy on Friday afternoon.

Sarah's body was found at 12:00 noon on Friday.

Dr. Roy first observed the body at 2 P.M.

The autopsy was performed at about 3:40 P.M. on Friday.

*Three variables could possibly alter a patholotist's opinion regarding the rigor mortis: the warm ambient temperature; the victim's physical exertion/stress at the time of death; and the victim's youth. If any of these variables had any effect, that effect would have hastened the onset and the passing off of rigor mortis, providing a shorter span of time for the rigor mortis, which would put the time of death at a later hour.

was in private practice as a consultant. She agreed to waive her $1,000 retainer but she'd still charge her fee of $150 per hour. Carol Waltman mobilized Trial & Error to provide the funds. I sent all of Dr. Roy's reports and testimony to Dr. McQuillen. Her cautious report opened, "The only accurate method of determining the time of death is to be there when it happens; even then there is a small chance of error." Unwilling to take a positive stand either way on the basis of the evidence presented by the state, Dr. McQuillen did assert, "I believe that the autopsy report in this case is preliminary with one page of microscopic added, not final."

But she'd been furnished everything the state had turned over to Tom Connolly—legally, everything there was. So the prosecution never gave Connolly the state's entire report. Nothing the state furnished him on discovery said anything whatsoever about the time of death.

The one valid indicator of that fact presented by the state was the progress of rigor mortis. While rigor mortis is regarded as a consistent, reliable indicator, there are other factors scientists assess. One is the development of fly larvae but, as far as the state's reports show, the larvae in this case were discarded without examination. And there is a test of the victim's eye fluid, generally considered an excellent indicator but, unless the results were concealed, that test was never conducted. Nor, if temperatures of the crime scene and the body were recorded, were these facts ever revealed by the state. Dechaine's prosecutors relied solely on the state of rigor mortis—the one factor they could most easily obfuscate in a courtroom—and the progress of hot dog digestion which, considering the circumstances of this case, was totally bogus.

It just seemed incredible to me. So I drove to Augusta, showed my authorizations by Connolly and Dechaine to clerk Sandra Hickey at the chief medical examiner's office, and asked to see the file on Sarah Cherry's autopsy.

Ms. Hickey said she'd have to check with the office of the attorney general.

She went to a phone at the far end of the file room and returned a moment later.

Ms. Hickey told me, "Mr. LaRochelle [Chief of the AG's Criminal Division] said to show you what we gave Connolly, and nothing else."

Nothing else? There wasn't supposed to be anything else!

First, I saw how the experienced, methodical Eric Wright led Dr. Roy through a uniquely odd method of declaring the time of death. Next, he dragged in that meaningless hotdog allegation. Now I saw obstruction by his boss, Fernand LaRochelle.

In Bangor, Dr. George Chase, retired chief of pathology at the Eastern Maine Medical Center, reviewed all of the specific facts regarding Sarah Cherry, as reported by the state's medical examiner and other state witnesses. Dr. Chase stated, in writing:

> Considering the conditions described above, it is my opinion that the undigested food may not be relevant, since terror induced by torture can retard or halt the digestive process. The fact of residual rigor in the pres-

ence of warm ambient temperature could argue that the rigor might have disappeared in twenty-four hours. It is my opinion that death occurred between eight and twenty-four hours prior to the time the above factors were noted.

George Chase, M.D.

Dr. Chase's opinion puts the time of death even later that Dr. Roy's finding.

❖

Dechaine's truck proved to be irrelevant, too. As Tom Connolly pointed out in his summation, police found no blood, fiber, or fingerprint from Sarah in that vehicle. More than that, after sealing the Toyota and towing it to their laboratory, after a thorough search, after vacuuming its interior and subjecting its contents to microscopic examination, the police experts hadn't even found a single hair from Sarah's head.

Hair loss is natural. Our hairs fall out when a new hair, growing in the same follicle, enters the "anagen phase." Natural blondes have somewhere between 80,000 and 140,000 hairs. Each day, the average blonde loses sixty-six hairs even without being kidnapped, wrestled into a truck, or struggling with anyone.

But beyond the laboratory's failure to find anything incriminating, Bowdoinham Police Officer Jay Reed (no relation to Deputy Sheriff Daniel Reed) had watched while Trooper Bureau had his tracking dog sniff Sarah's clothes, then Dechaine's truck. Officer Reed told me this startling fact, and signed a statement certifying that the dog had "found no scent [of Sarah] from the vicinity of the Toyota."

Perhaps that's why the state never mentioned this topic either way. This fact could also explain why they withheld dog officer Bureau's report from Tom Connolly.

One thing is certain: if Sarah didn't even lose a single hair in that truck, and the police tracking dog couldn't detect her presence, she was never there.

Which leads to the question: how did papers from the truck find their way to the Henkel driveway? How were ropes from that truck used to tie Sarah's wrists? Once the scientific evidence proves that Dennis Dechaine couldn't have committed this crime (because he was with the police when Sarah was strangled), and it becomes clear that his truck wasn't used to transport the victim, the answer is obvious. Those papers got in the Henkel driveway the same way property from your house or car might later be found in the home of a thief.

15

State Secrets

DOUGLAS SENECAL, SUBPOENAED BACK to Maine by Connolly, drove his twenty-year-old white Chrysler with its long, pointed tailfins out of the Devil's Highway to a country store. I snapped a few photos.

He strode over to me. I introduced myself and informed him I was looking into the case.

"Praise God," he replied without smiling.

"Some people say you're the bad guy. Mind posing for a straight-on picture?"

Stone-faced, he looked me up and down and stared into my face for a moment. "I think you have enough," he said, and walked back to his car.

Detective Westrum exercised his right to remain silent when I offered to hear his version of events, but it wasn't difficult to discover the few significant points in his life. He began his law enforcement career as a "cadet" with the Bath Police Department. In 1981, he was hired as a patrolman by the Topsham Police Department. A detective who knew him then considered Westrum "a good boy who would always tell the truth," but the same detective had serious doubts about Dechaine's guilt. "The state police get onto one suspect," he told me, "and they focus everything on that suspect. Besides, the kind of man who murdered that little girl took his time torturing her, tying her up, and gagging her, hiding her in the woods. That kind of man doesn't leave things with his name on them at the crime scene."

Arnold Hordeman, the clerk who actually sold that saw blade to Senecal on the day Sarah vanished, was the only witness who might say whether it was Senecal or one of Senecal's workers who had made that purchase. Interviewed at the town landfill, where he now worked, he had no memory of the sale which had occurred four years earlier. But he was certain of one thing: he'd never been interviewed by police. Detectives had contented themselves with another clerk who told them, based on the sequential number of Senecal's receipt, approximately what time the sale was probably made.

Sheriff Haggett told me that his office had no record of the radio logs for the days of the investigation. Nor, he said, did they have any record of the case at all. Still wondering whether it would have been even remotely possible for Dechaine to have snuck back and strangled Sarah Cherry after the cops took him home—but not wanting to let Haggett realize my train of thought—I asked the sheriff about the knife. He said the entire area had been searched with metal detectors but no knife was found. And none had been in Dechaine's possession when the officers encountered him, interrogated him, and searched him.

"Do you think he could have snuck back into the area the next morning, after the detectives took him home? Come back to retrieve the knife?"

"Impossible!" Haggett asserted. "We had officers all around there. We were searching. We knew the body was around there somewhere. He couldn't have gotten in without being seen. He was all screwed up, anyway."

"On the drug?"

"I don't know. Just all screwed up. He didn't know what he was doing or what was happening."

Then Haggett delved into his pond of opinion. "This isn't the first time," he said.

"Oh?"

"The Green River Murders. Same m.o. And he was out there going to college when they happened."

The absurdity of that rumor had already been disproved by detectives in the State of Washington who were investigating those murders. The m.o. was different, the killer's profile was different and the victims were vastly different—older, and most were prostitutes. In 2001, police arrested a man whose DNA matched that of the Green River killer.

During visits to the Senecal home, former friends observed Senecal's constant displays of affection toward his wife Maureen—hugging her, touching her. Maureen hadn't reacted or reciprocated. She seemed embarrassed when Senecal told them that he and Maureen skinny-dipped, and described how they made love in the pond behind the house. Once, Senecal told them, Maureen had left deep scratches on his back. During these interludes, a towel would be draped over the fence between the house and pond to notify the children not to intrude.

Maureen's love for daughter Erin seemed to be mutual, but the friends noticed that the younger daughter, the one called Peanut, deliberately avoided proximity to Senecal.

Summing up, the former friends—both the man and his wife—assured me that Senecal was a man who played on their friendship and Christian beliefs to cheat and lie to them. "He's a planner, a conniver. Crafty. Capable of planning a frame-up."

Just the sort of firsthand testimony Eric Wright would make sure was never spoken in open court. The facts would be classified as hearsay. The former friends' opinions were mere speculation. Nothing they said had anything to do with the murder of Sarah Cherry.

Legally, none of this was admissible in an effort to win a new trial.

❖

In his private life, Judge Carl Bradford plays the trumpet in a jazz band. He's a tennis player with a penchant for blue blazers. Noted by many for his cultured manner, he is married and has a son in the navy.

On the last day of July, Judge Bradford delivered the twenty-three-page decision he'd taken three weeks to craft. He called Margaret Steele's testimony about Lapierre's statements "irrelevant" because she never said Lapierre claimed that Senecal admitted killing Sarah. He dismissed Ralph Jones's testimony about the two men with the little girl, and his reporting the tire tread impressions to the police, as "not credible." He didn't believe Pamela Babine's testimony, either.

Judge Bradford went on to state, "The contention that scratches seen on Senecal by [Gerald] Paradis are evidence that Sarah Cherry was fighting off Senecal is rejected." And, he concluded somehow that, "Nothing said by Douglas Senecal to Patrick Senecal related in any way to Sarah Cherry or her murder."

The law required that, in order to succeed with a motion for a new trial on the grounds of newly discovered evidence, a defendant must establish all of these criteria:

1. The evidence will probably change the result if a new trial is granted;
2. It has been discovered subsequent to the trial;
3. Due diligence would not have sufficed to discover this evidence before trial;
4. The evidence is material to the issue; and
5. It is not merely cumulative or impeaching unless it is clear that such impeachment would have resulted in a different verdict.

Having ruled during the hearing that much of Connolly's evidence was hearsay and inadmissible, Bradford concluded:

The evidence which has been presented is no more than speculation and conjecture.
The motion for new trial on the grounds of newly discovered evidence is DENIED.

Eric Wright, on vacation, had a spokesman tell reporter

John Madden, "Finally, the charade is over."

Wright underestimated Carol Waltman, Tom Connolly, and Dechaine.

❖

Carol Waltman and her *Trial & error* friends produced an in-depth analysis of Judge Bradford's Decision and Order to deny Dechaine a new trial. Comparing Bradford's conclusions with evidence documented in the trial transcript, they listed twenty-eight points of disparity.

For the most part, these were errors of little consequence with respect to the legal issue bearing on the requirements for securing a new trial. An example is the first item:

> According to the Decision and Order, page 2 line 6, Judge says, "Mrs. Henkel called her neighbor, Holly Johnson." Trial Transcript, page 345, lines 5 through 7: Holly Johnson says, "I did not receive a call from Mrs. Henkel."

But even these less important discrepancies served to suggest Bradford's poor grasp of the facts or, perhaps, his preference for interpretations proving that the trial—over which he had presided—was flawless.

Aside from the judge's mischaracterization of various facts, Trial & Error's incisive report pointed out (complete with page and line citations) that:

> Officer Scopino testifies he used the notebook to write notes, he wrote Sara's [sic] name and birth date.
>
> Officer Reed testifies that he never realized that Officer

Scopino had used the notebook to write notes in it. He then handed the receipt and notebook to the state police. No fingerprint testing was done. Very little was done to preserve the integrity of the scene.

The judge says that when Dennis was asked about the auto body receipt, he denied they were his. [Decision and Order page 4, lines 2 and 3.] Officer Reed testifies that in his *original notes,* Dennis *did not deny* that the receipt was his.[Trial Transcript page 308.]

If the ropes from Dennis' truck were used to tie her up to be able to torture her, why is it that there are no rope burns on her wrists? If a person is tied up and being tortured and sexually abused, a struggle would occur, this would cause rope burns.

Decision and Order page 5, line 19: The officers' so-called admissions. Why would the officers not record his statements if it was true that he had confessed? When they interrogated him there was a recorder in the room next door for the purpose of recording any confessions. Also they never had him sign any confession slips. The officers who said that Dennis had confessed admitted to filing their reports 2 weeks to 6 months after they had arrested him.

When the defense for Dennis asked the state for the blood samples they had taken from Dennis, they said they had *lost* and *misplaced* it.

Decision and Order page 7, line 4: During the trial, all evidence pointing towards the alternative suspect was suppressed from the jury.

Decision and Order, page 8, line 2: Doug [Senecal] did not know Dennis Dechaine. Would Doug have to know Dennis? Couldn't he simply be covering himself?

Dennis Dechaine's first few weeks at the Maine State Prison were spent alone in a tiny, windowless room with no books or radio to take his mind from his fate. For the next eighteen months, he was locked in with various inmates, one of them that frightening multiple murderer. Threats predicted by guards failed to materialize, largely because some inmates believed him innocent. Avoiding the prison hazards of sex, drugs, and gambling, he got a job in the upholstery shop earning enough to keep himself in snacks from the prison canteen, buy his own clothes, and enjoy the few available prison amenities. As he told *Portland Press Herald* reporter Tess Nacelewicz, "I have certain standards. If you don't have money, you have to live like a pig." And some of his weekly salary of seventy dollars went to a children's charity for the support of a Philippine boy.

❖

Carol Waltman's Trial & Error members began a campaign of letters to the editors of Maine's newspapers because, as she told them, "It is very important to keep the public aware of the inadequacies in our judicial system." She laid out for them the plan of legal action from Maine's Supreme Court to the United States Supreme Court. There were *Trial &*

error lapel buttons for a dollar each and T-shirts for eight dollars. She provided every member with that comparative analysis of the trial transcript with Judge Bradford's written reasons for denying Dennis a new trial.

❖

Court records showed that in 1977 Douglas Senecal was divorced from his first wife after five years of marriage. The grounds: cruel and abusive treatment. I traced her to Rhode Island. She wouldn't talk about Senecal.

❖

Eric Wright ignored my phone messages but he answered my letter requesting access to trial exhibits—a part of the public record—advising me that Tom Connolly had been given access to all these materials before the trial. He alluded to alleged complaints by persons I'd interviewed and accused me of attempting to get witnesses to alter their testimony. Were that true, of course, it would constitute the crime called "subornation of perjury." The fact that Wright never pursued this allegation, assuming someone really said it, suggests that he knew I'd done no such thing. Eric Wright's letter concluded:

> Before you become entirely enraptured of Tom Connolly's theories, at least ask yourself, out of a sense of human decency, don't you think the Cherrys and the Crosmans have been through enough?..."

And no, he said, I could not see the trial exhibits.

The state didn't give in until I filed suit in superior court demanding access to this public record. Then Eric Wright showed me the evidence—except for those two fingerprints they'd lifted from the Henkel home and never identified. They were "somewhere else." Eric Wright said he didn't know where.

Stonewalled on my request to view the state police files on the case—accessible under Maine law after a case was closed—I filed another lawsuit in superior court. This time, determined to maintain their secrets, the attorney general's office dug in its heels. In court, they informed the judge pompously that yes, while police reports were accessible under the statute, files of the attorney general were confidential and not accessible. And *this* police file had been designated part of the AG's records and thus was protected from scrutiny.

The judge thought that sounded reasonable.

Score another point for the secret-keepers.

❖

Retired Maine State Police Lieutenant Peter McCarthy, who'd been part of the entire investigation, was eager to convince me I was pursuing an ignoble quest. He told me pointedly that Eric Wright was so convinced of Dechaine's guilt from the outset that he'd decided, whether or not Sarah's body was ever found, to charge their suspect with murder. McCarthy believed that the motive for the crime was, "Dechaine's antagonism toward women. He'd failed as a man and breadwinner—as a man." The absence of semen or the transference of hair or fiber between them was easily explained by Dechaine's "impotence" which "prevented him from mounting the girl." Peter McCarthy told me with a straight face that the boarder, Richard Bruno, lived in the

Dechaine home for the express purpose of "satisfying Nancy's physiological and biological needs." Moreover, police had come across women who reported that Dechaine showed "an unusual interest in their jewelry." Hence, McCarthy said, Dechaine had gone to the home of Henkel the goldsmith to steal jewelry.

Aside from the Dechaines' normal sexual life attested by both husband and wife, and the fact that Nancy had once termed Bruno "slovenly and gluttonous," all I could wonder as Mr. McCarthy prattled on was how a retired ranking officer in the state's legendary state police—a man I'd come to like and respect when I was with ATF—could believe, much less speak such whimsical tripe. And he did believe it. Some may say that Peter McCarthy is tedious, perhaps even easily gulled or prone (as we all are) to believe what he wants to believe, but Peter McCarthy is no liar.

It was interesting, though, that the decision to prosecute Dechaine was made even before Sarah's body was found. There had to be some basis beyond the flimsy evidence for Eric Wright's intense confidence. What that was remained a mystery to me for a very long time.

Trial & Error members broadened their suspect list to include the boarder, Richard Bruno. A witness reported seeing Dennis's red pickup on Lewis Hill Road the day before the crime when Dechaine and wife Nancy were on their way back from Madawaska, 300 miles to the north, in their car. The truck keys were at the house; Bruno had access to them. "Could it be," Carol asked fellow group members, "that while Bruno was out trying to dispose of the body that

Doug [Senecal] would have had the perfect opportunity to take Dennis's Toyota truck to set him up and also to keep him from leaving the woods, he would have been on foot and no way to leave the area. Also that would explain why Dennis could not find his truck."

A Toyota mechanic in Augusta with sixteen years' experience showed me how quick and easy it was to start a pickup like Dechaine's without a key. "Anybody could do it," he said. And Bruno owned a Toyota pickup like Dechaine's, except Bruno's was tan.

At the trial, Bruno had testified that he had no alibi for the day of the crime.

❖

Trial & Error sent reports to Professor Alan Dershowitz and the *20/20* television show. Carol Waltman and her members had no intention of giving up.

❖

Detective Mark Westrum—the officer who testified to Dechaine's most loquacious "confession," also the officer whose unprofessionalism was "established *ad nauseam*," according to Judge Bradford—ran for sheriff of Sagadahoc County citing former boss Haggett's mismanagement. Westrum lost by thirteen votes to Phippsburg Police Chief Russell Alexander and demanded a recount. During the interim, Westrum told *Portland Press Herald* reporter L. Mercedes Wesel that the delay created tension in the sheriff's department. And, "I know no other trade but law enforcement. It's been my whole life and career . . . . I'm faced with the prospect of being out on the street after thirteen years as a full-time law enforcement agent."

The recount gave him the election by twelve votes.

❖

Sheriff Haggett, still in office until the end of the year, became the object of an investigation into his handling of official funds. Haggett termed the accusations a "smear." Some said they were instigated by Westrum. The probe came to nothing.

My visit with Chief Medical Examiner Henry Ryan brought me his solemn assurance that, despite the apparent superficiality of the autopsy—no toxicology test, only one histology slide—that "these were sufficient, considering the nature of the case." So I asked why Dr. Roy hadn't even taken the temperature of the body at the scene.

Ryan replied, "It wouldn't do any good. She'd been dead too long."

"How did he know that?

After some hesitation, Ryan mumbled, "He could tell by looking at her."

❖

Trial & Error sent members an analysis of the psychic consultation with George Anderson two years earlier, along with seven piquant questions wondering whether various Anderson comments indicated involvement by Senecal and the boarder, Bruno.

Homicide detectives, like federal agents, have been romanticized in books and movies. But statistics show that the great majority of murders are committed by someone close to the victim—a friend or family member. Often, the killer is waiting for the police, head in hands, moaning his regret or his excuse. Mysteries arise when the murder occurs as an unintended by-product of another crime—the nervous bandit, the startled burglar. But, even while mysteries are the minority among murder cases, the statistics show that in 1999, as in most years, the slice of willful homicides cleared by arrest—including those by friends and family members and any others which are easily solved within hours—is only about 70 percent. And some of those "cleared by arrest" are never prosecuted because district attorneys don't think the police brought them enough evidence. And, of those brought to trial, some—whether innocent or guilty—are acquitted. That's every year, year after year. That leaves one hell of a lot of killers on the loose out there.

❖

Jim Pinette, retired from the state police homicide unit and licensed as a private investigator, had worked on the Dechaine case for Connolly. Now he told me that "a murder is just what it looks like." Maine's police didn't get complicated cases, he said. "Not as complicated as what Tom [Connolly] is talking about" regarding a frame-up.

Pinette would be right if anyone was thinking of a frame-up deliberately aimed at Dennis Dechaine, because nobody murders a little girl just to get somebody else in trouble. But Pinette continued, "If Senecal did it, Dechaine would have been just—uh, the opportunity was there and he took it" by using items from the truck to divert suspicion from himself.

Regardless of who the killer was, there is nothing far-fetched about that scenario.

Pinette went on to recall times when he and his fellow detectives had a murder that was hard to break, "we'd go down different avenues but invariably we'd come back to the simple explanation and that just about always worked out. I say 'almost' because there was a case of a little girl in Kennebunk we never solved, and a woman in Lewiston we never solved. But the ones we did, and all the cases I've been on, I've never seen the complication that you would have if Senecal was in the picture.

"It's straightforward to go with Dechaine," Pinette continued. "He's at the right place, he's got the right truck, he's running wild through the woods.... Let's say he did commit the homicide and he all-at-once realizes what he's done. He's not normal any more. Not going to act like you and I. And yes, he's not going to know where his truck is and he'll go backtracking through the woods. That, to me, is a normal reaction for a man that gets involved in a murder. From what I've seen of most defendants, after they do that they just don't act like you and I. They do crazy stuff, and I call that normal in terms of after you've killed somebody."

❖

A conversation with Detective Hendsbee in November 1992 was equally interesting, equally disturbing. "I'm sure Dechaine is guilty," he said. "Unfortunately, I liked the guy. I got wrapped up in him and I tried to find someone else who would have done it. There's only so much you can look at. You eliminate the family, the people who hired Sarah, you look at the evidence of what took place in the woods and then talking to him that night—you look at all that stuff and you can draw a conclusion on it. I'd much rather someone else had done it. As a matter of fact I was hoping someone else had done it up until the point that I went to do a search on the house. And he made me a total believer. His admissions there were just profound. I was shocked out of my shoes. I didn't even get out of my car and he was babbling all that stuff out."

Then Hendsbee told me, "The guy to talk to would be George Carlton. I'm sure that Dechaine told him everything because, uh, the indications I got at a visit there was that Carlton knew the whole story on it. I got this from Dechaine, even to the point where his wife even knows the whole story behind it.

"To me, personally, he's a serial murderer and there's conclusive evidence in another state there. Not the Green River murders. The m. o. wasn't the same and everything was different. There's three or four unsolved murders of teenage girls in Washington State, the next town to his town. I talked with the detectives out there.

"But the detective in this town, he's an Oriental guy, he just doesn't want to be bothered with it. His partner wanted to be bothered with it. She's a female. She called me seven times. But he was the chief of the detective force and he says, 'No, it wasn't him,' and it stopped right there."

And Hendsbee said, "There's a lot more evidence there than Connolly has that I'm sure you're not aware of. More admissions not used in court because it would be overkill. Admissions made in [the prison at] Thomaston, even to the point of where he put the knife. One was a notorious murderer and his credibility wasn't too great. There were a whole bunch of admissions of him telling just what took place. Where the knife went and what happened.

"The biggest rumor that went around the whole time was, 'the father killed her.' The one she was living with, Crosman. The whole thing was, Crosman murdered her and that's just the way he is. And that floored me. Then it jumped from Crosman to the real father. Then it jumped from her real father to Doug Senecal's name was brought up at a real early state, and he was eliminated.... You're never going to tie him in with that. He wasn't there.... He was too far away. He had people that seen him, and his actions that day...he just wasn't there. Nothing about him would even fit into that whole operation."

Asked about the deer sounds in the woods that night while they searched with the dog, Hendsbee said, "I didn't hear it. He [Trooper Bureau] thought it was deer up ahead and the dog was cowering off from it . . . . What it was, was the body the dog sensed and he wasn't [sic] afraid of it."

Asked why the dog didn't pick up a scent after sniffing Sarah's clothes, Hendsbee said, "You got me on that one and I was there when we went around the truck, and the dog hit on something...right out in front of the truck area, and then it beat feet across the road.... He was on a scent, he was taking us to the body. That body couldn't have been fifty feet from where we stopped. That dog was hitting right toward that place. That dog got a scent but what it was, when he got a deer scent he backed off. That's when [Trooper Bureau] said he picked up a deer scent and pulled him off. What it was, was the dog was pulling himself off because he didn't want to go in that direction."

Asked whether the dog could simply have been following Dechaine's trail from the truck and through the woods, Hendsbee replied, "Well, it was definitely following a scent but we had Sarah Cherry's clothes so I'm assuming it hit on her clothes."

Detective Hendsbee discussed his interrogation of Dechaine that first night. "He denied being in the area Sarah Cherry lives and I knew that was kind of a lie because I had the notebook there that kind of says differently. But I wasn't about to interrogate him after he had sat in that cruiser all that length of time because I had reservations about his Constitutional rights. So my whole purpose was to save what was remaining, but primarily to take him home.... What happens if Sarah Cherry did run off with somebody? What happens if he's not involved? My whole thing is, if that's the case, I had reasonable doubt although I didn't quite go along with him not saying he saw the house 'way up there and parked by the house. So I just basically interviewed him, lock him into a statement and conduct my investigation from there....

"The only thing that was held out at trial was more conclusive evidence that he did it.... The only thing I don't know is how he approached her, though. I can see how he approached her because of his personality. But that's the only thing I don't know. Everything else leads right to him."

Defects in Senecal's alibi were pointed out. Hendsbee responded, "That's gonna happen, though."

Even though there was insufficient evidence for warrants, I asked Hendsbee why he hadn't even asked Senecal, or anyone else, to provide blood or hair samples for comparison with the unidentified blood and hairs on the body, fingerprints for comparison with the unidentified latent lifted from the Henkels' door, or permission to search the vehicles of anyone else for traces of Sarah.

Hendsbee hesitated. "Well," he said finally, "there was no reason. There wasn't at the time...and there's nothing that says Senecal's truck was in the area.... And if Doug Senecal did it, no one knew it."

Hendsbee's statements left numerous questions unanswered. If Dechaine had told someone what he'd done with the knife, why hadn't it been recovered? If Senecal's actions on that day were so certain, why had his alibi fallen apart when Jim Pinette interviewed those alibi witnesses, and again when I talked to them?

Official reports detailed what those prison inmates had told Hendsbee. One claimed Dechaine had told him he'd "report[-ed] his truck stolen so the police would think someone stole his truck and killed the girl." But Dechaine hadn't reported the Toyota stolen, and no trace of Sarah was ever found in it.

The other inmate told police that Dechaine "needed sex because his wife wouldn't give it to him.... And he was saying he went out with this thirteen-year-old girl, he wanted to have sex with her. She wouldn't give it to him and he, ah, she kept saying, 'I'm gonna call the police.' This is the way I heard him saying it." This prisoner also claimed that Dechaine had laughed about the killing.

Hendsbee had given me a clue to the mysterious secret

behind the state's confidence in Dechaine's guilt, but I didn't catch it.

❖

On November 27, 1992, Tom Connolly filed an inch-thick brief—118 pages with nearly a hundred more pages of exhibits—arguing to Maine's highest court that Judge Bradford had been wrong to deny Dechaine a new trial.

❖

When I stopped for gas at a service station where Douglas Senecal had supposedly gassed up on the day of the murder, its owner—one of Senecal's alibi witnesses who, months before, had acknowledged to me that he had no idea whether Senecal had actually been there on the day of the murder—told me he wouldn't answer any more questions. "I got in enough trouble the last time I talked to you." Trouble, he said, from state police detectives.

Others expressed fear, too. And there were people who had spoken to detectives following the crime, witnesses whose statements were never included in the discovery material handed over by the prosecution to Connolly. Among them was the lady who observed suspicious activity by a man in a green pickup truck on the night of Sarah's abduction—this on the Dead River Road, a mere hundred yards from where Dechaine's Toyota had been parked. There were witnesses detectives should have interviewed, but didn't—people who'd contacted police to report sexual deviates in the area that week. But the police ignored these reports, probably because none of these suspects resembled Dechaine. Police had found a scrap of paper in the Dechaine kitchen bearing the name "Sarah" and a phone number.

Bruno the boarder and self-proclaimed antique dealer told them that was just someone he'd called to inquire about antiques. Police never contacted the subscriber to that telephone. I did; they'd never heard of Bruno. They'd never offered to buy or sell any antiques.

❖

The witness who'd told of seeing Dechaine's Toyota in the Henkel neighborhood on the day before the crime couldn't recognize Dechaine as its driver. He was never shown photos of anyone else.

Bill Connor, reporter for WCHS-TV, confirmed to me his quote of Eric Wright on the day of Dechaine's conviction. Wright had told reporters he "was convinced of Dechaine's guilt from the day I entered the case."

Wright entered the case the morning after Sarah's disappearance; this statement seemed to confirm Lieutenant Peter McCarthy's claim that Wright had vowed to prosecute Dechaine for murder that day—"even if we never find a body."

The boarder, Richard Bruno, was willing to tell me anything I wanted to know until I asked about his whereabouts on the day of the murder. He'd been with friends, he said now. They'd gone to an art exhibit at Bowdoin College. When I asked for the friends' names so I could inquire of them whether police had ever tried to confirm his alibi, he refused. He didn't want to get them involved, he said.

Bowdoin College had no art exhibit that day.

Most peculiar, however, was Bruno's change from the trial, three years before, when he'd testified that he had no alibi. And I wondered why police hadn't checked him more closely.

❖

Winter in Maine is usually described as stark, austere, bleak. The adjectives fit. The earth is so hard, we can't bury our dead. But winter is also a season of rest for the land and for the people. Crime is practically dormant.

It was freezing but sunny in January 1993 when I sat down at private investigator Ron Morin's kitchen table in Madawaska to hear about his experiences on the case.

Back in the summer of 1988, Morin had contacted a psychic in Connecticut who gave him detailed information about a murder he was investigating in Aroostook County, and her information had checked out, later, as amazingly accurate. At about 3:30 on the afternoon of July 7, 1988—the day after Sarah's disappearance; the day before the body was found—Morin phoned this psychic to tell her that the state police couldn't bring their tracking dog to aid in his local probe because the animal was being used in "another case, in southern Maine."

At this point, the psychic stated that a little girl, "wearing something lavender, was tortured, and had died from fear."

Sarah Cherry wore a lavender T-shirt that day.

The psychic went on to say, "there's something about an old, restored automobile, primer gray. She knows her killer but it's not a relative. Right now, she's lying down facing a wall. There's something about an aunt, somewhere between forty and fifty-eight years old. The girl is blonde."

It occurred to me as Morin spoke that this psychic could have heard news reports of Sarah's disappearance. But State Police Detective Graves, assigned to join Morin in his local murder case, was present at the time and heard the psychic's statements. He immediately telephoned the state police command post in Bowdoin and told Detective Hendsbee what the psychic had said, then relayed the psychic's statement that, "I see a man with a bushy mustache and pot belly, wearing Bermuda shorts, sitting in a lawn chair next to a camper. He's saying, 'It shouldn't have happened.'"

Morin said Hendsbee stepped outside the Silver Bullet command post and saw a man there who matched the psychic's description: Sarah's stepfather, Chris Crosman.

When Morin contacted the psychic again, she came up with a reddish, two-color pickup truck (Senecal owned a red and white pickup); she said there was a pond nearby and she saw a wooded area. Hendsbee told Morin to ask the psychic about the knife. She told him the crime took place in a blue-and-white trailer, and the knife was around there.

When Morin interviewed Ralph Jones—the Dead River Road resident who'd reported hearing Senecal talking to a young girl that day—Jones informed Morin that on the day after the body was found, police had roped off a blue-and-white trailer down the road from him and conducted a crime scene search.

Nothing about this was ever given to Connolly with the discovery material. It seems the prosecution didn't consider anything "relevant" for discovery unless it implicated their chosen suspect.

Morin said he'd contacted the task force investigating the Green River murders in the state of Washington and a detective there had informed him that he "got a hit on the name Richard Bruno," living in the state of Washington or northern California at the time, "but the day and month of his birth date were reversed." Morin had phoned Bruno at his current home in Massachusetts to ask whether he might drive down there and take Bruno's fingerprints. Bruno declined.

When Ron Morin tried to interview Rose Knodt, John Henkel's employer, "she became unglued. Very upset. Wouldn't meet me, wouldn't talk with me." Jennifer Henkel was cordial and cooperative the first time he talked with her but, when he called her back, she stated she'd talked with her ex-husband [the Henkels were divorced by this time], and he'd told her not to speak with Morin.

Morin said he found three women who reported being sexually abused by Senecal when they were girls. He asked Senecal for his side of these stories, Senecal told him, "I will never trust you. The only man on the face of the earth I will ever trust is Eric Wright."

❖

February was cold and gray. On the 24th, armed with my authorizations from Dechaine and Connolly, I visited George Carlton, the first lawyer Dechaine contacted that Thursday morning after his all-night interrogation by police.

Carlton told me he "really can't bring myself" to state guilt or innocence. "I sometimes say to people that they have been genuinely fucked.... All I can say [about Dechaine] is, the evidence *seems* to be overwhelming."

Carlton's secretary, who sat with us as we chatted, said that Dechaine came in at about 9:30 that morning. Carlton thought they'd talked for about half an hour that first day and then "I kind of hustled him on his way." Dechaine and his wife returned together, later that day. "Dechaine started out with a rather nebulous story" but, as the new client continued, it became apparent to Carlton that this was serious. Dechaine told him about acquiring the drugs, and showed Carlton track marks on his arms.

Carlton told me, "[Dechaine] said he couldn't remember everything that happened that day." The lawyer assumed a man-of-the-world expression and a superior smile. "When they say they can't remember, that means they did it."

"I've heard rumors you disclosed something to someone in law enforcement."

Carlton laughed. He couldn't imagine what I'd heard. "I'm sure you've been around all your life with these local small sheriff's departments, who are 90 percent assholes," and "I don't know how that [rumor] could have happened because I've even had Judge Bradford...I see him all the time, and he's said, 'When are you going to tell me the truth about that case?' And I said, 'You'll never hear anything from me, Judge.'"

The honorable judge, asking a fellow member of the Bar to violate his client's privilege of confidentiality? Hard to swallow, but I wasn't surprised. No one had to be with George Carlton for very long before they'd see that the poorly groomed, sixty-five-year-old man with booze on his breath in the early afternoon was easily given to snap judgments and was somewhat of a braggart. I wrote him off as a small-time bullshit artist and mentally congratulated Dechaine for having the good sense to dump Carlton and get Tom Connolly.

16

Friendship and Blood

RALPH WALDO EMERSON ONCE SAID, "A friend may well be reckoned the masterpiece of Nature."

Carol Waltman in the town of Madawaska on the Canadian border, three hundred miles north of the central action, knew in her mind, in her heart, and in her soul that nothing—not drugs, nor hypnotism, nor even a gun to his head—could cause Dennis Dechaine to inflict those atrocities on anyone. Carol and Dennis had been friends from childhood and they stayed in touch, remained close. It didn't matter how the state presented its puny, problematic evidence. It didn't matter, either, that police and prosecutors had fooled twelve jurors into voting "guilty." It would make no difference that every court refused to examine the facts and see the truth.

Dennis was innocent!

Dennis was her friend.

Carol was a good person but she was no amateur do-gooder in search of something to fill her empty hours. She had her husband and children. She had her elderly parents to care for. She had her business to run. She did all of those things but she pushed herself harder to wage this war simply because never giving up on justice was the right thing to do.

❖

Carol went undercover. And she went alone, despite a bone infection resulting from an injury to her elbow. She telephoned the Dechaines' former boarder, Bruno, posed as a woman with an antique bowl to sell, made an appointment to meet him near his new residence in Massachusetts, and she journeyed nearly 500 miles to keep that appointment. She met him alone—this man whom she suspected just might possibly be a murderer—met him at the spot he'd chosen in the parking lot of a country restaurant and handed him the bowl to examine. As expected, Bruno declined interest in buying the bowl at the price Carol quoted. Then she returned to Madawaska and called a friend, a former CIA man. He lifted Bruno's fingerprints from the bowl and had them checked against the latents the police had lifted, but never identified, from the Henkel house.

No match.

Bill Clinton was elected President. Los Angeles officers were acquitted of the videotaped beating of Rodney King. Dennis Dechaine was old news, forgotten by almost everyone.

All through 1993, Carol drove Trial & Error with an implacable determination. She kept supporters informed through newsletters. She reported on Connolly's brief to Maine's supreme court, discussed contacts with the *Unsolved Mysteries* television show, and distributed copies of the lawsuits I'd filed for access to the state's records. She managed a letter-writing campaign, solicited funds for the lawsuits and to pay for DNA testing of the victim's fingernails—and on and on, tirelessly.

In June, members received a transcript of one member's session with a "spiritualist minister" named Arlene Sikora. This and encounters with other psychics were equally fruitless. In July, Carol prevailed on me to accompany another psychic to the area where Sarah's body had been found.

❖

On September 9, 1993, CBR Laboratories reported to Professor Barry Scheck of the Benjamin N. Cardozo School of Law in New York on their analysis of the blood adhering to Sarah Cherry's fingernails:

> The DQ Alpha alleles 1.3, 2 and 4 were detected in CBRL item 12384, suggesting that there are two or more donors to the DNA extracted from this item.

The presence of two or more "donors" to the blood under the thumbnail 12384 proves one thing: even if some of the blood was Sarah's, some of it was someone else's. And, since the blood type wasn't Dechaine's, he couldn't possibly be that other donor.

This was more than a year before Professor Scheck became widely known for his association with the O. J. Simpson case, but he and the Innocence Project had already used DNA evidence to free many innocent men from unjust imprisonment.

❖

Carol appealed to her state legislator. Representative

Douglas Ahearne proposed a resolution to require the attorney general's office to release documents regarding Dechaine's case to defense attorneys. The legislature turned him down.

Ahearne and State Senator Judy Paradis met with Attorney General Ketterer to request that the AG's office surrender a sample of Sarah Cherry's blood for DNA testing to determine whether either of the bloods under her nails was her own. In a spirit of cooperation and hoping for reciprocation, Ahearne told the AG's people the results of the DNA test on the blood from Sarah's nails.

But they didn't reciprocate. Instead, on December 20th, they summoned Connolly to appear before Judge Bradford. They wanted the fingernails back, *and* they wanted the lab's test report.

But Tom Connolly, unaware that the AG's people already knew the test results, resisted—ready to "take a bullet," i.e., go to jail, in defense of his client's rights. It was shortly before the court hearing when Connolly discovered that his opponents already knew the bottom-line results of the tests on those fingernails.

But they didn't have the lab report.

❖

"May it please the Court," Eric Wright said to Judge Bradford, "I had not supposed after all this time that I would have had reason to file a motion again in criminal case 89-71. We are here however after five-and-a-half years since Sarah Cherry's death because of Mr. Connolly's actions. We are here because it came to the attention of our office ... that the defense had in its possession evidence which had been obtained by the state during the investigation of this case including, one can say fairly, body parts of the victim, namely her fingernail cuttings."

That was true. When Dechaine's trial had begun back in 1989, Tom Connolly intended to have DNA tests conducted on that blood. So the fingernails, which the state had no intention of introducing, were labeled as defense exhibits. But Connolly's plan was short-circuited by Judge Bradford's decision to agree with Eric Wright that "the short delay [to perform DNA testing] isn't worth the gamble" of delaying the trial for a month or two.

When the trial concluded, the court clerk notified each counsel that they could retrieve their exhibits or leave them to be routinely destroyed. The clerk packed the fingernails among Connolly's exhibits because that's how they were marked. He picked them up.

A few weeks before this motion was filed, Fernand LaRochelle, head of the AG's criminal unit, telephoned Connolly in an effort to get the fingernails back. Connolly refused. LaRochelle asked how the fingernails had come into Connolly's possession.

Considering how forthcoming the prosecutors had *not* been throughout this case, Connolly felt no obligation to satisfy LaRochelle's curiosity. Always happy to leave his adversaries wondering, Connolly tossed off a casual, "Oh, just tricks of the trade."

Now, in court, LaRochelle took the witness stand and quoted Connolly as stating that, "When the court had refused to turn [the fingernails] over to him, he had employed his own tricks in order to obtain those items...."

LaRochelle decided to convey "tricks of the trade" as a synonym for legal trickery. Or perhaps LaRochelle had a poor memory. More likely, Fern LaRochelle was a man who chose to hear the words of others with a spin he preferred, rather than quoting whatever might actually have been said. And this peculiar proclivity (in my opinion and based on facts I uncovered much later) is the unfortunate defect which ultimately had the most profound effect on the whole Cherry–Dechaine saga.

Wright told Judge Bradford, "The testimony you have just heard makes it evident that Mr. Connolly has been desperate to obtain these fingernail clippings," and his act of marking them as defense exhibits "was a conscious design. He plotted to do that as we now know and it is unimaginable that he could suppose after that hearing he got the right to obtain this evidence by means of a clerk's form letter which was sent to him about fifteen months later...saying essentially come pick your exhibits up or we will be getting rid of things within two weeks...."

Wright acknowledged that he had not responded in a timely manner to that notification by the court clerk. Had Connolly not retrieved the fingernails, they'd have been lost forever, a fate which wouldn't have harmed the AG's interests.

"Certainly we can suppose," Wright went on, "Mr. Connolly has done something with them.... And what has he done? I don't know, but I know what could have been done." This was the prosecution's new tack: if the test results expose holes in the state's case, attack those results. He couldn't fight the expertise of the scientists but he could, and would, imply that Tom Connolly had somehow altered this evidence by an unspecified contamination. Wright would like his "might have" to equal the weight of credible evidence.

Eric Wright demanded the return of the fingernails, and he wanted the officially documented reports of any testing that had been performed.

Connolly argued that "The fact that the prosecution did not respond to the order [to pick up their exhibits] for a period of greater than a year is a complete waiver to any claim that they have to those items." He also argued that "questions as to what has been done with those items are clearly work product [lawyer's notes, confidential communications, et al.]" and exempt from premature disclosure to the prosecution.

Wright countered that, "As to the notion of work product, it just...it's got to be borne in mind that this is not his property. This was originally the court's property...and before that was evidence acquired by the state during the investigation."

Judge Bradford banged his gavel angrily and ordered Connolly to return the fingernails to the state. Connolly complied. But the judge, perhaps in the grip of his fury, neglected to order the surrender of the report documenting the results of the DNA test.

Connolly phoned his secretary, Ida, from a courthouse pay phone: "Prepare an appeal of this to the high court."

Ida worked swiftly. Connolly filed the appeal.

An hour later, Judge Bradford phoned Connolly at his office. "Get back here with the results of those tests."

"Sorry, Judge, the case is out of your hands."

"Out of my hands? What are you talking about?"

"I've filed an appeal."

Wright and LaRochelle—and Judge Bradford—could only wonder whether the allegation by Representative Ahearne regarding those tests was true.

❖

On January 26, 1994, Dechaine wrote an official request to the warden of the Maine State Prison:

> Respectfully request that I be permitted to provide blood and hair samples to a certified DNA testing laboratory...enabling the selected laboratory to match my DNA characteristics with the DNA characteristics obtained in DNA testing of samples obtained from Miss Sarah Cherry's nails....

It took nine days for Warden Martin Magnusson to reply:

> Your request is denied. The Maine State Prison medical staff does not have the time to do anything but provide medical care to prisoners.

On February 6th, Dechaine wrote back:

> Since your denial hinges on your inability to provide medical staff to do the testing...perhaps you will be kind enough to reconsider if I provide medical professional(s) and agent(s) of the court at my expense. I thank you in advance for your thoughtful consideration

of this urgent request.

This time, seven weeks of Magnusson's cogitation produced this decision:

> I am this date sending your request through the Department for Attorney General review and recommendation as to how we should proceed with your request. I will let you know as soon as a decision is made.

On June 24th, Dechaine wrote to Connolly:

> I called Carol tonight and she told me how upset you were at learning that she'd shared the DNA report with the Attorney General. I want you to know that I was unaware of her intentions when I called to ask you for a copy of the report. I didn't tell you because I knew that you would not send it knowing that it would be shared. I'm sorry if you feel betrayed. However, I am approaching my sixth year in this cesspool and I am slowly realizing that I do not have the intestinal fortitude to endure much longer.... I have to say that I was tremendously impressed with [AG Michael] Carpenter's input in allowing me to give blood and hair samples. Tom, think for just one moment what that sort of gift means to me. Carpenter more than likely saved me a couple years of prison and perhaps an entire lifetime.... If giving him a copy of the DNA report gives me a chance of getting Sarah Cherry's frozen blood samples, then it is a risk well worth taking. I am desperate to move forward, to

show that I am willing to deviate from the confrontational style if only it will speed the process. Carol Waltman responds to my desperation by doing her best to help me.... Sometimes, her practical ways conflict with your lawyering mind.... I am just one of many who pushes Carol. Try to understand the difficult situation she is in as she tried to assuage the various interests that impose upon her and credit her for her remarkable successes despite the stresses of being involved in such a demanding endeavor....

Carol Waltman met with the AG's people and she foolishly believed their promise that, in exchange for giving them a copy of the lab report regarding the DNA tests, "all you have to do is file a court motion for a sample of Sarah's blood. We won't oppose it."

But they reneged on their word. They did oppose it. And they prevailed. It was not a move that engendered confidence in the integrity of the AG's people—assuming that anyone involved in this case still harbored a delusion of their integrity. But the AG's people, and the Maine courts, had no intention of risking the objectivity of science.

In its July 9–10, 1994 issue, the *Bangor Daily News* reported:

DECHAINE SUFFERS SETBACK IN APPEAL TO HIGH COURT
Bid To Retain Evidence In Baby-Sitter Slaying Denied

The Maine Judicial Supreme Court denied Dechaine's appeal of a Superior

Court Order that he return fingernail
clippings that investigators took from
the body of Sarah Cherry....

In November, Michael Carpenter announced he would not seek re-election to the office of attorney general. He said he wanted to spend more time with his family who'd remained back home, 196 miles north of the state capital. The area of achievement he cited with pride was "enforcement of civil rights."

Alfred Hendsbee, retired from the state police and licensed as a private eye, was running for sheriff of Somerset County promising "clean uniforms" and a reduction of the "frills," whatever they were. He told *Bangor Daily News* reporter Sharon Mack, "I believe that it is not what we do to the people but rather what we do for the people that makes law enforcement great."

Hendsbee lost.

Eric Wright's son found some money in a men's room and turned it over to the police. Six months later, in December, Wright felt that the boy's honesty hadn't been sufficiently recognized. He prevailed upon the police department to give the boy a certificate. The ceremony was reported with a color photo above the fold on the front page of the *Brunswick Times Record*.

In December, Dechaine became aware that new limits on judicial reviews of criminal convictions imposed by the U.S. Supreme Court left but one avenue to attempt: ineffective counsel. He began a list of "deficiencies" in

Connolly's representation.

Tom Connolly made a move virtually unheard of in the annals of trial advocacy. He joined in Dechaine's efforts by stating that he had, indeed, been ineffective.

He hadn't anticipated the testimony of dog officer Bureau, but how could he? The AG's people withheld Bureau's report from the discovery material. Connolly failed to anticipate the testimony of storekeeper Knight, who swore that Dechaine was at his Bowdoinham store when, in fact, Dennis and Nancy were still a hundred miles north of there with scores of witnesses to prove it. But Wright had withheld Knight's allegations from the discovery material, too. And if Connolly missed the impact of Dr. Roy's finding which proved that Sarah was murdered while Dechaine was being interrogated by police, so did the jurors and the media and the spectators and everyone else. Wright had cunningly manipulated the presentation of that testimony. And the medical examiner's conclusion regarding time-of-death had been withheld from the discovery material.

Connolly's real deficiency was naiveté. He never suspected that prosecutors would adopt an arrogant belief that concealing evidence was justified. He thought they'd obey the law. Connolly believed in a spirited fight, but a fair one. He thought Eric Wright & Company felt the same way.

❖

For Dennis Dechaine, Christmas 1994 came and went just like the previous five Christmases.

Connolly's secretary, Ida Bilodeau, spent hours transcribing the long-ago interview with the state's psychologist. After studying the entire transcript, Dechaine wondered in a letter to Ida:

> Why would Eric Wright and Mike Carpenter *both* tell my family and friends that I admitted to having confessed to Mark Westrum when it makes no part of this taped interview? Westrum's name never even surfaced.... More of the AG and his assistant liars? What in heaven's name is going on here?... I am so utterly confused by this and find the idea that our chief law enforcement officers are malicious liars completely unfathomable. What trust can one possibly place in law enforcement if they're bad top to bottom?

Portland lawyer Paul Boots began the task of appealing Dechaine's conviction on the basis of ineffective counsel, but Dechaine's letter to Ida continued:

> You know I'd live without any hope were it not for Tom Connolly. I owe him everything. I hope we can get this ordeal rolling soon. I do hope this finds you and Tom well.

In March, dog officer Tom Bureau, after seventeen years with the Maine State Police, was elevated to detective and assigned to the attorney general's office.

In May, Maine's highest court agreed with defendants in another murder trial—this case arising from a barroom brawl—that prosecutor Eric Wright had "made inappropriate statements to jurors" during his summation. But the justices concluded that Wright's improprieties didn't matter because, they said, "the trial judge either gave, or offered to give, curative instruction to the jurors." These justices' uncertainty as to whether such instructions were offered, or actually given, was apparently unimportant.

In October, Dechaine petitioned the Maine courts again, this time giving examples he believed constituted Connolly's ineffective representation and citing the DNA test results as justification for a new trial.

On November 5th, Carol Waltman mailed a letter to Trial & Error members listing the grounds for Dechaine's latest petition to the court. She continued:

> Having listed the grounds, it is important to state that despite the claims of ineffective counsel, Dennis continues to hold Tom Connolly in high regard. The fact of the matter is that though Tom should have applied more pressure to compel the truth, the state continually hinders him. Unfortunately, for post-conviction reviews to be successful, failings at trial must be assigned to trial counsel.
>
> We are fortunate to have secured a DNA specialist to assist him in his efforts at justice. Barry Scheck and his associates at the Cardozo Law School's Innocence Project have agreed to assist in the case pro bono, (free of charge). Mrs. Judy Potter, a law professor at the University of Southern Maine Law School, has agreed to serve as local counsel and to work with Mr. Scheck. Judy is also working pro-bono.
>
> Despite the generosity of lawyers in this case, *Trial & error* continues to incur expenses in the fight to reveal

the truth...must be prepared to pay for potential expenses of DNA testing and expert witnesses.

In our efforts to secure needed funds, we are conducting a raffle....

Time took its toll on witnesses. In the nearly eight years since the trial, the man who saw Dechaine emerge from the woods around 8:30 died of heart disease. The man who encountered Dechaine minutes later and tried to help him find his truck, and stayed with Dechaine until the sheriff's men took him into custody, died of lung cancer. The warden who led the search and was the first to check Sarah's body died in a plane crash. Forensic Chemist Judith Brinkman moved to Texas, then to Wisconsin. Former State Medical Examiner Dr. Ronald Roy departed to Canada. Former Deputy Sheriff Clancy retired in Florida. Former Sheriff Haggett was doing something unrelated to law enforcement in New Hampshire. The state would contend that the distances or demise of these witnesses rendered it impossible for them to mount a retrial in this case. The plain fact was that the state wouldn't have to present these witnesses. The defense could easily have stipulated that all of these witnesses' testimony at the original trial be entered into a new trial record without dispute. The only one who'd provided anything vital was Dr. Roy, and his sworn testimony proved Dechaine innocent.

In January, 1997, Fern LaRochelle was demoted from his position as chief of the AG's criminal division. Eric Wright departed that office altogether.

A year or so later, recognized from his old TV appearances by a man at the Joshua's Tavern in Brunswick, Eric Wright explained why he hadn't been seen on television news in recent months. "I've left the attorney general's office."

"Oh? Why'd you do that?"

"We had a difference of opinion."

"Oh. So what did you do after that?"

"I went to work for a law firm in Portland."

"Uh-huh. You like it there?"

"I'm not there any more."

"Why?"

"We had a difference of opinion."

"Oh." The man bid Wright a pleasant goodbye and returned to the booth where his friends waited.

Dennis Dechaine wrote a poem:

> I am a prisoner—
> a universe away from
> the quiet of my country home,
> the melodious songs of
> morning birds, the sweet gentle
> greetings of my mate.
> I am a prisoner!

Dechaine watched his life ebb away with every prospect of eroding forever, as if all the sands of the Sahara would have to trickle through an hourglass before he'd see justice. The men who'd withheld and concealed evidence worked hard to preserve their image of rectitude and virtue. But the filing of that allegation—ineffective counsel—eventually solved one of the mysteries that had plagued me ever since the scientific evidence proved that Dechaine couldn't possibly have committed the murder. And the solution to that puzzle was even more distressing—with its impact on an even broader scale—than the knowledge that Sarah Cherry's killer was still roaming free to repeat his depravities.

In 1995, prosecutor Eric Wright used DNA evidence to convict the rapist-murderer of an eighteen-year-old woman; in 1996, Wright bemoaned delays in DNA tests, stating that "only the guilty benefit from delays."

In January, lawyer Gene Libby of the prestigious Verrill & Dana law firm took Dechaine's case to the Maine Superior Court seeking DNA testing of the blood under Sarah Cherry's fingernails.

Lawyer Tom Connolly ran for governor on the Democratic ticket. In 1998, The *Village Voice* wrote:

> Connolly may have thought he could use a term in the state's highest elective office to rectify his own mistakes. Asked two years ago by *Casco Bay Weekly* whether he'd exercise his authority as governor to pardon Dechaine, Connolly said he'd consider it. "I'm inclined to," he told the paper. "I believe he didn't do it, and I'm unlikely to back down on my beliefs."

Connolly lost the election to the incumbent Independent candidate.

❖

Throughout the decade of the 1990s, Dennis Dechaine's fate was in the hands of lawyers, awaiting the interminable deliberations and decisions of judges. As for me, working alone I couldn't hope to solve a ten-year-old murder after the state police had done their bit and prosecutors had caged the police reports under locks as strong as those that imprisoned Dechaine. But if waiting and frustration were hard on me, they must have been literal hell for the innocent man serving life in prison.

For those of us outside the walls, summers with daisies and sunflowers waving in the breezes and the multi-hued greens of the forests fly by swiftly. Autumns bring the vivid brilliance of reds and yellows to those trees, then the wind-blown swirls of brown leaves scraping across our streets. Winters turn Mainers' thoughts to vacations in sunnier climes. Bears and bats and field mice hibernate. In the woods grosbeaks squabble and squirrels chatter, moose browse in a peaceful bog and the fearless weasel dons its ermine coat.

And then the spring. Moths flutter around porch lights again. Cyclists wearing shorts as they wheel along the roads take note of turkey tracks in the muddy stretches, and the snowbirds begin their annual re-migration back home. After a November rut, and the cold and hunger of winter and the March thaw, May arrives. Does bear their fawns.

Maine is a wonderful land for those of us who can enjoy it.

By 1998, all those seasons had turned over ten times since Dechaine was arrested.

A mere week can be a long time. Dechaine had spent 624

weeks behind bars. If you've ever waited an hour to meet a lover, you know how long sixty slowly-ticking minutes can seem. By July 1998, Dennis Dechaine had endured 105,120 hours of state-dictated despair inside the walls of that old penitentiary, closely confined among men most of us would do anything to avoid.

It took Judge Donald Marden nearly a year to say "No" to Dechaine's DNA plea.

From there, the case went to federal court where I assured Dechaine that justice would finally prevail.

17

Myth-Conception

Murder was so alien to Dechaine's nature that anyone who knew him—even the most jaded keepers at the prison—believed him innocent.

David Brannon, a former corrections officer at Thomaston, didn't like Dennis Dechaine. "Because of his crime," Brannon told me.

"You think he's guilty? Why?'

"Twelve people said he was."

Brannon explained that junior corrections officers assigned to evening and night shifts took their cue from their leadership, seeing every inmate as guilty. Brannon's co-workers on the day shift—the prison's most senior, most experienced guards—were "men who form their own opinions of what's going on."

"What do they think of Dechaine?"

Still amazed, several years after having left state employment to become a mailman at nearly twice the salary, Brannon said, "Dechaine gets more room and leeway than anybody I've ever seen in prison. He's the only inmate I ever witnessed come and get keys. They don't allow anybody to even *view* keys, much less touch them.

Except for Dechaine."

Top guards had a list, Brannon told me—prisoners they'd release if the power was theirs. "There were three inmates on that list. One of them was Dennis Dechaine."

There had to be something deeper, something stronger, more convincing than papers in a driveway and those so-called confessions to explain the prosecution's implacable determination to convict Dechaine and keep him in prison. Most of their "evidence" said nothing about the murder. Their most reliable evidence, the indisputable scientific facts, proved him innocent.

Any degenerate who'd inflict such bestial acts on a helpless little girl, any lawbreaker cunning enough to snatch a few items from an unoccupied truck and use them to send the police sniffing after someone else—and do all this without leaving an atom of hard evidence or a single eyewitness to anything incriminating—this man was either an experienced criminal or the luckiest man alive.

No one had nominated Dechaine for any Lucky Man awards, lately.

❖

So, why did Prosecutor Wright present Dr. Roy's scientific opinion regarding time of death in that peculiar manner? Why conceal the medical examiner's conclusions concerning time of death? Why did that medical examiner—Dr. Ronald Roy, currently practicing his profession in Canada—tell me when I spoke to him that "the Dechaine case is why I left the state of Maine" and refuse, under any circumstances, to return here?

Why did the AG's people fight so hard against having DNA tests on the blood under Sarah's nails? Why ignore the hair found on Sarah's body, a hair totally unlike Dechaine's? Why have their own psychologists examine Dechaine, then make sure that neither they, nor the defense doctor, could testify to the jury? Why did Prosecutor Wright fight successfully to keep mention of Senecal away from the jury and suppress the state's files regarding Senecal's prior abuse of a young girl, then summon the gall to assure jurors that, "there is no evidence, ladies and gentlemen of the jury, in this case, of an alternative perpetrator"? Why did Senecal himself tell private investigator Morin that the only man he'd ever trust was Eric Wright?

Why tell jurors the Toyota was locked when police found it? That was untrue. The trooper readying it to be towed to the state lab gained access via its unlocked rear window. Besides, anyone could have locked the truck's doors after taking the items he'd need to frame its owner simply by closing the Toyota's doors with the lock button down.

For that matter, why did Wright withhold even more evidence the court had ordered given to the defense as discovery? The report of dog officer Bureau; notes taken by county detective Westrum, follow-up interviews of Julie Wagg, the contemporaneous notes taken by Detective Hendsbee, Warden Service reports regarding their efforts with scent dogs—all of these were illegally concealed by the state. Why conceal evidence regarding the fingerprint lifted from the Henkel house—proof that it didn't belong to the Henkels or anyone else known to investigators? It wasn't Dechaine's. Whose was it?

Why did the state refuse me an opportunity to review public records, the trial evidence? Why did they destroy items from Dechaine's truck which didn't serve to implicate him—Dechaine's personal property—without his permission? Why were they still going to gargantuan lengths to make sure no one could see the complete police file? Was there even more evidence they'd unlawfully concealed? Were there even more lies they'd told? Why did they persist in preventing DNA evidence from coming before a court?

Prosecutors violated the court's discovery order, they violated due process of law, and they violated Dechaine's constitutional right to a fair trial. In the federal system, we have a name for that crime: obstruction of justice. But why? What could have really motivated prosecutors to commit all the improprieties they had perpetrated before and during Dechaine's trial? Eric Wright and Fernand LaRochelle were experienced and intelligent. They'd apparently served the people of the State of Maine satisfactorily for decades, too long to have suddenly transformed into Satan's minions. Detective Hendsbee was clearly in over his head, but I wasn't seeing him as a bad person. And yet, they all knew something, or thought they knew something, that justified their illegitimate actions. My answer came when Dechaine filed his appeal based on ineffective trial counsel.

Dechaine's motion mentioned Tom Connolly by name. Connolly alone handled every facet of the case. Old George Carlton was allowed to string along because no one had the heart to fire him and Connolly hoped Carlton's friendship with Judge Bradford might tip the scales now and then in courtroom situations where the judge had discretion.

Carlton's role was plainly that of an affable, volunteer water boy. Except for being shown as present, he's totally invisible in the trial transcript. So why, now, were the attorney general's people suddenly and vociferously insisting that the "ineffective counsel" allegation also embraced Carlton?

They answered that question with their next move: they cited a Bar Rule and a court decision holding that "by order of court" a lawyer may "reveal a confidence or secret of the client...as necessary to the defense of the lawyer . . . against an accusation of wrongful conduct...."

The AG's people believed that Dechaine had confessed the crime to Carlton during that initial consultation. They wanted to say that in open court. Of course! Rumors of Carlton's betrayal had been around for years. He laughed and denied it when I braced him about it in his office. He denied it to Tom Connolly. But even Detective Hendsbee had suggested that I "get in touch with George Carlton" for the inside, untold story. And then, when I asked Medical Examiner Ronald Roy why he'd lent himself to this peculiar and misleading presentation of his findings, Roy blurted, "He's guilty. Even his own lawyer admitted it."

Whether or not Carlton said anything to anyone, the belief that he'd certified his client's guilt must have contributed to Dr. Roy's participation in Eric Wright's chicanery and, hence, to Dechaine's conviction. The rule allowing a lawyer to reveal confidential client information if he's fighting an accusation of impropriety is codified in the American Bar Association's Model Rules of Professional Conduct as an exception to the primary rule, which states: "A lawyer shall not reveal information relating to representation of a client unless the client consents after consultation . . . ."

Had Dechaine really admitted something to Carlton?

Carlton couldn't testify, couldn't even be interviewed. His disability following a stroke was such that he could only communicate by blinks of the eye, and the only person capable of translating those blinks was his daughter. Carol Waltman and I journeyed to interview Carlton at Johns Hopkins Hospital in Baltimore, but his daughter refused to permit us any questions whatsoever. She said she'd been informed by the AG's people that we wanted to harm her father's reputation. George Carlton would die without ever giving testimony to anybody about whatever Dechaine had said.

When lawyer Gene Libby and Barry Scheck's Innocence Project entered this case and launched their legal efforts to get a new trial and have the DNA evidence considered, Libby asked for copies of the reports I'd given Tom Connolly. I supplied them, we met, he asked for my take on the evidence, and I gave it to him. The case was in their arena now. There was nothing else I could do.

Maine's high court rejected their appeal for a new trial based on the new DNA evidence. After reviewing Bradford's decision, the assigned justice wrote, "We find no error in the record, and we affirm the judgment." And, "based on the evidence submitted to it, the jury rationally could find beyond a reasonable doubt all the elements of the offenses with which Dechaine was charged." The assigned justice quoted the decisions in previous cases and stated, "We review the trial court's denial of a motion for a new trial for clear error." Somehow, the justice adopted the perception of the prosecution that, "Several separate admissions to the crime were made by Dechaine." And, with respect to the testimony of the trial jurors who had expressed doubts, "Clearly it is the trial court, not a juror, that possesses the superior knowledge and experience for determining whether any new evidence offered on a motion for a new trial meets the five well-established criteria for granting a new trial...."

❖

Other explanations for that court's judgment may have been revealed in an article for the January 1999 issue of *Maine Bar Journal* by Justice Leigh Saufley, the woman who would be appointed Chief Justice in 2001 when Chief Justice Daniel E. Walthan resigned. "Simply put," Justice Saufley wrote, "the caseload of the court is so high that there is very little time for reflection, discussion, debate, or even heated argument . . . . The press of business can result in equal time for issues of unequal importance and can lead to inconsistent or shallow analysis." She also acknowledged in the article that she'd had "simply no time to read the transcripts in (most) cases to which I am not assigned."

So, in practice, one justice examines a case brought to the court—the one to whom a case is assigned. And, in effect, his or her colleagues go along with whatever conclusion that justice has reached. It's an explanation, if not an excuse.

A new round began in the federal court. Years passed while lawyers struggled to find persuasive arguments, and judges struggled to lessen their backlog faster than new matters piled their caseload higher.

. In August 2000, curiosity and a lack of communication from the lawyers prompted me to visit the federal building and review the court file. Documents filed by the state's office of the attorney general gave me a real surprise. According to the AG's people, lawyer George Carlton hadn't merely muttered an indiscreet word to some cop. Affidavits filed by three other lawyers—one of them from the AG's office—claimed that Carlton came right out and told them Dechaine was guilty!

The AG's people had launched this latest effort with the affidavit of Assistant Attorney General (and chief of the AG's criminal Division) Fernand LaRochelle. He swore that Carlton's first betrayal occurred on the morning of July 8, 1988, two days after Sarah Cherry's disappearance. LaRochelle was well acquainted with Carlton. As one of Carlton's former law partners put it, Carlton and LaRochelle had once "worked together" on a murder case—LaRochelle prosecuting, Carlton defending. Carlton's client, "an eighteen- or nineteen-year-old who'd strangled his father's girlfriend, got sixty years."

LaRochelle's affidavit stated that he picked up his telephone on the morning of July 8th, called Carlton, told him he'd heard that Dechaine had consulted him, and added, "that investigators felt that if Sarah was still alive, it was important that we find her soon. So I have just two questions: is she alive? And, are we searching the right area?"

LaRochelle continued, "Attorney Carlton replied that Sarah was not alive and added something to the effect that we were looking in the right area.... I reported this information to Assistant Attorney General Eric Wright."

That did it! Little wonder that the AG's people felt sure of Dechaine's guilt.

A second affidavit by a former prosecutor named Edmund Folsom recounted a conversation with Carlton when, "in that discussion, George made it clear to me that he knew Dennis Dechaine had committed the murder from having discussed it with Dechaine in George's office." He remembered Carlton calling Dechaine "a sick little bastard" and making other comments on how "demented" he was.

Lawyer (now judge) Joseph Field's affidavit—the third—recounted a conversation with Carlton during which Field asked, "Do you think Dechaine actually did it?" Carlton's response "Yes."

My appraisal of LaRochelle was low, based on his order to the medical examiner's clerk when I requested a copy of the autopsy report—"Show him what we gave Connolly and nothing else." But, in the pragmatic, ends-justifies-the-means mind, LaRochelle's take on Carlton's statements would justify the rule-breaking, even perhaps a blood sport approach to convicting Dechaine. And two other respected attorneys confirmed similar versions of Carlton's treachery. A defense lawyer's (hopefully rare) betrayal of his client's confidentiality would be seen by anyone as powerful evidence.

Mark Twain once said, "A lie can travel half-way around the world while the truth is putting on its shoes." But, was Carlton lying?

George Melvin Carlton, Jr., was born in Philadelphia to

George Melvin Carlton, Sr., and Elizabeth Leona Ryan Carlton on December 5, 1924. By the time he'd reached his early teens his family had moved to Maine. At the age of nineteen, he was drafted to serve in World War II. He served with the headquarters company of the 327th Glider Regiment and he was awarded the usual decorations given to soldiers serving in Europe. Stories of his heroic wartime exploits, however, are not borne out by the official record. Carlton remained with the occupation troops in Germany for a while, and was discharged in January 1946 as private first class. In 1988, as a lawyer, he had many friends in the legal community. Former partner William Leonard called him a "genius."

Interesting conclusion. I asked Leonard, "What do you base that on?"

Leonard cited one incident. Carlton walked into a courtroom one day and predicted to an onlooker that the case in progress would end in a mistrial. Later, it did.

After Carlton's death, lawyers with a stake in the weight of his word invested him with a status approaching sainthood. Incidents illustrating a towering arrogance were now recounted as endearing examples of a vigilante dedication to honor and justice. Carlton's tossing of a minister down a flight of stairs became a demonstration of his princely unwillingness to stand for anything he perceived as "bullshit." Threatening to throw a judge named Rubin "out the window into the parking lot" was portrayed as a courageous act to protect a young attorney named Carl O. Bradford from Rubin's "abuse." Carlton's desk drawer, crammed with unpaid fee statements, was offered by former partner

Leonard as an example of Carlton's pragmatic fatalism—"They'll get in trouble again," Leonard quotes Carlton as telling him, "They'll need me again. They'll pay."

Former clients explained the unpaid fees as the logical consequence of Carlton's submitting exorbitant bills for weak service. In Dechaine's case, he charged the family $3,000 for those two first-day half-hour consultations in his office. They paid it. He'd wanted a cool $50,000 to defend Dechaine at trial—plainly excessive in a world where the highly successful Tom Connolly saw his own $30,000 fee as "more than I'd ever received for any case before." Then, after the trial, George Carlton sent Nancy another bill, wanting more than the $3,000 he'd already been given. But he'd been told up front the family couldn't afford two lawyers for the trial.

Lawyer Joseph Fields' affidavit made a delicate reference to his association with Carlton after Carlton's "return from Australia." That "return" was actually a surrender from several years as a fugitive from a federal indictment. The IRS had charged Carlton with evading his income taxes for the years 1966 through 1977.

Former law partner William Leonard mentioned this seven-year interlude in Carlton's life with a chuckle. "People all over were getting postcards from George with kangaroos, weeks before the U.S. marshal came around hunting for him."

Upon his return, in 1983, Carlton worked out a compromise and paid $38,495.54 to settle his debt to the federal government. Lawyer Leonard says, "a nice deal was worked out. There were people who knew him and were well-placed.

He served thirty days in jail as a cook—he was a good cook—and was suspended from the practice of law for six or nine months." Leonard also told me that Carlton "drank too much" and "he rarely cracked a law book," but he was "loved by lawyers and judges."

Some lawyers agreed with Leonard. But one characterized Carlton as a "braggadocian drunk," and several saw him as "just plain useless in the courtroom." Among the varying opinions I heard, "soaring vanity," "reckless egotism," and "a profound depth of cynicism preserved by frequent doses of alcohol."

A more objective assessment came from one of the most knowledgeable observers of Maine's legal scene: "a decent, garden-variety do-your-will, do-your-mortgage lawyer with no particular expertise in criminal matters beyond the occasional OUI (operating under the influence) case."

Sagadahoc County records for 1988, the year Dechaine consulted him, reveal Carlton's "expertise" as somewhat dubious with respect to anything. He represented clients in thirty-eight superior court cases that year. One client was acquitted of unlawful sexual contact—a "victory" most likely attributable to the client's refusal to talk to police and his rejection of Carlton's advice that he plead guilty. Several of Carlton's clients had some charges dismissed, but only after he pleaded them guilty to more serious crimes. All the rest of Carlton's clients, mostly drunk drivers, were convicted, jailed, fined, and had their drivers licenses suspended—the same penalty they'd have received if they'd come to court without a lawyer.

During the years 1987 and 1988, the civil court docket

listed 278 cases. Carlton was counsel in two of them. Both were dismissed for Carlton's "failure to file docket entries." Carlton dropped the ball and his clients forfeited whatever justice that may have been due.

Considering Carlton's age at the time, his dubious record as a defender, and the timing of his alleged comments to the three other lawyers, it seems prudent to examine those lawyers' affidavits more closely.

Edmund Folsom, a county prosecutor at the time, stated about the crucial conversation, "When George first took the [Dechaine] case, he spoke to me on the phone, and I jokingly told him he was too old to be dealing with a case of that nature. At the time, George seemed to be considering getting co-counsel, and he asked me about the lawyer in Portland who wore the hat all the time. I told George that lawyer's name was Tom Connolly, and I thought he was very competent and would be a good prospect. Also in that discussion, George made it clear to me that he knew Dennis Dechaine had committed the murder from having discussed it with Dechaine in George's office."

What a phony! Carlton's claim of considering the enlistment of a co-counsel after Folsom chided him on being too old, and posing his counterfeit question about Tom Connolly's suitability, was a "lawyer's lie"—falsehood by inference. Carlton didn't *say* he hadn't been cast off, he implied it through his question to Folsom. He was implying to a fellow lawyer that he was still involved, still trusted, still important. The fact is, Tom Connolly was recruited with the assistance of Professor Orlando Delogu because Delogu's son was among Dechaine's circle of friends. And

Carlton had already been told that the family couldn't afford two attorneys.

This lie made me wonder precisely how Carlton had "made it clear" to Folson that Dechaine was guilty. Perhaps Carlton's actual word to Folsom was something based on the same condescending comment Carlton gave me: "When they say they can't remember, that means they did it."

"As time went on," Folsom continued, "and Tom Connolly went through numerous post-conviction proceedings with Dechaine, I had a number of discussions with George about those proceedings. During those discussions, George repeatedly made disparaging comments about Tom Connolly's conduct in pressing those post-conviction matters. George remarked to me about having seen with his own eyes and heard with his own ears as Dechaine sat in his office and described events to him."

By the time of those appeals, George Carlton had reason for resentment. He'd been rejected as defense counsel, tolerated in the side chair by Tom Connolly for whatever benefit his friendship with Judge Bradford might yield, never mentioned in the press, never quoted, and never shown as having made any contribution anywhere in the trial transcript, including those conferences with the judge out of the jury's hearing. The egotism attributed to Carlton would motivate a fumbler of his ilk to invent some noble explanation for his non-participation at trial and throughout the appeals. Creating an impression that he was "too good" to defend a heinous killer was better than admitting he'd been rejected, ignored, and so pathetically useless.

Considering Dechaine's denials during seven hours of

police interrogation, his denials to Tom Connolly over the years, and his denials to me, it seems incredible that a broken-down braggart like Carlton could possibly have "seen with his own eyes and heard with his own ears as Dechaine sat in his office and described events to him."

Then, too, we have Dechaine's ramblings quoted by Detective Westrum. "I told my lawyer I remember being on a dirt road and coming out of the woods but nothing else."

Ironically, Dechaine recalls Carlton fondly as, "always smiling, always encouraging, constantly telling me that everything will come out fine."

While there is no reason to doubt Edmund Folsom's word, there's ample justification to question his gullible acceptance of Carlton's allegations. It's unlikely that any veteran attorney would have swallowed the unsupported word of anyone like Carlton against anyone he knew and respected. But I don't know Folsom. Perhaps he would.

Joseph Field's affidavit places his conversation during a lunch with Carlton while Dechaine's trial was in progress. "I asked George what it was like for him trying a big case like this one in the second seat, especially with Tom Connolly in the lead seat. I did this in a clearly humorous tone . . . ." Later in the conversation, Field "asked him whether he thought Dechaine had actually done it, and he answered strongly in the affirmative. Although I don't recall his exact words, he told me that Dechaine had even told him [George] that he [Dechaine] had committed the murder...."

Field's and Folsom's affidavits support Assistant AG LaRochelle's affidavit attesting to Carlton's betrayal. LaRochelle's is the most important because it was Carlton's words to him that let prosecutors rationalize withholding discovery material from Tom Connolly, manipulating the presentation of evidence, and concealing evidence. This was the conversation prosecutors used to secure the cooperation of other witnesses. Medical examiner Ronald Roy actually stated, when I questioned his peculiar presentation regarding time of death, "Well for God's sake, his own lawyer said he did it!"

No one will ever know how many times cops or prosecutors have bumped a dubious expert into certainty by assuring the witness that "we know this guy did it, so don't give his lawyer an edge to get him off. We'll all look stupid. Think of the victim's family. They deserve the closure of a conviction. Think of the future victims if your wishy-washy testimony gets him off."

So they told Roy that Dechaine's own lawyer had admitted the man's guilt.

But LaRochelle's account only states: "Attorney Carlton replied that Sarah was not alive and added something to the effect that we were looking in the right area."

How did Carlton actually phrase his reply? Was it offered as one of his "genius" divinations? Did he say it plainly, "She's dead."? Or perhaps he came across in a manner LaRochelle might interpret as Carlton's attempt at discretion—more like, "Well, I wouldn't expect to find her alive, and if it was up to me I'd say you're looking in the right place." Nothing in LaRochelle's affidavit even pretends to quote Carlton's actual words. Today, according to what LaRochelle told me, he can't remember the details of that conversation. This lawyer's denial reminds me of some comedian's Watergate-era joke, "What did the President know? And when did he stop knowing it?"

Whatever Carlton actually said, LaRochelle's inference sufficed to convince him of what he desperately wanted to believe, that the state had the right man in their sights. From then on, we can only wonder what "clarification" or "amplification" was added as Carlton's betrayal was passed on to Eric Wright, to Roy, and to others.

Assuming that all three of these lawyers are telling the absolute truth about what Carlton said, it seems incredible that they'd place credence in his words. Carlton's braggadocian nature, his character, his status as a third-rate loser even in minor cases, his egotistical confidence in his hunches, and his humiliating rebuff in favor of another attorney—all of these attributes, added to the scientific evidence regarding time of death and DNA results—combine against believing George M. Carlton, Jr.

This episode raises a more vital question. Here's an attorney, claiming to betray his client's secret to the prosecutors and others, a clear violation of a lawyer's trust and the rules of the bar association. But no lawyer seems even slightly surprised. Attorneys are required to report such violations to the Board of Bar Overseers. None of them did.

It was twelve years after the murder when I interviewed Fernand LaRochelle. He said, "Um, my purpose was, as I've indicated, uh, to hopefully—if she was still alive—uh, have him tell us that if he knew so we could save her...."

"Since he was thinking she wasn't alive," I pressed, "why do you think he told you? We think about lawyers and they never tell anything."

"Yeah, well I don't remember what, to be honest with you, I don't recall his answer. I think he basically, he may have said that, uh, uhhh, I don't know. Uh, what does my affidavit say?"

"I think it said he said she's dead and you're looking in the right place." (Actually, it states: "Attorney Carlton replied that Sarah was not alive and added something to the effect that we were looking in the right area. There was no further conversation....")

"Okay, okay, uh, and your question to me is what again?"

"Oh. Well, uh, why would he.... I guess it seems like betraying a client."

"Uh, well he was probably answering my, probably—I mean I can't speak for him obviously but he is, uh...I mean my question was 'Is she still alive?' Uh, I guess you can't dance on the fence on that too long. Either she is or she isn't."

When I asked whether LaRochelle would have answered such a question, were he the defense lawyer, Mr. LaRochelle said, "I don't know. I haven't thought about it. There are probably pros and cons, uh, to that, and, uh, so, uh, it's a difficult question. Don't know."

"It just surprises me," I said, "and I think it would surprise readers that a lawyer did that."

"Really?"

"Yeah. I guess it doesn't surprise you guys. Hey, while I got you on the phone can I ask you one other thing?" I asked about his order to the clerk in the medical examiner's office to show me what they'd given Connolly regarding the autopsy, "and nothing else."

Mr. LaRochelle said, "No no, there shouldn't have been, and so I'm not sure what she means.... I don't know what I said to her and I don't know how she took what I said to her but certainly Connolly got everything that we had." Mr. LaRochelle assured me that they always pass everything along, and "we don't sit there editorializing." He denied ever seeing the autopsy reports since he wasn't the prosecutor, and he denied being present at the autopsy.

Dr. Roy's report lists LaRochelle as being present. Perhaps he's forgotten.

❖

Even if LaRochelle regarded his question to Carlton as legitimate in the hope of finding Sarah Cherry alive, Carlton was saying the girl was dead. How, if he believed the girl to be dead and beyond help, could LaRochelle see Carlton's answer as anything but the most egregious betrayal of his client? How could Field and Folsom view Carlton's babblings with such a cavalier disregard of the lawyer's oath? How could any of them put so much credence in the word of a man who demonstrated so little reason to be trusted? Their credulity prompts the question: were they really that stupid, or were they simply doing what so many of us do: believing what they wanted to believe?

Joseph Field is now a judge. When I asked him about lawyers revealing clients' secrets, he cleared his throat and told me, "Particularly when you're practicing law but even if you're practicing alone, um, it is not uncommon for people to have, uh, seek legal advice, and I did this all the time when I was practicing law. In fact, I do it all the time now on the bench...not uncommon. As for the ethics of it, I don't know. There was always the understanding that it was in confidence and you just sit there and ask him for advice.... It'd be damned hard to practice law in a small town, in a rural area running a small practice. Even in big cities you have some of that."

"It didn't seem he was asking for advice," I said. "It just seemed [from your affidavit] he was talking. Did I miss something? Was he asking you for advice or counsel or something?"

"Well, uh, you know I, uh, it wasn't exact—I don't, uh, was he asking for advice? No, he wasn't asking, specifically asking for advice. Was he asking for, uh [clears throat] uh, I suppose you could, it's hard to answer."

I offered a thought that this bit about lawyers keeping clients' secrets was just a myth. Judge Field said, "Well, I'm not going to sit here and pass on other peoples' ethics without knowing the facts." He suggested I take up the question with someone on the bar association's ethics board, and wished me good luck.

In 1999 the Board of Bar Overseers was asked some questions on the topic of keeping clients' secrets. They acknowledged in the January, 2001 issue of the *Maine Bar Journal* that:

> ...the scope of the Maine Bar Rule on confidentiality is not as broad as its counterpart in the ABA [American Bar Association] Model Rules.

It's okay, Maine's Bar Overseers said, for an attorney to reveal a client's secrets without the client's knowledge if the lawyer is seeking advice from a fellow lawyer, as long as that fellow lawyer isn't representing interests adverse to the client *and* the fellow lawyer undertakes an attorney client relationship with the client.

Disclosure to prosecutors is still forbidden. Unless, of course:

> ...they are reasonably necessary to avoid violation of the Bar Rules or to defend [the attorney] against an accusation of violation of the Bar Rules.

But the Bar Overseers extended this license to disclose beyond the situation where a lawyer has actually been accused of wrongdoing:

> ...The Commission concludes, on the contrary, that the scope of the permission to disclose set forth in paragraph (3) of Bar Rule 3.6(h) also allows disclosures that are necessary to obtain advice in *anticipation* of a *possible* accusation of wrongful conduct or to prevent wrongful conduct from occurring at all. [Emphasis added.]

Do attorneys betray their clients' secrets in casual conversations with colleagues—even to courtroom adversaries—like old hens clucking a neighbor's peccadilloes across a back yard fence? It's not a crime. It's merely a violation of the Bar Association's rules—offenses which rarely, if ever, bring any meaningful penalty. Reasons for this, and for those lawyers' silence about Carlton's betrayal, may lie in the culture of clubby tolerance among many members of Maine's bar—chiefly in rural areas. Or it may lie in a sense of omnipotence some lawyers get, described by the winning lawyer in author Jonathan Harr's *A Civil Action*, as feeling "we are kings in our castles, deciding the fate of others."

❖

Carlton countered his humiliating non-person status in this case by offering an image of the righteous attorney, too good to sully himself defending a repulsive fiend. For police and prosecutors, accepting Carlton's disloyalty let them rationalize every act they committed. They did it to fulfill their duty, to satisfy a screaming citizenry, and of course, like the terrorists we've come to know so well, they did all those things in a noble quest for justice.

That made it okay.

18

What Really Happened?

THIS CHAPTER IS NOT EVIDENCE. But hard evidence leads to logical deductions. And Sherlock Holmes already said it: "Once you eliminate the impossible, whatever remains, no matter how improbable, must be the truth.

Sarah Cherry was alive and well at noon when she spoke with Mrs. Henkel on the telephone. Not a girl who'd abandon the baby in her care, she must have been forced to leave. A conclusion that she was in the living room when someone compelled her to leave with him is predicated on Sarah's sneakers and socks in that room, the television set playing with its volume low, and the presence of baby Monica in her crib.

The downstairs and upstairs doors were unlocked. Anyone could have entered.

He may have come to steal. Anyone casing the premises would know that the Henkel house was often unoccupied. On July 6, 1988, he saw no car in the driveway to suggest otherwise. Whether he knocked or simply opened the door and mounted the steps is irrelevant. A grown man would have no trouble forcing ninety-eight-pound Sarah to come with him—whether by flashing his knife, making threats to her or the baby, or by inflicting that powerful blow under her chin leaving a deep mark which Dr. Roy noted in his report, a blow that would have rendered Sarah unconscious.

The man took her somewhere where he felt safe. A place where no one would hear the girl's screams. Psychologists and FBI profilers say that carnal barbarians who commit these risky and reprehensible acts—kidnapping, torture, sexual abuse, and murder—are no neophytes in the sexual abuse of children. They are men with a history of ever more serious crimes, acts of ever-increasing seriousness that culminate in the monstrous depravities perpetrated upon Sarah. This breed of criminal craves power and control over another human being. They often demand that their victims demonstrate subservience by performing sexual favors.

He was older than she, more experienced, physically more powerful. But little Sarah Cherry was stronger spiritually, strong enough to reject his depraved demands, tough enough to resist no matter what inhumane tortures the man perpetrated upon her.

The disarrangement of her brassiere, pushed up but not removed, and her shirt, still on the body and bloodstained when she was found, suggests that these garments were never taken off. The absence of her underpants indicates that they and her jeans were removed completely. The panties were never found, not in the woods, not in Dechaine's possession. Predators of this sort keep such items as a "trophy." The jeans, pulled up but not higher than her knees, suggests that her attacker tried to replace them after she was unconscious, or dead, and awkward to handle.

The tiny knifepoint cuts on her head and around her breast indicate the predator's cruel, slow, determined attempts to make Sarah submit to his demands, surrender to his total control. Contusions from hard blows and her bruised lips suggest his fury and frustration at her adamant refusals. The birch sticks rammed into her vagina and anus were revenge for his defeat by the might of this little girl's indomitable character.

Whether he committed all these acts in the forest where the body was found, or he tortured Sarah in some safer place and took her to the woods to get rid of her, a man with a record for sexually assaulting little girls would realize that he'd become a suspect in this case. His only hope lay in diverting investigators toward someone else. Previous encounters with policemen may have left him with an impression that some cops will seize upon the most obvious clues, and take pride in the most elementary deductions. All he needed was a patsy. Anyone would do.

Dechaine's truck stood unoccupied on a remote road with no house in sight. Perhaps, as he drove Sarah from the safe haven where he'd tortured her, he deliberately chose the spot near that deserted Toyota pickup to dispose of her. It wouldn't have taken much, during the course of tormenting the girl, to find out that Mrs. Henkel wasn't expected home until after three o'clock. It didn't require the brilliance of a brain surgeon to tie Sarah's wrists with a rope he found in that truck, gag her with the bandanna and scarf, to take a few items bearing the truck owner's name and plant those "clues" outside the Henkel house. All it required was cunning and a desperate fear of being caught.

He must have carried Sarah to that woods before Wednesday evening when the area grew populous with policemen. The time-of-death evidence tells us she didn't die until after midnight, so he must have left her there, bound and gagged, while he took those papers to the Henkel driveway. He may also have sought to create an alibi for himself—make some innocuous purchase, engage the store clerk in some memorable conversation or argument, and keep the store receipt to prove where he'd been that afternoon.

He returned to Sarah—parked far enough away or down some abandoned logging trail so that no happenstance passer-by would notice and remember his vehicle later as having been near this spot. But the hours he'd spent abusing Sarah, and the time it took in transporting her to the woods, and driving those papers back to the Henkel house, and creating an alibi, and getting back to where he'd left his victim—all these had consumed the afternoon. The killer hadn't planned on his patsy meeting up with the Buttricks. He couldn't have guessed that Helen Buttrick would hear of the search for Dechaine on her police monitor and phone to tell the sheriff's men where he was. He couldn't predict the deputies finding Dechaine nearby so soon, and more officers homing in on this area. Sheriff's cars were already speeding up and down the nearby roads. The proximity of police exacerbated the anxiety brought on by Sarah's defiance. He couldn't leave now, mustn't let himself be seen walking back to his vehicle, wouldn't risk driving away and being stopped by officers near here. His chances of escape would be better under the cover of night. He had to wait. It was during these early evening hours with renewed efforts to dominate this girl, that total defeat and blind vengeance probably moved him to violate her with the sticks. Dr. Roy would testify that Sarah was still alive when these outrages occurred.

❖

By the time darkness fell, there were even more cops cruising past the woods where he hid with Sarah. Her killer stayed with her, afraid to move. But the sounds of police entering the woods with a tracking dog left him no choice. He had to make sure that Sarah would never talk. He strangled her. Then he heaped brush over her body. In the darkness, he couldn't see that this hasty effort to conceal the body left the top of her head exposed. He could sneak away now. The cops were no longer looking for a killer. They had Dechaine, and the dog was taking officers along a trail—the route Dechaine walked when he left his truck—a trail that led away from the killer and the body.

The scientific testimony regarding time-of-death—a conclusion supported by every forensic medical text and every pathologist I interviewed—certifies that Sarah died during the hours specified by Dr. Roy's findings. The *earliest* she could have been strangled was at two o'clock on Thursday morning. That's the precise time, according to the state's police reports, when Detective Hendsbee and Trooper Bureau followed the tracking dog into those woods, and when they heard noises emanating from the direction where Sarah's body would be discovered the next day. The officers attributed the noises to deer. Were they, instead, the sounds of Sarah's desperate struggle as her killer tightened that scarf around her neck?

This sequence fits more facts than any theory advanced

by the state. *This* scenario is supported by all of the state's evidence, including their scientific findings. It accounts for the total absence of any forensic clue linking Sarah Cherry to Dechaine or his truck. And it accounts for the fact that the intense police search of the woods, and Dechaine himself, never produced the knife, or the "trophy" panties that her killer saved.

One mystery remains: the identity of the killer.

19

Who Killed Sarah Cherry?

BY THE TIME THE MILLENNIUM ARRIVED, Dechaine's vain quest for justice had trudged its tortuous path through the lethargy of our legal system for twelve years. Each judge proceeded with leisurely propriety in his deliberations. Twelve *years*!

The history of this case speaks to me. It tells me that jurists reviewing appeals from a conviction may give lip service to the basic issue, but they really have no interest in a defendant's innocence or guilt. They act like robotic regulatory functionaries, concerned solely with whether the case they're reviewing touched all the bureaucratic bases. It's all about process. That's all. If a trial didn't violate any law, "Petition Denied." Go away and quit bothering us because trial judges and juries never make mistakes.

Professor Orlando Delogu of the University of Maine's School of Law offers a more scholarly and probably a more realistic view: "Appellate courts look for procedural errors or errors of law because that's their bailiwick; [such errors] are also easier to spot on the basis of the record before them. It's not that they are not interested in guilt or innocence—it's a fact though that they did not see first-hand the witnesses, the defendant, etc. They were not present when the jury was picked, they did not hear the argument, the objections of counsel, etc. They will sometimes second-guess the conclusions of those that did, but it's got to be pretty blatant for them to do so—but it does happen. When they are nervous about an outcome, finding a procedural flaw or an error of law is a useful shorthand way of overturning the outcome and sending the matter back for a new trial."

❖

In the year 2000, Dennis Dechaine's cell in the West Block faced south into the prison compound. His corridor housed eight men and a shower. Every morning at 6:30, a scratchy recording of reveille blared through the prison loudspeakers. Guards lumbered thunderously across the grated walkway above his cell on their way to the dorms and the mental health unit.

At seven o'clock, his cell door opened. Sometimes, he'd go to breakfast. More often, he'd eat a banana in his cell and take a morning shower before work. At eight, he'd head to his job as a clerk in the upholstery shop where ten men worked, "a good group," he says, "happy to have something creative to do and comfortable with each other." He prepared job packets for upholsterers and refinishers from assignments received through the prison store. He helped keep track of backlogs and inventory. He ordered supplies.

And, he said, he earned "enough to cover living expenses with a bit left over to bank. I also get to keep a few houseplants there which pleases me more than I can say: a huge spider plant, a variegated philodendron, Christmas and Pond Lily cacti, an ancient poinsettia, a kalanchoe, and several shorter-lived species. To have such beautiful things to care for is good for my soul."

But inmates were awaiting transfer to a new prison in Warren, currently under construction. "Sadly," Dechaine said at the time, "shop plants will have no place at the new prison. Our production will be more streamlined in a building that has no windows."

His persistent complaints and suggestions to the warden regarding the housing arrangements planned at the new prison earned him several write-ups, but the only "charge" thus far was that of being "an administrative burden." Although later dropped, the threat of it persists.

He worked a six-hour day and considered work "a gift in a place like this. The mind-numbing monotony, the stress and ignorance—all of it often makes me wonder how in God's name anyone can exist here for any length of time."

And yet, immediately after this brief detour into the misery of his surroundings, he'd say, "This place also gave me the chance to tinker with flowers and especially rose bushes, which I love (probably comes from growing up where only a handful of varieties could survive the sub-arctic winters). I am conflicted when it comes to growing anything in here. Beauty in such an ugly place is sometimes unsettling, and my rebellious streak makes it hard for me to participate in anything that makes my keepers look good... Some day I hope to lay to rest the pettiness that causes me to think like this and enjoy a rose for its sake instead of mine. I've got a ways to go."

But he could also describe the reality of prison life. "The truth is that the day-to-day drudgery of prison does not begin to express the myriad of emotions evoked by being in a place that is at once intensely social and cruel. I struggle to find balance here, never knowing how human to be, who to trust, who to avoid. Every day I know the stress of surviving a day in prison and I am so weary of it, so indescribably weary. When I open my eyes from a night's sleep to see the bars that cage me into my forty-two square feet, I feel anger, sadness, and sorrow. What a damn waste, what a damn shame it is to suffer years of diminished opportunity, friendships lost and never known. I try not to dwell. I open my eyes every morning, beat back the cascade of emotion, and begin occupying myself in any way so I don't have to think about the tragedy of my imprisonment. Thankfully, most of my dreams are a satisfying departure from this place."

He kept a picture in his cell titled, "Brooklyn Boat Dock Window." Inscribed beneath the photo are these words: "How wonderful the window is that frees our sight to find, the country all behind the wall that otherwise is blind...."

Twelve years: 4,380 days, 4,380 nights. Twelve Christmases. Twelve birthdays. He was thirty when he entered the state system. He had a loving wife, friends, a beautiful home, a farm, a good life. He turns forty-three in 2002. He has new friends—felons convicted of almost every crime imaginable who've come to give Dennis Dechaine more respect, more kindness, more protection from harm than have our official organs of virtue and integrity. While guards once allowed him to soften the iron and concrete habitat with flower beds, that work generated antagonism among those corrections officers who didn't believe a prison should harbor anything that wasn't harsh and ugly.

Dennis Dechaine had come to terms with his fate. He could hate those who did this to him, but he said hatred only hurts the hater. So he works at forgiving them.

How far he's come from the "Mouse" he once was. Today, he has an inner strength like steel. I admire him enormously. After making a career of dealing with mobsters, murderers, and terrorists, taking guns and bombs away from the most vicious predators I could find, I thought I was tough. Until I came to know Dennis Dechaine.

❖

Douglas Senecal was well acquainted with Sarah. He could easily have lured her out of the Henkel house and into his clutches. There is the pending indictment for sexually molesting Sarah's stepsister, the strange fact that he was the only family member to skip Sarah's funeral, and the disturbing detail that Senecal's alibi doesn't hold water. There's the Department of Human Services agent, quoting Senecal as saying, "this family takes care of its problems in its own way." There's Ralph Jones's statement of hearing Senecal with a young girl who was "laughing or crying" not far from where the body was found; and Pamela Babine's testimony of having seen him in a truck identical to Dechaine's.

Detective Hendsbee lacked the requisite probable cause for warrants but he could have asked for blood and hair samples, could have asked to search Senecal's truck. If Senecal acquiesced, it might establish his innocence; if he refused, it might suggest more probing. Were it not for Hendsbee's inane excuse for inaction—"We had no proof he was in the area that day"—he might have conducted a real investigation. Senecal's statement to private detective Morin—"The only man in this world I'll ever trust is Eric Wright"—strikes an uneasy chord in many minds.

But there is absolutely no evidence placing Senecal near Sarah that day. Not a single clue proves any link to her murder. Were it not for the authorities' eager acceptance of Carlton's words—whatever he actually said—they might have proved Senecal's innocence, or his guilt.

John Henkel knew where Sarah would be that day: at his home. He knew she'd be alone, and he knew for how long. He'd have had no problem entering the house. When he returned home after his wife's report to police, he was quick to note and mark out the tire tracks, which he knew hadn't been made by his own vehicle. His only alibi rests on the hazy memory of his employer. But she wasn't quite sure, when Detective Hendsbee interviewed her seven months after the crime, whether he'd gone out for lunch that day.

A waitress where he often dined described him as a "weird pervert" who seemed to be stalking another waitress. She also told Hendsbee that, "All the people in the restaurant used to feel real creepy about Henkel."

But the police probe of Henkel was vacuous and superficial. All they wanted was enough to say, "We checked him out." They already "knew" their killer.

The Henkels divorced after Sarah's murder. Mrs. Henkel was cordial when I interviewed her. Then she wrote me a letter threatening legal action if I ever trespassed on her property. The most I could get out of John Henkel when I talked to him, years after the crime was, "The Lord will forgive anything."

"God can forgive any crime a man commits," I responded, "if the man repents and tries to repair the damage he's done. If he stole, he has to give back what he stole. Somebody has stolen Dennis Dechaine's life and the Lord can't forgive that without repentance, can't forgive the continuing sin of stealing a man's life. The man who stole it has to give it back."

Henkel shook his head. "The Lord will forgive anything."

But there is absolutely no evidence placing Henkel near Sarah during the period when she was abducted. Not a single clue proves any link to her murder. Were it not for the authorities' eager acceptance of Carlton's words—whatever he actually said—they might have proved Henkel's innocence, or his guilt.

The Dechaines' boarder, Richard Bruno, never knew the Dechaines before he answered an ad offering a room for rent. He'd lived with them for only a few weeks when the crime occurred.

If that trial witness really had seen Dechaine's Toyota pickup near the Henkel home the day before the crime—when Dechaine and his wife were still so many miles north of Bowdoinham, driving home in their Tercel station wagon from the July Fourth celebration in Madawaska—it might be significant that the Toyota and its keys were in the residence, accessible to Bruno. Also accessible to Bruno on the day of the crime, while Dechaine was driving the Toyota

Tercel and Nancy was at work, was the Dechaines' Chevy pickup, identified by Susan Norris as the one in which she saw a man and a young blonde girl that afternoon. He admitted to police that the scrap of paper with "Sarah" and a phone number they'd found discarded in the woodbox was in his handwriting but, he said, that note concerned a potential buyer or seller of an antique. Bruno claimed he'd been in the antiques business for fifteen years. But police never contacted the subscriber to that phone. I did. Those people told me they'd never heard of Bruno. Nor had they ever offered to buy or sell an antique.

Bruno refused to let police search or photograph his room. At the trial, he testified that he had no recollection of where he'd been on the day Sarah was abducted. Years later, he told me he'd attended an art exhibit with two friends at Bowdoin College that day. But Bowdoin College records showed that no such exhibit had been held. And Bruno refused my many requests to name the "friends" who could substantiate his claim.

Bruno's self-professed business as a small dealer in antiques left him free and accountable to no one for his daily activities. The source of his income was unknown and police theorized early on that Sarah's killer had happened upon her when he went to burglarize the Henkel home. But the police also assumed, without a scintilla of evidence, that Dechaine was that would-be burglar.

No one mentioned any woman in Bruno's life. A neighbor characterized him as "weird." Bruno knew the Dechaines would be away over the preceding weekend and he knew when they'd return. He had access to that Toyota pickup, its keys and everything inside it: the papers dropped in the driveway and the ropes used to bind Sarah's wrists. He almost certainly knew from Dechaine on Thursday where the Toyota had finally been found, and—since he was unknown to the police—he could easily have taken Sarah's body there that night to finish her off and cover her corpse while Hendsbee and Trooper Bureau floundered through the forest behind their dog.

But there is absolutely no evidence placing Bruno near Sarah that day. Not a single clue proves any link to her murder. Were it not for the authorities' eager acceptance of Carlton's words—whatever he actually said—they might have proved Bruno's innocence, or his guilt.

Twelve years would pass. A half-dozen tempting suspects and a dozen or more less inviting possibilities came to my attention. I investigated all of them, and cleared each one, or ran through all leads without finding evidence of guilt.

Then, on April 5, 2000, Dechaine sent me a letter he'd received from an inmate at the state's other penitentiary, the Maine Correctional Center—known simply as MCC. This prisoner named an inmate who had a friend who "knows for certain" that Sarah Cherry was murdered by "Jason Fickett . . . a scum, in for child molesting."

Fickett. Fickett? Sounded familiar.

Combing back through the mound of mostly worthless material turned over to Tom Connolly as discovery data, I found a report by State Police Detective Drake dated 7/7/88, the evening after Sarah's disappearance and the day before her body was found:

Det. HENDSBEE and I arrived off the Lewis Hill Road. A [searcher] found the footprints off what is known as the Fickett Road, a dirt road up into the woods.

And, at 7:38 P.M.:

Det Hendsbee and I checked the footprints on the Fickett Road and tracked them to a trailer by the name of Fickett. The tracks were barefoot but showed two different sizes going right into this trailer . . . . Det. Hendsbee advised he would advise the wardens about this location in the morning.

Hendsbee's own report of the incident agrees with Drake's: seeing the two pair of bare footprints and deciding to "have the wardens check it out in the morning." This at a time when Sarah was still missing and known to be barefoot.

A letter to the MCC prisoner, the one with a friend who "knows for certain" that Sarah Cherry was murdered by Fickett, brought this response:

Mr. Moore,
I tried to get your number put on my phone list but by the time that happens in here I believe Hell will freeze over.

So I utilized a ruse to circumvent the prison's rules, and spoke with him. He gave me the name of the inmate who knew about Fickett. I found that man, now released, chatting with workers unloading fish from a delivery truck. He had known Fickett in prison. He had no hard evidence. All he could tell me was that Fickett was deathly afraid when the word circulated that every inmate would have his DNA checked and recorded.

Considering the Hendsbee and Drake reports, Fickett was worth exploring.

Back in 1994 when I'd first read those police reports, I'd tried to find the Fickett Road. But no one I interviewed on the Dead River Road or the Hallowell Road had ever heard of it. None of the small roads I drove past in the area was marked with that name. There was no Fickett Road on the official town map. There were other leads to pursue. I lost sight of this one.

Now I acquired his date of birth from the motor vehicle bureau and submitted a request to the state police for his criminal record. Conviction data is public information. The fee is $8.00. My request came back with this purple stamp:

> NO RECORD AGAINST ABOVE
> NAME & DESCRIPTION IN
> FILES OF STATE BUREAU
> OF IDENTIFICATION
> APR 10 p 12:36
> Dorothy Morang
> MAINE STATE POLICE

How could Fickett have been a "scum, in [MCC] for child molesting," without having a police record? At MCC, a clerk told me, "Jason Fickett? He's been released."

When I confronted the State Bureau of Identification with this peculiar fact, a clerk said, "Oh, really? Well, I'll check again." And then, a day later, "Oh yes, here it is."

Fickett, a hulking six-foot-five-inch, 270-pounder born in 1961, exhibited the casual detachment of a man rarely ruffled. When Sagadahoc County sheriff's deputies raided his trailer in August of 1995, searching for drugs, Fickett and a male companion were asleep in separate rooms.

The other man, taken outside, informed deputies of a trip they'd made to Connecticut to buy drugs. Detective John Burne reported:

> At 8:45 A.M. I re-entered the trailer and sat down next to Jason. I read Jason miranda. Jason stated he understood and waived his rights in the presence of [deputies] Temple and Ackley. I asked Jason several questions regarding his trip to Conn. and the whereabouts of the heroin I believed him to have transported back to Maine. Jason listened carefully, but denied everything in short careful answers. I told Jason that I wasn't going to sit and provide him with the whole case if he wasn't going to answer questions. Jason shrugged me off.

Fickett was still dressed in his underwear. A deputy found a bag in the jeans beside his bed. Inside the bag: 100 packets of heroin wrapped in blue druggist paper. Also in the jeans: $140 in cash, and Fickett's wallet.

Detective Burne asked Fickett for an explanation.

Fickett shrugged, "What's to say? Can I have my pants when you're done?"

According to Burne's report, the man arrested with Fickett stated that Fickett didn't use heroin, himself, "but instead used it to control people around him and, of course, sold it for profit." The man named a woman whom Fickett "would make [her] perform sex acts on Jason while he videotaped these sessions."

That woman admitted performing those sex acts while Fickett videotaped her and she reiterated that "Jason never uses heroin and uses it only as a tool to control people." Fickett had a penchant for controlling people. Interesting.

In September 1993, Sagadahoc County Deputy Sheriff M. Erik Baker reported: "I responded to the Bibber residence on the Lewis Hill Road for a complaint of a juvenile acting in a suspicious manner." The juvenile, a young girl, had come to the Bibbers' home wearing a sweatshirt and shorts. She'd asked if she could use their phone to call her boyfriend. But no one answered the boyfriend's telephone, so she left the house. Moments later, the Bibbers saw a green Ford pickup stop, its driver shouted something and the girl yelled "No!"

When Deputy Baker found the girl, she said she'd been partying at her boyfriend's place the night before. When she got mad and wanted to go home, Jason Fickett offered her a ride. But Fickett detoured to his cabin in the woods. He got her inside on a pretext and there, according to Baker's report, "Jason grabbed her in the ass. He then told her that she was not leaving until she fucked him." The girl refused and went into the bathroom.

Jason said to her that she was not leaving until she made

him cum. [She] told him No. She said she became scared and frightened for her life. She came out of the bathroom and told Jason she wanted to go home. [She] said she would call the cops if he did not take her. Jason grabbed her by the throat and hit her on the back. Jason said he would kill her if she called the cops.

It wouldn't have been wise to kill her. Everyone at the party had seen her leave with him.

[She] stated he calmed down once she convinced him she would not call the cops. [She] stated that she went to run out the door and Jason grabbed her by the arm. She struggled with him and got away. [She] said she ran down the tote road. [She] saw him coming down the road in his truck and she ran into the woods.

Fickett was arrested. He claimed he'd only stopped at his cabin because he was too drunk to drive the girl home. He admitted grabbing her arm, "because she was too drunk to stand up." Baker states, "I asked him if he asked her to fuck him. He said no, but he asked for a blow job." He alleged that the girl had performed sexual acts for one of the boys at the party, earlier. But, when he asked her to perform fellatio on him, Fickett claimed "she said no, and that was the end of the topic."

Other men at the party acknowledged that the girl had performed oral sex on one of them. The prosecutor apparently saw this juvenile as a problematic witness. Fickett was held on charges of Terrorizing, Criminal Restraint, Assault, and Furnishing Liquor to a Minor—a series of misdemeanors. He got sixty days in jail, to be served concurrently with the penalty for violating his probation. In other words, the incident with this girl cost him nothing.

On the drug charges arising from the heroin in the pocket of his jeans, he'd get four years in prison and six years' probation.

Fickett's criminal record included more interesting entries: convictions in Skowhegan, Maine, for two rapes. The first was committed on September 25, 1986. Court records show that this victim "submitted to compulsion." In the second rape, committed on September 1, 1987, his victim was an eleven-year-old girl. He wasn't indicted for either attack until more than a year after raping this little girl. Fickett pleaded guilty to both crimes.

The conviction that aroused my intense interest was the one for Gross Sexual Misconduct in Sagadahoc County. His attorney was Joseph Field, the same lawyer who'd represented Douglas Senecal for sexually abusing his stepdaughter, the same lawyer who'd later swear that Carlton told him Dechaine was guilty.

And Fickett's judge was Carl O. Bradford.

Small legal community. Very clubby.

Convicted for all of these rapes in Somerset *and* Sagadahoc Counties, Fickett was sentenced to a grand total of four years' imprisonment and six years' probation.

The Sagadahoc County case interested me because it occurred so close—geographically and chronologically—to the murder of Sarah Cherry. On May 8, 2000, I asked court clerk Debbie Peabody for the transcript of Fickett's gross sexual assault trial. Ms. Peabody told me, "that's an old file, it's stored up in the attic" and "I'll dig it out for you tonight after work."

But one of the deputy sheriffs I'd been annoying to obtain legally accessible records about Fickett saw me now, heading for the court clerk's office. There may be no connection but, when I called the next day, Ms. Peabody gave me a very officious, "I have your telephone number. I'll call you when I have it."

A week passed. I phoned her again. She informed me with a snippy condescension that my request "is not high on my list of priorities."

Three weeks with no action. I appealed to the state court administrator. Trial transcripts are, after all, public records. Court Administrator Deborah Hjort instructed Ms. Peabody to give me the transcript, and ordered her to apologize. The next day Ms. Peabody handed me the transcript, turned her back, crossed to the far side of her office and muttered a barely audible, "I'm sorry."

First the state police told me Fickett had no record. Then a court clerk tried to keep me from seeing the trial transcript. These acts, combined with the facts I found in these files, lead some people to interpret these official obstructions as deliberate.

Fickett's victim in this case was twelve years old. He'd had intercourse with her at least eight times. The last time he had sex with her was on June 10, 1988.

The detective who investigated this case heard the victim describe coitus, and fellatio, and "penetration by a foreign object" by Fickett. This detective also received the doctor's report showing this victim with "abrasions on both knees, hymen not present." That detective's name was Alfred Hendsbee, and he'd questioned Fickett about these crimes on June 12th, only twenty-four days before Sarah Cherry was abducted. Fickett wasn't indicted for this crime until July 12, 1988. On the days when Sarah was kidnapped and murdered, Mr. Fickett was on the loose.

So, when Alfred Hendsbee saw large footprints and small bare footprints leading into "the Fickett trailer" owned by Jason Fickett, he already knew all about this man. But he didn't smash his way into that trailer to see whether the missing barefoot child was inside with a known pedophile. According to his official report, he didn't even knock on the door. He turned to his partner and decided he'd "have the wardens check it out tomorrow."

But of course Hendsbee "knew" that Dechaine had done it. There were those papers in the driveway. And Eric Wright had vowed to prosecute Dechaine for homicide even if no body was found. And Dechaine's own lawyer had already told LaRochelle enough to convince them that Dechaine admitted the crime.

For what it's worth, there's one thing Hendsbee couldn't have known at the time: Lawyer Gene Libby's efforts would eventually identify one of the two blood samples under Sarah Cherry's thumbnails as her own, but the state's evidence produced at Fickett's trial showed his blood type as identical to the mystery blood found under Sarah's nails.

Nevertheless, there is absolutely no evidence placing Fickett with Sarah that day. Not a single clue proves any link to her murder. Were it not for the authorities' eager acceptance of Carlton's words—whatever he actually said—they might have proved Jason Fickett's innocence, or his guilt.

❖

The Carlton treachery explains Hendsbee's indifference to the screaming clue of small bare footprints before his eyes, as well as the numerous violations by the prosecution around the time of the trial. But to persist in that conviction today, in the face of the immutable proofs of Dennis's innocence, indicates gross incompetence or some very dubious motives.

Questions, questions. How could Hendsbee ignore those small, bare footprints, leading directly into the remote residence of a man he'd just finished investigating for sexually assaulting little girls? How could he presume that those little footprints hadn't been made by a mysteriously missing barefoot twelve-year-old girl? Even if he believed that Dechaine was involved, how could he be sure that Fickett—a man he knew had recently been sexually assaulting a girl the same age as Sarah—was not also involved? How could he resist smashing his way inside to see whether Sarah was there? How could he simply walk away?

But he did.

He didn't even knock.

All through this case I'd believed every word Hendsbee said or wrote in his reports. After all, he was a cop. These prosecutors had obviously lowered themselves into the depths of dishonor but, even when a cop harbors wrong conclusions, I always assume that he or she is honest. Hendsbee, I believed, was simply viewing the evidence from the wrong vantage point. I continued to nurture this comfortable faith for a very long time—until July 25, 2001.

Tom Connolly had been naïve in trusting all lawyers.

I was naïve in trusting all cops.

We were both wrong. We know better now.

20

"Cheer Up, Things Could Be Worse"

SURE, THERE ARE BAD LAWYERS. But every profession, from medicine to the clergy, has harbored renegades. Most attorneys are honest, honorable, intelligent, and hardworking. They protect us from those who do us harm. We need them.

On February 10, 1999, Maine's high court rejected Dechaine's effort claiming ineffective counsel, on the basis of a statute providing that such petitions "may be dismissed if it appears that by delay in its filing the State has been prejudiced in its ability to respond to the petition or to retry the petitioner." If the delay is more than five years, "prejudice is presumed...." The court also said that "Connolly's lack of success" in having the fingernail clippings tested for DNA "cannot be blamed on his defective performance, but rather upon the volume of incriminating evidence against his client." In conclusion, the court stated, "The dismissal of the Dechaine...petition on procedural grounds will not result in a manifest injustice because the Petitioner cannot show that no reasonable juror would convict him even if he could get DNA test results of the victim's fingernail nail [sic] clippings into evidence."

❖

On April 26, 2000, a habeas petition was filed in federal court. The lawyers for Dechaine in the federal effort were the renowned Professor Barry Scheck of the Cardozo School of Law's Innocence Project in New York, and local lawyer Gene Libby, a partner with the respected firm of Verrill and Dana.

U.S. Magistrate David M. Cohen, whose job it was to review the petition and make a recommendation to the federal judge, rejected arguments that Maine's high court should have granted Dechaine a new trial because, Cohen said, "[Dechaine] came knocking too late," i.e., after that five-year limit had expired. As for the grounds of ineffective counsel, the magistrate said:

> A claim of "fundamental miscarriage of justice," in turn, requires a showing "that it is more likely than not that no reasonable juror would have found petitioner guilty beyond a reasonable doubt...." Paradoxically, the court in assessing the strength of such a showing *may take into consideration evidence that would not come before the "reasonable juror."* [Emphasis added.]

Magistrate Cohen stated that the federal court could consider relevant evidence that had been excluded or unavailable at trial without regard to the rules of admissibility because the emphasis here was on actual innocence. But he wasn't troubled by the absence of forensic evidence linking Dechaine to the crime, the evidence regarding the tracking dog which he termed "ambiguous," and the absence of any incriminating detail in what he called the "purported confessions." He alluded to the AG's claim of "possible contamination" of Sarah's fingernails and concluded—with respect to the DNA arguments forming the foundation of briefs filed by Barry Scheck, et al.—that "There is no evidence that the mystery DNA necessarily or even likely transferred to the nail clippings during commission of the crime. Indeed, the only evidence of record touching on the subject remains that of [state chemist] Brinkman and [state pathologist] Roy to the effect that the blood of the assailant would not have been expected to be found on Cherry's nails." And, "This evidence [that two people contributed DNA to the Cherry thumbnail clippings, neither of whom was Dechaine] standing alone, simply does not suffice to place this now twelve-year-old case 'within the narrow class of cases...implicating a fundamental miscarriage of justice.'"

When it came to considering all evidence, whether or not it was admissible or available at trial, Magistrate Cohen cited ten elements in support of his opinion that:

Nonetheless, the evidence of Dechaine's guilt remains substantial:

Dechaine's papers were found in the Henkel driveway; a neighbor thought she saw a red Toyota pickup truck heading north (in the direction in which the body later was found) shortly after the last known contact [by Mrs. Henkel] with Cherry; Dechaine's truck was found near the body; Dechaine himself emerged from the woods in the general vicinity of the body; a rope from Dechaine's truck was found in between the truck and the body; the rope used to bind Cherry's hands was consistent with that in Dechaine's truck and that found in the woods; the dog evidence indicated that someone headed from the passenger side of Dechaine's truck toward the spot where the body was found; [Mrs. Dechaine] was surprised that the penknife was not on her husband's key ring; and four police or corrections officers testified that Dechaine made incriminating statements on three separate occasions within the space of several hours on July 8, 1988—the pivotal day on which the body was found and Dechaine was placed under arrest. Finally, three attorneys aver that Carlton indicated to them that Dechaine was guilty; most chillingly, that Carlton conveyed to LaRochelle of the Attorney General's Office on the morning of July 8, 1988—before Cherry's body was found—that Cherry was no longer alive and that searchers were looking in the right place.

For the foregoing reasons, I recommend that the Petition be DENIED without a hearing.

There's an old Irish saying, "Is this a private fight, or can anyone join in?"

On August 14th, I filed a Declaration with the court describing my involvement with the case. I detailed how Magistrate Cohen's conclusions indicated the state's lack of candor in describing the trial evidence. I also detailed evidence concealed by the state, including the state's own evidence regarding time-of-death proving the impossibility of Dechaine's guilt, and even the facts about Jason Fickett—in short, virtually all of the essential information revealed in this book.

The AG's people responded with a motion to strike my Declaration from the record. Since I was a "non-party" to the case, they said, they shouldn't have to answer the evidence I'd presented.

Lawyer Gene Libby explained, in laymen's terms, the reasons why it was legally inappropriate to focus the court's attention further on the evidentiary facts of the case:

> Since ours was a habeas corpus appeal, the issues were limited to those raised in the Petition. The two issues raised asserted the State court erred in 1) Concluding it lacked authority to order third parties to submit to blood testing; 2) the applicability of the "miscarriage from justice exception" to excuse Dennis from the procedural default under the State's Post-Conviction statute. These issues were mainly issues of law and did not depend so much on the particular facts of the case. We had set out in detail the facts in our initial filing with the court and, since the Judge made a de novo ruling, he had available and stated he did consider the entire record (including our original factual analysis in the Petition). It was our judgment that a long rendition of the facts was unnecessary to the legal issues before the court. You should recall that The Innocence Project and I collaborated in the appeal. It was the decision of all the lawyers participating in the appeal to focus on the legal issues before the court and not extraneous factual issues which would not ultimately effect the courts ruling.

The U.S. District Court judge issued his terse decision on November 21, 2000. My Declaration was struck from the record without comment and:

1. Petitioner's objection is hereby DENIED;
2. The Recommended Decision of the Magistrate Judge is hereby AFFIRMED;
3. The Petition is hereby DENIED without a hearing.

Lawyer Libby sought Dechaine's permission to appeal this decision, but Dechaine wanted no part of any more attempts. Libby argued, "This is your last chance to contest the conviction."

Still, Dechaine was consumed by a fatalism. He said that brother "Phil had suffered another heart attack, for which I am blaming myself, and I was so utterly discouraged by the court's response to my pleas for justice that I couldn't imagine any good coming from any other efforts."

Libby says, "It is indeed unfortunate that Dennis was so consumed by the pain others were feeling that he elected not to appeal. However, it was his decision, not mine." Left with no choice, Gene Libby withdrew from the case. Later, when Dechaine did finally gather the strength, he filed an appeal on his own, *pro se*. But he'd had the opportunity to file a timely appeal, and his solo effort was rejected, too.

❖

With the last legal avenue closed, friends with whom I shared my disappointment invariably suggested, "Write a book about the case."

To each of them I reiterated a decision I'd made during

the early days of my involvement. I'd already had two books published but I needed to decide, when I first became involved in my quest, whether I was working this matter to find the truth, or gathering material for a book. Dissimilar goals require different approaches. I'd opted for finding the truth, and I'd kept myself on that track with a vow not to write a book about it. My friends understood.

All except teacher and bookstore owner Gary Lawless. He listened to my excuse and shook his head. "A lot of good that does Dechaine."

❖

During the course of gathering material for this book, I encountered lawyers—even the state's attorneys—who withheld information. Some lawyers showed a cavalier tolerance toward breaches of lawyer-client confidentiality. The Bar Association's so-called enforcement arm, the Board of Bar Overseers proved indifferent to misconduct by its members connected with this case.

But this wasn't a conspiracy against Dennis Dechaine. He's merely someone they don't care about. All of this egregious conduct adds up to preservation of that clubby atmosphere, avoiding the necessity of stepping on a fellow lawyer's toes, safeguarding the image of their profession at the expense of the reality. After all, one might ask, what's a little hypocrisy among friends?

The University of Maine Law School's Professor Orlando Delogu sees a broad spectrum of students—wide-ranging in ages and backgrounds—commencing the study of law each year. "Sixty to seventy-five percent of first-year law students," he says, "are motivated by the highest ideals of justice. By the time they've survived three years of law school, often with considerable outstanding student loan debts, and passed the bar exam, we're lucky to have ten or fifteen percent who remain primarily motivated by those ideals. The rest, whether motivated primarily by money or power, aren't bad. They just have different priorities."

❖

Eric Wright lost my respect when he misquoted witnesses and made false statements to jurors during the trial, but that's not illegal—Wright wasn't under oath. He refused to be interviewed for this book.

Twenty-five years in law enforcement left me with certain beliefs. One "given" is that officers tell the truth. As with any rule, however, there are the inevitable exceptions.

My disillusionment with Detective Al Hendsbee came on July 25, 2001. I began by telling him, "There's something in one of your reports that's going to confuse the readers. You remember those big and little footprints on the Fickett Road?"

Hendsbee began to describe the scene and, "I think it's got a camp on the end of the road." He was right. A small camp stood just across that dirt road from Fickett's blue and white trailer.

"Let me read from your report." I quoted what he'd written about the footprints, and the Fickett trailer, and I came to the point: "You say these footprints were 'believed not to be involved,' but how could you be sure, since the girl was barefoot?"

"Oh. We didn't know she was barefoot."

I explained that she had to be; her sneakers and socks

were left behind.

He said, "We didn't know that. The other thing was, I think it was, they were real small, small footprints or big ones. I can't remember. Either big or small."

"There were two sets, a big set and a little set."

"Yep, yep."

"And I was just wondering why you thought they weren't involved."

"I don't know, at the time."

"Oh. Okay."

"Yeah, I don't know. There's a reason for it, uh, I don't know at the time."

"Okay, 'cause it says it was to the Fickett trailer."

"The Fickett trailer?"

"On the Fickett Road. The Fickett trailer."

"I don't know if there's a trailer. I know there's a camp up there."

"Yeah, well I don't know. It says in the report, 'the Fickett trailer.' It must have had a sign on it."

"Coulda been. Yep, yep."

"Well, do you know Fickett?"

"Nope."

"You don't know Fickett?"

"Nope."

"It's Jason Fickett."

"Don't know him. Am I supposed to know him?"

"Well, yeah. You investigated him a couple weeks before Sarah Cherry was killed."

"I did?"

"Yeah."

"For what?"

"For having sex with a twelve-year-old girl."

"I did?"

"Yep."

"I convict him?"

"Yeah."

"He's a big guy?" Hendsbee asked.

"Great big guy. You remember him?"

"Well, I don't know the guy's name but I remember he was screwing, she wasn't a twelve-year-old. I think she was older than that."

"Well according to the court things, she was twelve."

Hendsbee said he believed that was Fickett's first offense and he thought the girl was sixteen. But his testimony at Fickett's trial shows that he was aware that Fickett had known the victim's mother for quite some time, and he knew that Fickett had had sex with the child many times. He was also well aware of her age, since this factor added substantially to the seriousness of the crime.

Moving closer to the meat of the matter, I told Hendsbee, "I read the court transcript on his trial and you were investigating him. You interviewed the victim two weeks before Sarah was killed."

"It wasn't on that road."

"No, but it was Jason Fickett."

"It could have been. I have no idea."

Asked again why be believed those footprints to be "not involved with the case," Hendsbee said he couldn't remember. I asked whether he remembered Dr. Roy.

"I knew him well."

"Any good?"

"He always was good."

I explained how Roy's time-of-death evidence excluded Dechaine as the killer. Hendsbee alluded to the imprecision of time-of-death estimates. I agreed, told him that was why the pathologist couldn't state a specific time, just a six-hour range.

Hendsbee said the sheriff's men had "screwed things up." And, "My job was to find her alive, hopefully. And I was hoping she would be alive, but Dennis sorta confirmed that she wasn't. But that's, well, from then on it was, we had to find the body."

"Dennis confirmed she wasn't?"

"Uh, he indicated that through his actions."

"Oh."

"I had a strong sense that she was dead." Changing the subject, he said, "You know that time of death is not an exact science, and the other thing is . . forensic science is not exact, give and take hours. It all depends on conditions. There's a lot of variables there."

But the variables—the victim's age, physical exertion and stress, and the ambient temperature—if they played a part, they'd prove the time of death to be even later than 2:00 A.M. to 6:00 A.M. Thursday morning. I pointed out that Hendsbee's own reports stating that he and Trooper Bureau had been in the woods at exactly 2:00 A.M. with the dog, hearing noises coming from the spot where Sarah's body lay.

"Uh yeah," Hendsbee replied, "yep, that area, yeah."

"I'm just wondering if the guy was over there killing her."

"Nah."

"No?"

"Nah."

"How do you know?"

"Didn't happen that way."

"All I can go on is what's in the reports."

"No. Didn't happen that way. Did not happen that way. It didn't. There's too many other things leading up, and Dennis Dechaine being at the [Henkel] house, at being there, and her being with him. I really don't know. I'm gonna tell you something. Let me explain something. I was opposed to this Dennis Dechaine [being guilty] during this whole thing when everybody else was. I really liked this guy . . . . I really think the world of the guy. The sad part about it is, he had so much to offer." Hendsbee protested at great length about the tragedy for all concerned and how much he liked Dechaine, all the while assuring me that, "I know he did it." But, he said, "My thing was, disprove Dennis Dechaine 'cause I didn't really want to arrest the guy to be perfectly honest with you...."

Being perfectly honest? First he tells me Dechaine's actions convinced him the girl was dead, which (if true) would surely mean that Dechaine was at least involved but he goes on to drown me in assurances that he "was opposed to this Dennis Dechaine [being guilty] during this whole this...."

Hendsbee pointed out that, "It's thirteen years. I don't review my cases and I don't want to relive this whole thing.... I have a hard time with this case. I felt sorry for Sarah Cherry, I felt sorry for Dennis Dechaine. I just want to put this thing in my past.... I'm not shunning you or anything, but whatever I got in my reports, there's a reason why it's there, and I disallowed [the significance of the footprints] because it's disallowable. Fickett was a big guy?"

"Yeah, about six-five."

"Yeah," Hendsbee said, "three hundred pounds."

"Yep. A mean guy."

"Yeah, he is a mean sonofabitch. He didn't give me a hard time...."

Coming back to Dechaine, Hendsbee told me, "I was there. I was with him, I felt him, I know him and I got all the responses from him, and if one of my lieutenants hadn't opened his big mouth and shut him up, he'd have confessed the whole thing to me right then in even more detail than what there were."

Hendsbee seemed to be growing more and more agitated as he sought to explain how his instincts told him Dechaine was guilty but, "If I could have found a way to show the guy is innocent, I'd have found it way back then 'cause I liked the guy so much."

Asked whether he remembered Eric Wright, Hendsbee said, "I put the case together for him. Are you taping this?"

"Yes. I don't want to be misquoted—I've already been misquoted by certain people in this case—and I don't want to misquote anyone else."

"I thought you were," but he was annoyed, he said, that I hadn't warned him up front that I was recording our conversation. "You've heard everything I've got to say. And don't ever call me again."

Hendsbee's answers were a great disappointment to me.

First, "the sheriff's men screwed up." Then, he'd have obtained a detailed confession from Dechaine "if one of my lieutenants hadn't opened his big mouth." Hendsbee kept insisting that his prime desire was to prove Dechaine innocent, but he seemed to contradict that gallant motive when he told me that during his first interrogation, "I know him, I got all the responses from him." And then, when I first mentioned Fickett, "Am I supposed to know him?" Minutes later, although thirteen years had passed, he recalled the case, described the Fickett Road, and described Jason Fickett's physical appearance. But he couldn't connect these facts twenty-four days after interrogating the man about the rape of a girl the same age as Sarah Cherry. Perhaps Hendsbee didn't admit knowing of Carlton's prattle to LaRochelle because he thought that was still some sort of secret. But his reactions when the questions touched a nerve were too much for me. Then there was the claim that he hadn't known Sarah Cherry was barefoot when she'd been abducted. But Hendsbee's official report for July 6, 1988 at 11:30 P.M., ten minutes after he'd first been summoned to investigate the missing girl, stated:

> SARAH is described as five feet tall and about 90 lbs., blond hair, blue eyes, wearing blue jeans, a black and purple T-shirt and was barefooted.... BUREAU advised that this is suspicious and is requesting a CID unit assist him in the search. I advised I would be en route.

Once a man plays fast and loose with the truth, his credibility is destroyed. He can't redeem it with syrupy protestations of how much he liked and admired Dechaine.

Mark Twain, remembered largely for his humor, once made a cynical observation I find disturbing because I've come to believe it. "It is curious," he said, "that physical courage should be so common in the world and moral courage so rare."

❖

The man who murdered Sarah left a picture for the cops to find. Carlton applied a gloss. Police daubed some color around the edges. The prosecutor framed the picture and showed it to the jurors. They bought it. The authorities are perpetuating their indifference with no better motive than to preserve a phony image of themselves as society's protectors. It's a fraud that guarantees us more un-avenged murders, more innocents imprisoned.

Perhaps this is why, despite that former state police homicide detective's assurance that Maine "doesn't get complicated cases," the state legislature proposed a bill in 2001 to create a cold case homicide squad. It is needed, lawmakers say, to probe seventy-five unsolved murder cases collecting dust in state police files. Police reports show that of the thirty-seven homicides committed in 1988, thirty-one were "cleared"—a euphemism for "we're sure we know who did it"—which does not necessarily mean that anyone was ever charged with the crimes.

Sarah Cherry's case, of course, is among those carried as "cleared."

How many of those seventy-five were committed by Sarah's slayer?

How many more innocents languish in Maine's prisons?

Who's next?

No one is safe from Sarah's killer.

Worse yet, no innocent man, woman or child is safe from the state.

For me, though, the worst is not discovering that one scumbag lawyer betrayed his client with a lie. Nor the lawyers who seem to have condoned that treachery. It's not the unworthy machinations of the men we trusted to do justice on our behalf, nor even an innocent Dennis Dechaine being railroaded into life imprisonment. These are appalling and indefensible, but not the worst. Not for me.

My dreams are haunted by an image of an innocent, caring, athletic, optimistic, spiritual Sarah Cherry, bound and gagged in the dark forest. She hears the policemen and their dog coming into the woods—heaven-sent rescuers, only yards away. She struggles, squirms, thrashes about, kicking and gasping for breath. But the cops are following the dog that's sniffing along a trail that leads away from her—Dechaine's trail. The heartless fiend who has tortured and terrified her for more than ten endless hours tightens that scarf about her little throat. And the only mercy she'll know on that evil day envelopes her—the blackness, and death.

In my dream, I see his face. I find him. Filled with a rage that barricades my brain, I kill him. The police are coming for me when I wake up.

Afterword

ANCIENT NATIVE AMERICANS addressed everything in nature as "thou." Our modern society refers to a tree or animal as "it." Officials in this case—their eyes on career and image and their haughty view of what's good for the world—saw Dennis Dechaine as an "it." The same way Sarah's killer saw her.

As this book goes to the printer, Sarah Cherry would have been thirty. If childhood predicts womanhood, she'd have been a good and beautiful woman.

On June 16, 1992, Maine's attorney general, Michael Carpenter, answered a letter from two Trial & Error members. Carpenter glossed over their questions with a warning that the evidence offered by witnesses implicating a different suspect had "not yet been tested by the adversarial process," i.e., a hearing in open court where allegations can be challenged. Then he wrote:

> Since you neither are investigators nor have had access to all the information acquired by this office relative to Mr. Dechaine's guilt, I can assure you that your assessment of his claim of innocence is uninformed. Soon after I became Attorney General, I was briefed on this case. I have made it a point to understand both the evidence and the other matters, some of which concern you, which the jury did not hear...."

He'd been briefed by the chief of his criminal division, Fernand LaRochelle. And the "other matters" which "the jury did not hear" are nothing more than LaRochelle's conversation with Carlton. Attorney General Carpenter's action (or inaction) leaves one to wonder what decision he'd have made if he'd taken his own advice and had LaRochelle's report and Carlton's alleged statement "tested by the adversarial process."

It's too late for that, but maybe Mr. Carpenter will change his view some day. He claims to have undergone a conversion once before, from the days when he was a young ROTC officer facing anti-war demonstrators across a fence—a time when, he says, "I despised them,"—to his later years when he says he ultimately realized the peace groups' view was justified. Perhaps he still has the power, now that the dubious nature of his "evidence" has been exposed, to reassess his opinions.

Carpenter was naïve. Dechaine was naïve. Tom Connolly was naïve. For that matter, so was I. Even LaRochelle and company were naïve for a while, until they saw the truth and resolved to cover up their sins. Perhaps Sarah Cherry was naïve in allowing her abductor to get close to her. We all had faith in people we should have scrutinized more closely. But if our system of law can't correct its errors, we're doomed to the self-destruction we saw seventy years ago in Nazi Germany where nobody objected to the arrests of innocents until the secret police came for *them*.

Today, Dechaine's only hope lies with politicians. But many Mainers feel good believing that Sarah Cherry's killer is doing life in prison. And politicians who risk their careers merely to do the right thing are so rare that one of our former Presidents won a Pulitzer Prize for writing a book about them. He called it *Profiles in Courage*.

Friends tell me that this book might create an understanding that translates into cries for justice. One friend thought that people might even write a note to Maine's governor, even send him their copy of this book along with the note, and the governor might gather the courage to restore faith in our government with a pardon for Dennis Dechaine.

Clarence Darrow, the great defender, saw many events that fueled his often pessimistic statements. He told us once that: "You can protect *your* liberties in this world only by protecting the other man's freedom. You can be free only if I am free."

My friends believe that a lot of people might care enough about one victim of injustice to actually spend five minutes and first-class postage. My friends believe there might actually be a courageous politician. So this case *could* have a happy ending.

But, considering what this case has taught me, I think my friends are naïve.

What the Jury Never Heard

THE FOLLOWING PAGES EXAMINE the state's own evidence in the Dennis Dechaine case, and present new discoveries made since this book was first published in 2002.

The State's Case Against Dennis Dechaine: Why It Proves Nothing

Dechaine's papers were found in the driveway of the house where Sarah Cherry was abducted; her body was found 450 feet through a woods from his parked truck; he emerged from another side of that woods; and he allegedly made admissions to officers.

The state's theory *lacks:*
- *A credible motive.* No history of violence, crime, or perversion; not in a psychotic state on the day of the crime according to state psychologists.
- *Opportunity.* State medical examiner's opinion, supported by other pathologists and forensic pathology textbooks: Sarah Cherry was murdered when Dechaine had been with the police for five or more hours.
- *The trophy.* Victim's panties, presumably taken as a trophy (the usual conduct of sexual predators) not on Dechaine's person; never found. Since no one suggests that he anticipated being questioned and searched when he emerged from that woods, why would he have discarded the "trophy"?
- *Any forensic evidence* of contact between Dechaine and Sarah Cherry.
- *Any forensic evidence* (according to the police lab and the tracking dog, which couldn't detect her scent) that the victim was ever in Dechaine's truck.
- *Any DNA link.* DNA of some other male was in blood under Sarah's nails. Biological evidence which might

have yielded more DNA was destroyed by the state six days after the defense filed a motion for retrial.
- *Any witness or evidence* of any connection between Dechaine and Sarah.
- *A competent investigation* which probed all of the other suspects—two of whom were already officially alleged to have sexually abused little girls.
- *Ethical conduct* by prosecutors who obscured, withheld, concealed, and incinerated items of evidence.

Trial & Error's theory—that the real murderer used items he took from Dechaine's truck to divert police away from himself—is considered improbable by some, but this theory of the crime accounts for *all* the evidence, including facts concealed by the state.

> Once you eliminate the impossible, whatever remains, no matter how improbable, must be the truth.
> —Sherlock Holmes

No one has yet explained—*if* Dechaine committed this crime:
- How did he connect with Sarah Cherry/why did he go to that house?
- What made this nonviolent man with no record of crime, violence, or perversion commit Maine's most brutal crime in living memory?
- How could he kill her five hours after his time is accounted for by the state's own witnesses, including the police?

- Why is some other man's DNA in the blood under Sarah Cherry's nails?
- Why is there absolutely no scientific or forensic evidence to support guilt?
- Why do officers' own contemporaneous notes cast troubling doubt on their allegations that Dechaine made any incriminating admissions?
- Why did the state obscure evidence regarding time of death before, during, and after the trial?
- Why do members of the attorney general's staff make false statements?

The Complete Evidence in the Dennis Dechaine Case, Concealed During the Trial

The state's case rests exclusively upon the prosecutors' interpretation of circumstantial evidence, and the so-called confession—nothing else. (See below.)

Critical facts concealed by the state, including indisputable scientific evidence, prove conclusively that it is physically impossible for Dechaine to have committed this crime.

THE SO-CALLED "CONFESSIONS"

No "confession" purportedly made by Dennis Dechaine —*even if truthfully reported*—contains a single detail of the crime or the victim. Words quoted by officers shift from, "I couldn't have done it" to "I must have done it" when Dechaine was confronted with his papers in the driveway and the fact that the body was found in the area of his truck. Dennis Dechaine's documented personality included all three characteristics of innocent persons who tend to make such false "confessions."

The only extensive "confession" was reported by Mark Westrum, who had been a detective for two days. But experienced investigators in the next room with a tape recorder were not summoned to record or witness Mr. Dechaine's alleged words. And Mr. Westrum's original notes show that he first quoted Dechaine as saying, "How could I kill her?" then went back some time later, crossed out "How could," and wrote over those words "Why did"—changing the quote from "How could I kill her?" to "Why did I kill her?" His notes quote Dechaine tellings his wife that "something bad had happened," but his typed report and testimony changed this to Dechaine telling his wife, "I had done something bad." At trial, Westrum testified to his "improved" version. (See Westrum's original notes, Exhibits.)

Mr. Dechaine denies making the statements attributed to him by Mr. Westrum.

With no witness and no signed statement, we have only Mr. Westrum's unsupported allegation that Mr. Dechaine said anything.

Westrum's notes were withheld and concealed until the secret files of the attorney general were finally made public through an order of the Maine legislature.

Maine State Police Detective Hendsbee *testified at trial that he was reading from his notes* when he quoted Dechaine as saying, "It must have been someone inside me doing this." This was considered so important to the state's case that prosecutor Wright had Hendsbee repeat the phrase four times for the jury—even insisting that Hendsbee read the quote from his contemporaneous notes.

That statement is not in Hendsbee's notes. He did take the time to record various exculpatory statements by Dechaine at that time, but he never noted the alleged admission considered so important to the state's case—the words he testified that he was reading from his notes. These notes were withheld in defiance of the legislature's order until a lawsuit was filed in superior court demanding the file. (See Hendsbee's testimony, and notes, Exhibits, pages 393–95.

The Scientific Evidence

Science has no axe to grind, no client to defend, no wrong to avenge, no career to advance. *Science doesn't care who wins.* Scientific evidence, and the facts concealed by prosecutors, refute the state's interpretation of circumstantial evidence in this case.

- *Concealed Evidence Indicates that Sarah Cherry Was Never in Dechaine's Truck*

The victim's body was found 3.2 miles from the house where she was abducted. Chemical swabbing, thorough vacuuming, and microscopic examination of Dechaine's truck revealed *no* trace of Sarah Cherry—no fingerprint, no fabric, no hair, no blood. The police tracking dog, given the victim's clothing to sniff, detected no scent of her in that truck. The dog officer's report was concealed from the defense. These facts, revealed four years after the trial in a signed statement by Bowdoinham Police Officer Jay Reed, who witnessed this event, were confirmed in a tape-recorded interview with State Police Detective Hendsbee in 1992.

- *Items in the Driveway and from the Truck*

The state inventoried 180 separate items in Dechaine's truck—everything from bottle caps to magazines. Dennis Curley of Caribou consulted a statistician who stated that the *odds against* two items bearing Dechaine's name to be the *only* ones to "fall out" of that truck in that driveway are 1.57 : 10,000, or 99.9 percent unlikely.

Items *lifted from* Dechaine's truck were connected to the crime, no witness nor any scintilla of forensic evidence links

Dechaine, himself, or even his truck, to the crime.

The state's case depends totally on the prosecutors' *interpretation* of circumstantial evidence. It was sold to jurors *only by concealing evidence* that would have disproved that interpretation.

DNA Testing

Would any guilty defendant request DNA testing *before his trial?*

Dechaine requested DNA testing before his trial. Dr. David Bing of CBR Laboratories in Boston points out that Prosecutor Wright proffered misleading and factually incorrect testimony upon which the court relied to prevent DNA testing of the blood under the victim's nails before the trial. DNA tests were performed in 1993 by Dr. Bing. The nails were photographed upon arrival in their original package with the seals intact and Dr. Bing certified no sign of tampering. He discovered the DNA of two persons: Sarah Cherry, herself, and another person who is *not Dennis Dechaine.*

The Office of the Attorney General hired Dr. Harold Deadman, a retired FBI expert on DNA, to assess Dr. Bing's results. Dr. Deadman attested to Dr. Bing's character, reliability, and integrity, and to the correctness of Dr. Bing's procedures in analyzing the DNA under Sarah Cherry's nails. *Dr. Deadman's report was kept secret.*

The nails were returned to prosecutors. Tests on them performed recently by the Maine State Police lab found the DNA of a male person who is *not* Dennis Dechaine in the blood under Sarah Cherry's nails.

An AP dispatch reported Deputy Attorney General Bill Stokes as saying, "There is no logical connection between the DNA collected from Cherry's fingernails and her death." He suggested that the male DNA was probably that of an officer, or one of the medical examiner's staff who had handled the body. Attorney M. Michaela Murphy obtained a court order to test the victim's male family members and every official who touched the body after it was found, and before the nails were clipped. All were eliminated.

Mr. Stokes's next idea: the medical examiner used dirty nail clippers to clip Sarah's nails—clippers contaminated, "probably," (he said) with the DNA of some previous corpse.

His "dirty clipper" supposition moved attorney Murphy to obtain a court order for all of the autopsies conducted by the medical examiner for the year before the crime. The files were made available to her, and she'd be able to check them — ignoring female corpses since the mystery DNA was that of a male, and eliminating those whose autopsies hadn't involved the use of nail clippers. But, in order to secure Deputy AG Stokes's agreement that she review these files, she had to agree that no one would assist in this enormous chore except her licensed private investigator.

Psychologists' Conclusions

Undisputed testimony characterized Dechaine as a gentle man whose aversion to the sight of blood was so intense that this farmer had to pay others to kill his chickens. At age thirty, he had no criminal record and no record or reputation for sexual perversion.

But, because Dechaine used drugs on July 6, jurors may

have conjectured that drugs caused this gentle man to commit this crime of the utmost savagery, brutality, and depravity. Prosecutor Wright overcame defense lawyer Connolly's motion to have the state psychologists testify. Jurors never heard their official conclusion, that Dechaine "was not in a psychotic state on the day of the crime." (Trial transcript, page 1156, statement by Judge Bradford, out of the jury's presence.)

The real killer, according to those who have studied such predators, possesses a personality antithetical to Dechaine's.

In the book *Mindhunter, Inside the FBI's Elite Serial Crime Unit*, the author and former member of this FBI unit states:

> With most sexually based criminals, it is a several-step escalation from the fantasy to the reality, often fueled by pornography, morbid experimentation on animals, and cruelty to peers. (Page 114, *Mindhunter*.)

It may be relevant to this case to consider:

> With an incident like this, we see how pressure from many sources can corrupt an investigation, punish the wrong people, and damage trust in public officials. (Source: Page 132 of *The Unknown Darkness* by Gregg McCrary, another retired FBI profiler.)

Lawyer/novelist Scott Turow was a member of Illinois Governor Ryan's blue ribbon commission that discovered numerous wrongful convictions and death sentences in that state. Turow's experiences moved him to state, "When someone's on trial for a grotesque crime, jurors are registering their reaction to the crime. They'd convict anybody the prosecution puts before them."

Alternative Suspects Ignored by the State

According to official reports, the state's investigation focused *exclusively* on Dechaine from the moment the search for Sarah Cherry began on July 6, 1988.

Considering the facts known on July 6, that focus was appropriate.

The next day, however, Detectives Hendsbee and Drake followed small bare footprints beside large footprints leading into a trailer bearing the name "Fickett." They both knew Sarah Cherry to be barefoot—her sneakers and socks remained at the house from which she vanished. They both had already been investigating Jason Fickett for three weeks (and thereafter) for having sex with another twelve-year-old girl. (See page 396.) *This fact was concealed* from the defense and the public. Hendsbee decided they'd ask game wardens to "look into" this clue the next morning. Neither detective so much as knocked on that trailer's door. According to police reports, this was the only door in the area on which no officer knocked. This clue was never pursued. (See Exhibits, pages 398–401.)

Detective Hendsbee now says he didn't know that the owner of that trailer was the same Fickett he'd previously investigated.

Even if there had been no name on that trailer, Hendsbee's failure to take any action whatsoever—while searching for a barefoot twelve-year-old girl who vanished only a half-mile away—clearly demonstrates that official minds were firmly closed to the possibility of any suspect except Dennis Dechaine.

Jason Fickett was later convicted of having sex with that

twelve-year-old girl (which included insertion of objects, similar to acts committed upon Sarah Cherry); then he was convicted of having sex with an eleven-year-old girl; then convicted of sex "by compulsion" with a young woman. He has subsequently been arrested for at least two attempted rapes. After a year as a fugitive, he was recently arrested and awaits trial for the sexual abuse of another child.

Mr. Fickett recently told private investigator Tom Cumler that no officer has ever interviewed him about the Sarah Cherry case. (Documented with additional incriminating evidence in Attorney M. Michaela Murphy's motion to test DNA in the Dechaine case.)

Fickett's blood type (determined during Hendsbee's earlier investigation) is type A—the same as the "mystery blood" found under Sarah Cherry's fingernails. The state's claim that DNA tests eliminate Fickett as a suspect in the Sarah Cherry case does not alter the fact that—before this was known—he was not investigated. They probed no one except Dechaine.

Mr. Fickett was not the only person worthy of inquiry. The former wife of Sarah Cherry's stepfather had married Douglas Senecal who was, at the time of the crime against Sarah Cherry, under indictment for sexually abusing his step-daughter. Senecal's two step-daughters and Sarah Cherry visited back and forth at one another's homes frequently and were friends.

Senecal's "alibi" failed under scrutiny. Det. Hendsbee, in a recorded interview, admitted that he'd never even asked Mr. Senecal for hair or blood samples, or for permission to search his pickup. Asked why, Hendsbee offered this excuse,

"If Senecal did it, no one knew it." (Page 256.)

Despite defense lawyer Tom Connolly's presentation to the court of evidence implicating Mr. Senecal—facts the jury was never allowed to hear—Prosecutor Wright stated in his summation that, "there is no evidence, ladies and gentlemen of the jury, in this case of an alternative perpetrator." (Trial transcript, page 1489.)

Mr. Senecal told private investigator Ron Morin, "The only man on the face of the earth I will ever trust is [prosecutor] Eric Wright." Senecal also refused to answer his own lawyer's private question as to whether he was involved in the Cherry murder. (See Cumler affidavit, motion by Attorney M. Michaela Murphy to test DNA in this case.) Mr. Senecal still refuses to provide his DNA for testing in this case.

When the Office of the Attorney General finally made its files on this case available to comply with the order of the legislature, there were no lead sheets. Lead sheets list every clue—each lead which must be pursued; they are maintained as a sort of register where the lead is entered and, beside it, the name of the officer assigned to follow that lead. Behind that entry there's a space to note the results of the officer's inquiry—either "unfounded," or some reference to the report of that officer's findings. Often, the pursuit of one lead produces more leads, which are then entered on the register, assigned for investigation, and so on.

The state has explained that no such lead-sheet system was used in this case. Nor, although police had established a command center and publicized its phone number with a request for citizen cooperation, was there any log of tips phoned in by the public.

Without lead sheets or some similar method of keeping track of the widespread activities by many investigators and the numerous leads produced by their efforts, plus the various leads that always come in from citizens during the course of a high profile case, there is no way of controlling the overall probe or to make sure that all the bases have been covered.

Among other clues known to have come in, but not pursued, were allegations from several people offering information suggesting the involvement of the suspect Senecal. Another lead, known to have come in, reported a man in a small red pickup truck who drove up to a young girl within days of Sarah Cherry's murder and allowed her to see him—totally nude. It's impossible to tell from the reports the state ultimately revealed whether these leads were lost, forgotten or simply ignored. The report of the nude man in the red pickup, according to the woman who reported it, never even brought a return phone call.

As of this printing, Maine's Sex Offender Register lists sixty sexual predators within ten miles of where Sarah Cherry was abducted and murdered. (pages 399–400.)

None were questioned or investigated in this case.

Evidence Destroyed by the State

Evidence incinerated by authorities after Dechaine's trial includes the rape kit, a hair found on the victim's body (which they'd eliminated as being Dechaine's), and various other items. The evidence destroyed would have been valuable in future DNA testing. *This evidence was destroyed six weeks after Dechaine's appeal for a new trial was filed.*

But the state has preserved all of the evidence it sees as incriminating Dechaine.

Deputy Attorney General William Stokes "explained" that they simply disposed of evidence they "didn't need for our case against Dechaine."

Also missing from the attorney general's files are the fingerprints lifted from the door of the house from which the victim was abducted—fingerprints which do not match those of the victim, the residents of that house, or Dennis Dechaine.

QUESTIONABLE OFFICIAL CONDUCT

Numerous actions in this case raise disturbing doubts. Among them:

- Westrum's inexplicable alteration of Dechaine's words in his handwritten notes;
- Detectives' indifference to the small bare footprints, beside large footprints, leading to the door of a known sexual predator only half a mile from the abduction site;
- Concealment of that predator's record and crimes from the defense;
- Obscuring/concealing/suppressing the time of death (pages 367–75, 407) and other scientific evidence;
- Concealing confirmation of Dr. Bing's DNA evidence by the state's own expert;
- Concealing the tracking dog's failure to detect the victim's scent in Dechaine's truck;

- Concealing conversations with George Carlton, Dechaine's initial attorney, in which Carlton allegedly made comments which caused prosecutors to infer Dechaine's guilt.

See pages 379–87 regarding misrepresentations and falsehoods by officials.

JUSTICE IN THE APPEALS PROCESS

Officials tell us, falsely, that appeals courts affirmed Mr. Dechaine's guilt.

When Prosecutor Wright's 1988 conviction of another murder defendant was appealed, the state's attorney quoted *State v. Blier*, Maine, 1977, to remind the appeals court judges that "the reasonable doubt which will prevent conviction...must be in the mind of the jury, the trier of facts, and not that of the appellate courts."

The U. S. Supreme Court recently heard an appeal by Delma Banks, Jr. Lawyers for the State of Texas pooh-poohed the proof of prosecutorial misconduct.

Justice Ruth Bader Ginsburg: "Why wasn't it the obligation of the prosecution, having deceived the jury and the court, to come clean...rather than let this falsehood remain in the record?"

Justice Stephen Breyer: "What bothers me...is that if we were to say that defense counsel behaves unreasonably if he relies on the prosecution, that's to say that the justice system lacks integrity, and indeed it might contribute to a lack of integrity."

Justice Anthony Kennedy: "So the prosecution can lie and conceal, and the defense still has the burden to discover the evidence?" And, "Do you want us to say that the defendant relies at his peril on the representations of the state?"

On February 24, 2004, the U.S. Supreme Court blocked Mr. Banks's execution. Justice Ginsburg, writing for the majority, stated, "When police and prosecutors conceal significant exculpatory or impeaching material, it is ordinarily incumbent on the state to set the record straight.... A rule declaring 'prosecutor may hide, defendant must seek,' is not tenable in a system constitutionally bound to accord defendants due process." Chief Justice Rehnquist and Justices Stevens, O'Connor, Kennedy, Souter, and Breyer agreed with Ginsburg. Justices Thomas and Scalia also stated they would send the case back to the federal appeals court. (Sources: articles in the *New York Times* and *Washington Post*, December 9, 2003; AP wire 2/24/04.)

Former FBI Director William Sessions has joined distinguished judges and prosecutors supporting Mr. Banks because his claims, "by their very nature raise issues that threaten the ability of the adversarial system to produce just results."

Unfortunately, Maine's guardians of justice (who refuse to admit ever having erred) have concealed facts from courts in other cases, too. In July of 2001, regarding a case prosecuted by officials of the State of Maine, the Federal District Court "supportably found four reckless omissions and one intentional withholding of information." (Source: *United States v. John B. Stewart*, U.S. Court of Appeals No. 02-1938, decided July 29, 2003.)

Prosecutor Eric Wright was found to have made improper statements to a jury in still another murder case.

(*Portland Press Herald,* May 24, 1995, Page: 4B.)

Have we in Maine reached that point described by Daniel Patrick Moynihan as a "tolerance for impropriety"?

In the end, it doesn't matter how many remote possibilities prosecutors dream up to explain away the documented evidence. Science proves the impossibility of Dennis Dechaine's guilt. Concealment of vital evidence by prosecutors suggests that they *knew* the devastating impact of these indisputable facts.

Summary of Evidence Contradicting Guilt

Time of death, DNA of a male person (not Dechaine) under the victim's nails, knots binding victim different from all knots at Dechaine's farm and barn, police lab evidence (and tracking dog) that victim was never in Dechaine's truck; fingerprints at crime scene which are not Dechaine's; concealment by officials; and psychiatric examination showing Dechaine's personality (even on drugs) as inconsistent with perpetrator of a depraved crime.

If a killer concocted an alibi, "I was in the woods using drugs" is the worst possible story he could invent.

Getting the Answers

The questions posed in *Human Sacrifice*, published in 2002, have never been answered. Despite numerous vaguely negative allegations by various officials concerning *Human Sacrifice,* no one has ever specified a single evidentiary element in that book as being inaccurate, nor a single relevant bit of evidence as being left out, nor any evidentiary fact misstated.

Considering the fact that Trial & Error members support all allegations with documented evidence, it's reasonable to expect the same of anyone disputing them.

The vital evidence documented in *Human Sacrifice*, and in this report, is *not* the author's evidence. It's the *state's* evidence—much of which they concealed for fifteen years.

No one wants to believe that an innocent man is serving life imprisonment. Or wants to believe that our police did a poor job. Or wants to believe that our prosecutors would conceal evidence that proves a defendant to be innocent.

No one wants to believe that Sarah Cherry's murderer is free to attack other girls.

And we all tend to believe what we want to believe. It's only human.

Can anyone suggest a credible or moral argument against giving Dennis Dechaine a trial where jurors hear *all* the evidence?

> The only thing necessary for the triumph of evil is for good men to do nothing. —Edmund Burke

> Those who benefit from the status quo never want change. —NY Attorney General Eliot Spitzer, speech at National Press Club, 1/31/05.

Detailed Facts Regarding the Time of Death

If Sarah Cherry was strangled to death *after* Dennis Dechaine was with the state's own witnesses, including police officers, his guilt would be impossible.

The only known facts regarding the condition of the body are those reported by Medical Examiner Ronald Roy, M.D. According to his report (if it is complete), he discarded the fly larvae found on the body; he did not record body temperature or ambient temperature (near 90 degrees all that week, according to the weather bureau); and he did not perform the vitreous potassium test on the victim's eye fluid. The only details he reported which indicate the time of death are the rigor mortis (which he says was "still present but passing off") and signs of putrefaction (decomposition)—none of which he observed; nor is any sign of decomposition evident in the autopsy photographs.

State officials persistently allude to the opinions by the independent consultant, Dr. Eleanor McQuillen, whose services were requested by *Trial & Error*, i.e., her 10/29/92 statement that, "In summary, what's reported is consistent with Dr. Roy's conclusions."

Officials avoid mentioning the next sentence, i.e., "It's what's missing that could be important to confirm time of death and complete the autopsy findings."

Officials also ignore Dr. McQuillen's statement: "I believe the autopsy report in this case is preliminary with one loose page of microscopic added, not final.... Without the entire file on this case, I am not in a position to give an opinion further." (Dr. McQuillen was furnished what the state claims is Dr. Roy's entire autopsy report, the transcript of his trial testimony, and the state's photographs of the victim's body.)

Aside from the progress of rigor mortis observed by Dr. Roy, Dr. McQuillen stated, "Other than the description of 'good preservation' there is no description of early blue-green discoloration of the lower abdomen and by photograph I see none."

An "Outline re Time of Death" accompanied Dr. McQuillen's report. It states:

Postmortem decomposition
1. Sequence
   24 hours—blue-green discoloration of lower abdomen.
   36 hours—blue-green discoloration of entire abdomen.

No such discoloration was evident on the body of Sarah Cherry.

Dr. McQuillen stated during the recorded 2/23/93 interview with her that, "Well...at around 24 hours you should start to see the blue-green discoloration of the lower abdomen. But it's not there and it wasn't described and therefore one has to suppose that it was either a shorter period of postmortem time period, or there is a cool environment that preserved the body...being placed in a cool earth grave is one of the reasons."

Dr. McQuillen erroneously adds, "It was in the ground laying in a hollow of the ground."

That conclusion is based on a mistaken interpretation of Dr. Roy's testimony. The body was not buried. Police photos show that the body lay *on* the ground, partially covered by sticks and forest debris. The victim's head and thigh were exposed to air and light. Police photographs show the body lying in bright direct sunlight.

According to leading textbooks and other pathologists, both of the relevant reported markers—rigor mortis, and no sign of postmortem decomposition—indicate that death occurred less than 36 hours before Dr. Roy first viewed the body, i.e., sometime after two o'clock Thursday morning—*more than six hours after* Dechaine's actions are accounted for by state's witnesses, including police officers.

❖

The following are quoted from leading textbooks on forensic pathology:

From: *Unnatural Death* by Michael M. Baden, M.D., former chief medical examiner, City of New York:

> Rigor mortis begins to show two hours after death and takes twelve hours to peak.... The stiffness remains for twelve hours and gradually disappears. After thirty-six hours, the body becomes soft again.
>
> Between the time they are laid and the time they hatch, maggot eggs last less than twenty-four hours.

From: *Forensic Medicine: A Guide to Principles* by Doctors Gordon, Shapiro, and Berson:

> The two main factors which influence the onset and duration of rigor mortis are: (1) the environmental temperature; and (2) the degree of muscular activity before

death. In infants and children and in aged persons, the onset is relatively more rapid than in adults.

Putrefaction tends to be more rapid in children than in adults.

From: *Medicolegal Investigation of Death*, Werner Spitz, M.D., and Russell Ficher, M.D.:

The time of persistence of rigidity is greatly influenced by the temperature of the body and its environment. It may disappear as soon as nine to twelve hours after death if the body is in an extremely hot environment and decomposition begins. The original onset of rigidity is hastened by the presence of high fever, convulsions or extreme muscle activity in the period prior to death.

(Regarding decomposition) environmental temperature is the most important single factor. It is not uncommon to see advanced decomposition within twelve to eighteen hours.

Flies may lay eggs between the lips and eyelids of patients *in extremis* and certainly within a few hours after death. Certain species of blowflies actually produce live larvae so that tiny maggots can be seen moving within a matter of an hour or so after death.

From: *Investigation of Violent and Sudden Death: A Manual for Medical Examiners* by Robert C. Hendrix, M.D., Professor of Pathology, University of Michigan, Deputy Medical Examiner, Washtenaw County, Michigan:

The general rules indicate that rigor mortis begins about four hours after death, progresses to a maximum by eight to twelve hours, persists for about four hours, then gradually reduces over the same time span. [NOTE: This would have the rigor mortis *totally* dissipated by 20 to 28 hours.] It is a chemical change and is hastened by heat, retarded by cold.

Any wound, even a superficial one, will hasten putrefaction, as will severe local congestion such as occurs in strangulation. Heat will accelerate putrefaction.

The stomach usually empties itself in about three hours if not prevented from doing so. Great excitement, marked fear and actions of some drugs, severe injury, and death all delay or stop gastric activity.

State Medical Examiner Ronald Roy observed that rigor mortis was "still present...but passing off."

George Chase, retired chief pathologist for the Eastern Maine Medical Center, reviewed all the circumstances of Dr. Roy's observations and estimated that death had occurred around 24 hours before the autopsy, i.e., the day *after* Dechaine was questioned.

The evidence of Dr. Roy's *observations* must be accepted. But his report and his trial testimony suggest that his conclusions were based on information furnished by detectives and the prosecutor indicating that Mr. Dechaine could only be guilty if death occurred prior to 8:00 P.M. on the day Sarah Cherry was abducted.

Dr. Roy's bias toward the prosecution's case may be conjectured from his assertion (after jurors were informed that Mr. Dechaine once had a small pen knife attached to his key chain) that the shallow cut wounds were inflicted by "a small knife, like a pen knife that someone might carry." (Page 571, trial testimony.)

In truth, virtually any sharp instrument can make small, shallow cuts.

However, Dr. Roy also agreed with the experts who wrote the forensic pathology textbooks, when he testified: "Well, temperature, as I said, will hasten all the processes. An elevated temperature will speed it up and make its onset quicker and its disappearance quicker. Strenuous physical exertion may hasten the onset of rigor mortis. I would expect to find more fly activity." (Transcript pages 556–57.)

Concerning speculation that the victim did not actually expire until hours after being strangled, Dr. Roy testified that the ligature constricted her neck to a diameter of "Three inches, two and a half, three inches." (Transcript page 563.) No one, conscious or unconscious, could breath under that circumstance.

A scientific assessment of Dr. Roy's undisputed observations shows that:

1. Rigor mortis normally passes off thirty-six hours after death.
2. Passing off of rigor mortis and the appearance of abdominal discoloration is quicker in children, in high temperature, during extreme stress/terror/muscle activity. Thus the rigor would pass off and blue-green

discoloration would appear more quickly (i.e., a shorter time before the autopsy) when these factors are present.

3. All of these factors were present in this case.

❖

State officials persist in stating that the duration of rigor mortis can be affected by "variables," but they never specify any variable which could have extended the period of rigor mortis, or retard putrefaction—both of which would be necessary to indicate a time of death prior to 2:00 A.M. on the morning of Thursday, July 7, 1988.

In fact, every variable that might possibly have affected rigor mortis and putrefaction (temperature, fear, stress, struggling against the bonds, and the victim's age) would, if they had any effect, establish an even *later* time of death, making Dechaine's guilt even more impossible.

Based upon the on-site observations by Dr. Roy, the preponderance of expert opinion indicates that Sarah Cherry died at least six, and most likely more hours *after* it would have been possible for Dennis Dechaine to commit the crime.

Prosecutor Wright never asked the standard question routinely asked at all murder trials to show that a defendant had opportunity to commit the crime, i.e., "At what time, in your medical opinion, did the victim die?" Instead, he asked how long the victim had been dead when Dr. Roy saw the body. Dr. Roy testified that death occurred 30 to 36 hours before he observed that "rigor mortis was still present but passing off."

Dr. Roy's casual conjecture that the rigor's duration

"could have been longer" is contradicted by the views of other pathologists and all of the leading textbooks on forensic pathology.

Prosecutor Wright attempted to fix the time of death via progression of the victim's digestion—a factor pathologists know to be totally irrelevant in this case.

From *Investigation of Sudden Death: A Manual for Medical Examiners*, by Robert C. Hendrix, M.D., Michigan medical examiner and professor of pathology at the University of Michigan:

> The stomach usually empties itself in about three hours if it is not prevented from doing so. *Great excitement, marked fear, and actions of some drugs, severe injury, and death...all delay or stop gastric activity.* [Emphasis added.]

Even the state's own medical examiner, Dr. Roy, testified that: "There are many factors that can slow down digestion. Strong alcohol. Notably stress will do it. It's not uncommon for people under great stress to find out later that they still have not digested the meal from the six or twelve hours or the day before." (Transcript, page 585.)

The importance of this evidence is confirmed by the state's efforts to *hide* it.

When Medical Examiner Clerk Sandra Hickey was asked to produce the complete autopsy report, Deputy Attorney General Fern LaRochelle told her, "Show him what we gave

[defense lawyer] Connolly and nothing else."
Under the law, there's not supposed to be anything else!

❖

If time of death isn't important, why were prosecutors so determined to conceal it?

The Struggle to Uncover Evidence Concealed by the State

On November 30, 1992, following numerous denials of his requests for documents, James P. Moore filed a Petition for Review of Final Agency Action (Cumberland County Superior Court Docket No. CV-92-1348) concerning official denials of access under the Freedom of Access statute to the files and records of the Maine State Police relating to the investigation of the murder of Sarah Cherry.

That petition was denied on February 8, 1993, upon the court's acceptance of argument by Assistant Attorney General Leanne Robbin that these records of the Maine State Police (unlike other records of that agency, which would be accessible under the Freedom of Access statute at that time) had become part of the records of the attorney general which were deemed "confidential," and were therefore not accessible under the Freedom of Access statute.

That reason for denying access vanished on September 13, 2003, the effective date of an order by the Maine State Legislature (Chapter 18, S.P. 369—L.D. 1097) which rendered reports and records of the Department of the Attorney General "relating to the unlawful homicide of Sarah Cherry" accessible under the Freedom of Access statute.

On December 26, 2003, A new Freedom of Access request was submitted for the entire Maine State Police files of records and reports regarding the investigation of Sarah Cherry's murder. Lt. Anne Schaad of the Maine State

Police responded that the entire file of the Maine State Police regarding this case was available for review at the office of the Attorney General.

On April 28, 2004, following repeated assurances by the Maine State Police and Deputy Attorney General William R. Stokes that the complete police file was at the office of the attorney general and available for inspection in accordance with the Order of the Legislature, a copy of page 409 of the transcript of Dennis Dechaine's trial was submitted showing Assistant Attorney General Eric Wright's acknowledgment that a report had been filed by Maine State Police canine officer Thomas Bureau, and that this report had not been made available to Mr. Dechaine's attorney as part of the court-ordered discovery. This report was also not among those on view at the offices of the Attorney General.

On May 3, 2004, Deputy Attorney General William R. Stokes responded that he "checked the state police file myself and find no evidence that Trooper Bureau, in fact, prepared and filed a canine incident report." And, "It is quite possible that although Trooper Bureau believed he filed a report, he, in fact, did not."

Mr. Stokes's response went on to divert this discussion into an argument concerning Mr. Dechaine's attorney's "decision not to raise a discovery objection during the trial"—a matter totally irrelevant to this FOA request.

Mr. Stokes went on, in this same communication, to state that, "We cannot provide you access to a report that does not exist."

On May 6, 2004, it was reiterated to Mr. Stokes that this

was a request for the entire state police file concerning this investigation.

On May 13, 2004, Mr. Stokes released the report filed by canine officer, Trooper Bureau, proving his earlier assurances to be incorrect.

On May 20, 2004, in a telephone conversation with Mr. Stokes, Mr. Stokes asked several times that he be informed of what reports should be part of the state police file which had not been made available. In response, he was informed that specifying what reports were sought (based on witness interviews and T&E's investigation) and which should be part of this police file, would—based on his recent conduct—result in receiving only those reports specified; and further, that there was reason, based on investigation, to believe that additional reports were being withheld.

On June 24, 2004, Mr. Stokes surendered the VICAP report filed by Detective Alfred Hendsbee, lead detective in this case.

In August 2004, in response to a lawsuit filed in Maine Superior Court, the state finally made available the contemporaneous notes by Detective Hendsbee. These notes reveal that Detective Hendsbee's trial testimony was untrue: the alleged statement by Dechaine which Hendsbee *testified he was reading from his notes* is *not* in those notes. The only Dechaine statements quoted in those notes are totally exculpatory. (See Exhibits, Hendsbee testimony and Hendsbee notes.)

There remain a number of official documents known to have existed which the state persists in claiming it cannot find.

Misleading and False Statements

Dennis Dechaine's first attorney was George Carlton. Unfortunately, and unknown to Dechaine, Carlton's "better days" were long past. Former law partner William Leonard said that Carlton "drank too much" and "he rarely cracked a law book." Charged with evading his federal income taxes for the years 1966 through 1977, Carlton had fled to Australia. In 1983, after seven years as a fugitive, he negotiated a compromise with the government and paid $38,495.54 to settle his debt, served thirty days in jail, and was suspended from the practice of law for less than a year before being re-admitted to the Maine Bar and licensed to practice again. Court records demonstrate Carlton's abject incompetence. Every client throughout 1988 (except one, who ignored his advice to plead guilty) was convicted; every client who trusted him to litigate a civil case lost out because of the alcoholic Carlton's failure to file routine docket entries.

Why would any lawyer who knew Carlton trust his competence, his judgment or his credibility?

Nevertheless, on the Thursday after Sarah Cherry's disappearance, the day before her body was found, Deputy Attorney General LaRochelle telephoned Carlton. LaRochelle's affidavit states that he told Carlton he'd heard that Dechaine had consulted him, and "that investigators felt that if Sarah was still alive, it was important that we find her soon. So I have just two questions: is she alive? And, are we searching the right area?"

LaRochelle used that ploy in at least one other case. But *that* lawyer thought he was joking—asking a lawyer to violate client confidentiality is improper—so she'd given LaRochelle a snappy retort and hung up the phone.

This time, LaRochelle claimed better luck. His affidavit continued, "Attorney Carlton replied that Sarah was not alive and added something to the effect that we were looking in the right area.... I reported this information to Assistant Attorney General Eric Wright."

LeRochelle "can't recall Carlton's exact words."

Carlton denied to Tom Connolly and others that he'd ever said Dechaine was guilty. Perhaps his reasoning was best expressed when he told me, "Dechaine said he couldn't remember. And when they say they can't remember, that means they did it."

Whatever Carlton actually said to LaRochelle, LaRochelle and everyone to whom this secret was relayed—Eric Wright, lead Detective Hendsbee, Medical Examiner Ronald Roy— interpreted it as indicating that Dechaine had confessed to Carlton.

Carlton's treachery is undeniable. Later, he made more dramatic allegations to others. Did they truly believe him, or were they merely recounting what he'd said? None saw fit to inform defense lawyer Tom Connolly, Dechaine, or the court or let jurors learn of this perfidy. All of this was kept secret until July 2000, when Carlton was incapacitated by a stgroke and unable to confirm or deny the allegations, and prosecutors used Carlton's alleged comments as ammunition to defeat Dechaine's habeas corpus petition in federal court.

The prosecutor "may prosecute with earnestness and vigor—indeed, he should do so. But, while he may strike hard blows, he is not at liberty to strike foul ones. It is as much his duty to refrain from improper methods calculated to produce a wrongful conviction as it is to use every legitimate means to bring about a just one. —U.S. Supreme Court, *Berger v. United States*, 295 U.S. 78 (1935)

Trial & Error members support every statement with hard facts, from the state's own evidence, much of which officials had concealed.

Officials involved in this case, with cynical confidence that they'll be believed merely because they hold important positions, provide whimsical theories, vague possibilities, and outright falsehoods.

Or they simply change the subject.

1. Deputy Attorney General William Stokes has stated that there are false allegations and misrepresentations in the book, *Human Sacrifice*. *The fact is,* no one has specified a single falsehood, misrepresentation, or error in that book regarding evidence in the Dechaine case or the conduct of any official.
2. Mr. Stokes has told people that *Human Sacrifice* author James P. Moore "was paid to write the book," and that "he never investigated a homicide." *Both allegations are untrue.* (Even if they were true, what would that have to do with the evidence in this case? Officials wouldn't keep changing the subject if they

could explain the evidence establishing Dechaine's innocence.)

3. Mr. Stokes and ex-prosecutor Eric Wright have both stated publicly and falsely that the former chief pathologist of Vermont agreed with the state's theory that Sarah Cherry died a few hours after being abducted on July 6th, 1988. *The fact is* that the Vermont pathologist, who examined the state's entire autopsy report, said: "It's what's missing that could be important to confirm time of death. Without the entire file on this case, I am not in a position to give an opinion further." (See pages 367–75 and 407 for additional details on this subject.)

4. Eric Wright stated, "The state's psychologists would not have testified, as [Trial & Error] wants the public to believe.... [T&E] flatly misrepresents the doctor's opinion." *The fact is* that Judge Bradford stated, on the record (but outside the jury's presence) the state psychologists' findings: that Mr. Dechaine "was not in a psychotic state on the day of the crime."

5. Additional untrue statements by Mr. Wright regarding this case:

Wright: "Dechaine admitted to the state psychologist that he could have lost papers from his truck when he turned around in the driveway of the house where Sarah was babysitting."

FACT: Dechaine never stated he'd turned around in *that* driveway. He said he'd turned around in *a* driveway, *somewhere*, at some time during that day. (See page 402.)

Wright: "Dechaine confessed to the psychologists, and

we have it on video tape." (Stated to Carol Waltman, Dechaine's brothers, State Senator Judy Paradis, and State Representative Douglas Ahearne, on September 1, 1994; see Exhibits, page 403.)

FACT: Nothing on that video remotely resembles a confession. The video is in the AG's file, opened after fifteen years of official secrecy, available now for anyone to view.

Wright: "Nothing I've heard explains how Dechaine's tire tracks ended up in that driveway." (Brunswick *Times Record* interview, 12/5/03)

FACT: The state's expert reported: "The impression seen in the casts *could have been* made by the left front tire, however, *this does not exclude any other tire with a similar tread design.*" (Emphasis added) Dechaine's other three tires were eliminated as having made tracks in that driveway. (See Exhibits, page 404.)

Wright: "We await any sensible explanation for how someone other than Dechaine committed the crimes against Sarah."

FACT: The detailed answer in *Human Sacrifice*—unlike Mr. Wright's scenario—accounts for *all* the known facts, including the evidence he withheld.

Wright: "There is no evidence, ladies and gentlemen of the jury, in this case of an alternative perpetrator." (Trial transcript, Wright's closing argument at trial.)

FACT: One suspect, well known to Mr. Wright, was already under indictment for child molestation. Wright told Judge Bradford that requiring that man to testify was useless, because he'd take the Fifth Amendment. (Transcript, Motion for New Trial, May 4, 1992, page 62.)

Another suspect, a known pedophile, lived only half a mile from where barefoot Sarah Cherry was abducted. Detectives followed small bare footprints beside large footprints to that pedophile's very door, and never even knocked!

That man, recently arrested again for having sex with another little girl, has multiple convictions for unlawful sex with minor children, and for rape. (See pages 358–59, and Exhibits, page 356.)

It is ironic that Mr. Wright—a man who has made so many false statements in this case, told another jury only months before Dechaine's trial, "Concealment of evidence is always taken in the law as evidence of consciousness of guilt, and so of guilt. So, too, is lying. This principle is so simple, so logical, that I would be surprised if any of you would say during deliberations that the defendant's history of lying throughout this case is simply to be ignored." (*State v. Saunders*, 11/88)

Official misrepresentations of evidence persist today. Detective Hendsbee told reporter Christopher Cousins (*Brunswick Times Record*, 12/5/03) that Dechaine admitted being at the house where Sarah Cherry was abducted. That is untrue. Mr. Dechaine's actual words, quoted in Deputy Dan Reed's official report, were only that Dechaine stopped in *a* driveway, *somewhere*, to relieve himself that day. (See Exhibits, page 402.)

Deputy Reed, himself, told detective/interviewers from Court TV's "Wrong Man" program that Dechaine "described the house to a 't'." His official report states otherwise. (See Exhibits, page 402.)

Deputy Attorney General Stokes has stated, and written in letters to numerous people, that appeals courts affirmed Mr. Dechaine's guilt. That's not true, and he knows it. Prosecutors fighting appeals quote *State v. Blier*, ME 1977 to remind the appeals court judges that "the reasonable doubt which will prevent conviction...must be in the mind of the jury, the trier of facts, and not that of the appellate courts." (*State v. Saunders, 11/88*)

Why does Mr. Stokes imply that appeals court judges have weighed the Dechaine evidence?

Eric Wright and other officials continue to claim that Dechaine's truck was locked when officers found it. That's untrue. The trooper who prepared it for towing to the crime lab entered through the unlocked rear sliding glass window. Beyond that, anyone lifting the ropes and papers from Dechaine's truck in order to frame him could have locked it when closing its door.

Detective Hendsbee has stated that, since Dechaine had the keys to his truck in his pocket, he was the only one who could have locked that truck because it cannot be locked without the key.

Hendsbee knew that to be untrue. His official report, dated three days before Dechaine's trial, states:

"I arrived at Headquarters and tested the locks on DENNIS DECHAINE'S pick-up truck. The truck can be locked without a key by holding the latch inward and can also be locked with a key." The same page of the report shows that at 0945, "I called Eric Wright at his request and discussed the case with him." (See page 405.)

Statements by Detectives Hendsbee and Westrum alleging admissions made by Dechaine are discussed on pages 352–53; also see Exhibits, page 392–95.

State psychologist MacLean has told people during at least one social gathering that Dechaine confessed to him during his psychiatric examination. But the final paragraph of Dr. MacLean's eight-page report proves this to be untrue, stating that Dechaine maintained his innocence. (See Exhibits, page 406.)

Robert Dorr, formerly employed by the Office of the Attorney General, circulated a leaflet at the 2004 Democratic Convention containing numerous allegations, all of which are disproved by the state's own official records. (See Exhibits, page 408–09.)

❖

Standards of the American Bar Association for prosecutors prohibit:
- Avoiding the pursuit of evidence because it might damage the prosecution's case;
- Failing to make a diligent search to comply with discovery requests;
- Failing to make timely disclosure to the defense of evidence indicating innocence;
- Failing to report another prosecutor's misconduct;
- Failing to follow the standards of professional conduct and ethical codes.

The ABA Standards state: "The duty of the prosecutor is to seek justice, not merely to convict." (See Exhibits, page 410.)

The evidence provided here suggests that prosecutors from the Office of the Attorney General deliberately violated all of these standards.

❖

In October 2004, responding to growing public concerns, Attorney General G. Steven Rowe appointed a commission of attorneys to probe allegations of misconduct. (See Exhibits, page 411–12.)

Thirteen months later, Attorney General Rowe was reminded that he had established his commission more than a year ago, that he had promised to release their report when it was received, and asked to release that report now. (See Exhibits, page 413.)

Mr. Rowe's response is also in the Exhibits, page 414.

> Cowardice asks the question, Is it safe?
> Expediency asks the question, Is it politic?
> Vanity asks the question, Is it popular?
> But conscience asks the question, Is it right?
> And there comes a time when one must take
> a position that is neither safe, nor politic, nor
> popular, but he must take it because his
> conscience tells him that it is right.
> —Dr. Martin Luther King Jr.

> The truth is incontrovertible. Malice may attack it, ignorance may deride it, but in the end, there it is.
> —Winston Churchill

Detailed Facts Regarding DNA

Dechaine's attorneys filed a motion to have DNA evidence analyzed two months prior to his trial, i.e., January 1989. Dechaine offered to pay the costs of testing.

The trial court *denied* Dechaine's motion for DNA testing.

There was, back then, abundant DNA material available for testing:

1. Blood from under Sarah Cherry's fingernails;
2. Material extracted in a post-mortem rape kit;
3. Unidentified hairs found on the victim's body.

At the time, DNA testing was an accepted science in courts across the country. The cause of death was strangulation. It is archetypal in cases of strangulation that the victim will scratch her/his attacker.

But prosecutors *knew* that DNA tests couldn't help their case; their lab had already informed them that the blood under the victim's nails was not Dechaine's blood type.

In 1992 the State of Maine *destroyed* the rape kit and crime scene hairs while Dechaine's case was under *active appeal*. Prosecutors kept all of their own evidence intact.

Recent DNA testing proves that the DNA did not come from Dechaine, from anyone who handled evidence in the custody chain, nor anyone in Sarah's immediate family.

Is it morally defensible that Dennis Dechaine be denied a chance to prove his innocence *because* of actions by officials of the State of Maine?

On September 23, 2005, attorneys M. Michaela Murphy and Steve Peterson filed a motion for a new trial under the provisions of Maine's DNA statute. Judge Carl Bradford denied the defense the right to present any evidence discovered subsequent to the 1989 trial and the 1992 motion for a new trial (including the evidence concealed by the state), any evidence regarding time of death, and/or any evidence concerning alternative suspects.

Dechaine's defense attorneys conferred with him and decided to withdraw the motion due to Judge Bradford's restrictive interpretation of what evidence would be permitted under existing law, and because this was the defendant's last chance to get a new trial.

Deputy Attorney General William Stokes wanted the motion dismissed "with prejudice," which would prevent any such motion under this law ever being brought to the court again.

Judge Bradford: "I think it would probably be a dismissal with prejudice as to the current law."

Attorney Murphy argued, "There is absolutely nothing in the statute that says it cannot be withdrawn. There is no time limit for filing this motion for a new trial under the statute."

Thirteen days later, on November 9, Judge Bradford stated, in dismissing the defendant's motion for a new trial, that "Ultimately, however, the court does not have the statutory authority to dismiss this motion with prejudice."

With no legal alternative, Judge Bradford dismissed it without prejudice.

In January 2004, State Representative Ross Paradis sponsored "An Act to Amend the Law Governing DNA Testing." This was drafted with the assistance of the Innocence Project to bring Maine's DNA law into alignment with that of other states; only Michigan had a DNA law as restrictive as Maine's. Thirteen representatives and senators signed on as co-sponsors. As the committee hearings began, it was revealed that an assistant attorney general had been responsible for crafting the original restrictive statute. During negotiations at the hearings, the president of the Maine Prosecutors' Association succeeded in watering down the amendment slightly, and among the changes was the deletion of a provision permitting the assignment of a different judge.

The committee voted unanimously to send the amended bill forward to the full legislature. On April 13, 2006, the legislature voted for the new DNA statute, and Governor John Baldacci signed it into law on May 30, 2006.

Conclusion

Locked into a premature theory and unable to admit they're not infallible, officials stubbornly ignore the evidence that proves them wrong. Pressed for explanations, some change the subject; some make patently false statements.

The more one ponders the motives of the officials in this case—based on their actions, considering all the evidence—the more one becomes convinced that their priorities must have been:

1. Quiet the media;
2. Calm the citizens;
3. Satisfy the victim's family; and possibly,
4. To look like heroic professionals.

Dennis Dechaine? He was collateral roadkill.

We can easily forgive a child who is afraid of the dark. The real tragedy of life is when men are afraid of the light. —Plato

Because one of the main sources of our national unity is our belief in equal justice, we need to make sure Americans of all races and backgrounds have confidence in the system that provides justice. In America we must make doubly sure no person is held to account for a crime he or she did not commit. —President George W. Bush, State of the Union, 2005

I do not think much of a man who is not wiser today than he was yesterday. —Abraham Lincoln

Dante once said that the hottest places in hell are reserved for those who, in a period of moral crisis, maintain their neutrality. —President John F. Kennedy, Bonn, West Germany, June 24, 1963

Exhibits

Contemporaneous notes of Detective Mark Westrum

Aside from Westrum's inexplicable alteration changing Dechaine's words from, "How could I kill her" to "Why did I kill her," observe (above) that Westrum's contemporaneous notes quote Dechaine as saying, "I told my wife something bad had happened."

At trial, Westrum's testimony changed this to, "I told my wife that I did something bad."

Trial testimony of Detective Alfred Hendsbee

Page 799

1   THE COURT: 68 is also admitted.

2

3 BY MR. WRIGHT:

4 Q   Now, before we talk about how you conducted the search,
5 could you tell the jury, please, what time you arrived at Mr.
6 Dechaine's residence and what happened, with some precision,
7 what happened when you arrived on Friday afternoon at the
8 defendant's residence?
9 A   The time was 1:57 in the afternoon. I pulled into
10 Dennis Dechaine's residence and Dennis and his wife Nancy
11 were sitting on the front porch. When I pulled in, Dennis
12 came down off the porch towards my car, and at a rapid pace.
13 His wife was following him. Dennis stated that I know what
14 you are here for. I can't believe I could do such a thing.
15 It's not - -
16 Q   If you don't remember please refer to your notes.
17 A   He stated: I can't believe that I could do such a thing.
18 The real me is not like that. I know me. I couldn't do
19 anything like that. It must be somebody else inside of me.
20 At that time I hadn't even gotten out of my car.
21 Q   It must have been somebody else inside of me - -
22 A   Who is doing this.
23 Q   You hadn't said that. It must be somebody else inside
24 of me doing this?
25 A   Yes. At that time I hadn't gotten out of my car. I

asked Dennis to step away from my door so I could get out of my car, at which time he did. But he kept saying that there has got to be somebody else inside of me doing this. I couldn't have done such a thing.

When I got out of my car Dennis stated: do what you have to do. At that time I told Dennis I was there just to serve a search warrant. He said do what you've got to do. I just can't believe I could do that.

Q   You then conducted your search that went on for some period of time?

A   No. At that time I went in the house with Dennis and Nancy and also arrived there with me was the Peter McCarthy. It was very difficult for me to do the search because I couldn't secure one area and leave them in another area because things could change. I had to get some assistance in doing the search. So I basically stayed with Dennis and Nancy.

Q   Did you make any requests of them or have any conversation with them regarding how the search would be conducted?

A   I told them that the items on the search warrant were so small and the house was so big that I didn't know where to begin the search. And he asked if he could be of any assistance. Basically I asked for his sneakers and where the dirty clothes were. I was told at that time that the dirty

Contemporaneous notes of Detecctive Hendsbee

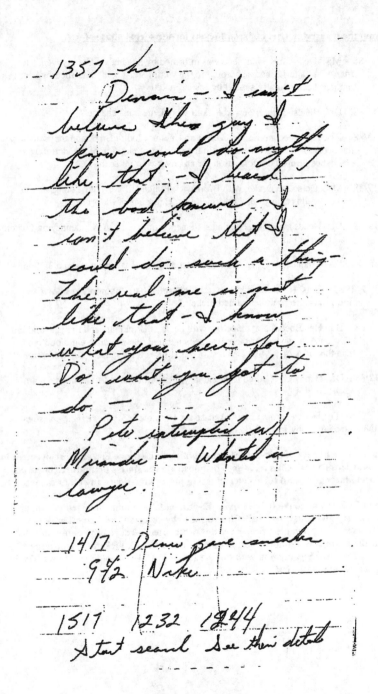

1357 hrs

Dennis – I can't believe these guys I know could do anything like that – I wasn't The bad knows – I can't believe that I could do such a thing – The real me is not like that – I know what you here for Do what you got to do –

Pete interrupted w/ Miranda – Wanted a lawyer.

1417 Dennis gave sneaker
9½ Nike

1517 1232 1244
Start search See their detail

Chronology, investigation of Jason Ficket re the "A.A." case

From the transcript, trial of Jason Fickett for the sexual abuse of A.A.

6/11/88 – MSP Det. Alfred Hendsbee was informed by Sagadahoc County Dep. Munsy that A. A., age 12, had, according to the victim and a complaint filed by her mother, been sexually abused by Jason Fickett.

6/12/88 – Det. Hendsbee interviewed Fickett who denied this charge.

6/13/88 – Det. Hendsbee advised by MSP Lab Chemist Judith Brinkman that semen had not been conclusively identified in the rape kit or clothing of the victim. Det. Hendsbee furnished information for an arrest warrant to the D.A.

6/17/88 – MSP Detective Drake, with Brunswick Police Officer Tom Young, arrests Fickett on this charge, and informed Det. Hendsbee of the arrest.

6/29/88 – Det. Hendsbee took a detailed statement from victim A.A.. identifying Fickett as the perpetrator.

July 6, 1988 – Sarah Cherry, age 12, is abducted barefoot between noon and 3:20pm

July 7, 1988 - Dets. Hendsbee and Drake follow small bare footprints beside large footprints into "a trailer named Fickett."

7/11/88 – Det. Hendsbee reports meeting with chemist Brinkman, and that she told him "that on A.'s underwear there was semen found that is a different blood type than that of A.A.'s." She also testified that Fickett is type "A" and a secretor.

7/12/88 – Det. Hendsbee testified to grand jury; Fickett indicted for having sex with 12-year-old A. A.

NOTE: facts regarding the A.A. case are from the MSP file re their investigation of the rape of A. A. by Jason Fickett.

While this sequence of events does not establish or disprove Fickett's involvement in the murder of Sarah Cherry, it <u>does</u> demonstrate the state's premature conclusion of Dechaine's guilt, and their determination <u>not</u> to investigate any other suspect.

Jason Fickett was convicted of raping 12-year-old A.A.; and convicted of raping an 11-year-old girl, and convicted of having sex "by coercion" with another female. Two arrests for attempted rape were not prosecuted because prosecutors decided that the victims would not make good witnesses. In 2003, Fickett became a fugitive from warrants charging him with having sex with a 14-year-old girl. He was finally apprehended in late 2005.

Report of Detecctive Steven Drake regarding footprints

MAINE STATE POLICE

Case No. LC 88-00203

Sagadahoc S.O.
Det. STEVEN DRAKE, mc
Code No. 1153
Homicide (SARAH CHERRY)
Bowdoin
Sagadahoc

CONTINUED:

1924 - I spoke to DEBBIE CROSMAN who advised there were no fingerprints taken at the school but would get a hairbrush for me so we could have a sample of SARAH's hair.

1938 - Det. HENDSBEE and I checked the footprints on the Pickett Road and tracked them to a trailer by the name of FICKETT. The tracks were barefoot but showed two different sizes going right into this trailer.

It should also be noted that one of the searchers advised that off one of the side roads which he marked with a big wooden arrow that he made from logs, they found a mud hole which had some barefoot footprints, a shirt and a chain and looked like some broken glass. Someone may have been four-wheeling and hit a tree and the tree had a scar on it. Det. HENDSBEE advised he would advise the wardens about this location in the morning.

2041 - I interviewed RICHARD DUNBAR in my vehicle. See attached Summary of Interview.

7/8/88

0532 - I received a wakeup call from Augusta as I requested. The officer advised that the Triple I check had been started yesterday.

0652 - I arrived at the C P in Bowdoinham and was advised to check on the babysitter for the HENKELS and who it was and to see if DENNIS DECHAINE had any tie in with that babysitter, to finish the neighborhood on the Dead River Road and to check with the Farmer's Market where DENNIS DECHAINE had his stand. It was also suggested that we check on Washington state and Oregon for DENNIS DECHAINE's background and the Madawaska area.

0744 - I received from CHRIS CROSMAN, dob 8/3/49 of RFD 2, Box 79, Topsham, Meadow Rd., Bowdoin, 666-3477, the following items:

One red hairbrush belonging to SARAH CHERRY

One sheet from SARAH's bed. It was advised that she slept with a sheet Monday and Tuesday night

❖397❖

Report of Detecctive Hendsbee regarding footprints

MAINE STATE POLICE — Case No. LC 88-00203

CONTINUATION REPORT

Complainant: Sagadahoc Sheriff's Office
Type of Case: Homicide (SARAH CHERRY)
Signature and Rank: Det. ALFRED HENDSBEE, mc
Code No. 2134
Town: Bowdoin   County: Sagadahoc

7/7/88

CONTINUED:

1845 - A person came into the command post and advised he had just found a white approximately three foot high fishing pole off from the side of the Lewis Hill Road.

1907 - Det. DRAKE and I arrived at a small dump that is located approximately two tenths of a mile from the Command Post up the Lewis Hill Road. I photographed the fishing pole described as an orange and white, approximately three foot high fishing pole. The line was in the pole; however, was not strung through the eyelets. The pole was leaning against a tree off the side of a dump approximately 50 feet from the roadway. It was unknown if it was part of the dump or whether someone had placed it there purposefully to hide it. I took photos of the pole and retained it to be examined by the Lab.

1920 - Det. DRAKE and I were at a private driveway leading to a FICKETT's trailer. This private drive in the upper half of the driveway which is located approximately a mile into the woods, a party had observed bare footprints in the roadway. Det. DRAKE and I examined the footprints and found that there was a small sized barefooted footprint as well as a larger sized barefooted footprint leading from the roadway into the FICKETT trailer. These were believed to not belong to the case as there were two different sized footprints and believed belonging to the people owning the FICKETT trailer.

1950 - I interviewed a LARRY YOUNG. See attached Summary of Interview. 257

2020 - I cleared the C P.

2140 - I called Wdn. BILL ALLEN in reference to the information received from LARRY YOUNG in reference to the footprints as well as material. Wdn. ALLEN stated he would take care of it in the A.M. Wdn. ALLEN also advised that throughout the night, there would be some warden scent dogs used to travel the various roads in the area to see if they can pick up a scent of SARAH.

Page 10

❖398❖

Registered sex offenders within 10 miles of Bowdoin, ME

DEPARTMENT OF PUBLIC SAFETY
Maine State Police

Maine Sex Offender Registry
ONLINE SEARCH SERVICE

Search Results

Results for: **Zip Code "04008 with a 10 mile radius"**

Please select the record you would like to view by selecting the person's name below.

New Search

Name	Date of Birth
Allen, Paul	03/01/1963
Anguiano, Guadalupe	05/13/1960
Bartlett JR, James	07/07/1948
Beckwith, David	10/30/1955
Beem, Frederick	03/15/1975
Bennett, Earl	07/23/1961
Bishop, Jeffrey	04/11/1963
Bonyun, Floyd	02/23/1979
Burton, Stephen	01/24/1954
Buxton, Peter	06/07/1960
Caron, Paul	09/21/1978
Chapman, Daniel	09/25/1973
Collier, Jeremy	01/22/1978
Coombs, John	11/06/1952
Currier, Kenneth	10/27/1950
Dauphin, Harold	12/11/1944
Doak, Warren	02/21/1959
Dubar, Wayne	06/17/1964
Dudley, Dustin	10/31/1988
Dunning, Rhonda	03/20/1969
Dunphy, Kevin	03/21/1959
Emmons, Brian	06/12/1976
Foster, Ralph	07/04/1976
Garshva, John	01/22/1956
Gordon, Joshua	12/27/1976
Graham, Richard	07/28/1963
Grant, Leslie	05/24/1966
Green, Langdon	09/22/1954
Hodgdon, John	11/25/1981
Jandreau, Steven	10/20/1972

Jewett III, Ernest	05/11/1954
Labonte , Charles	04/15/1964
Le , De	01/28/1964
Leavitt , Charles	01/02/1956
Lyons , Walter	07/14/1971
Mccown , Jeremy	08/17/1981
Merryman , Brian	06/18/1977
Michaud , Richard	12/14/1964
Mitch , Orrin	10/10/1956
Moody , Robbie	01/11/1982
Moore , George	12/19/1944
Nicholson , Daniel	12/30/1971
Nickerson SR, Alan	05/05/1947
Palmer III, Lewis	07/16/1964
Patterson , David	02/01/1966
Pelletier , Willard	08/10/1978
Pierce , William	01/24/1954
Pottle , Misty	09/15/1975
Pruell JR, Norman	09/10/1978
Racine , Gerard	07/30/1946
Salvadori , Scott	01/18/1967
Scott , Merritt	02/06/1921
Seigars , Robert	11/11/1943
Shorette , Theodore	07/06/1963
Sibley , Hiram	07/14/1932
Spencer , Richard	03/03/1936
St amant , Bryan	06/12/1963
Stone , Calvin	01/19/1971
Turmenne , David	02/01/1947
Welch , David	05/30/1964
Wright , Daniel	11/03/1971

New Search

Report of Detective Hendsbee regarding the tracking dog scenting deer

MAINE STATE POLICE

Case No. LC 88-00203

CONTINUATION REPORT

Sagadahoc Sheriff's Office
Homicide (SARAH CHERRY)

Det. ALFRED HENDSBEE, mc
Code No. 2134
Bowdoin, Sagadahoc

CONTINUED:

also stated he was told that DECHAINE had been interviewed and that his stories were not consistent. The interview was done by Dep. Sher. DAN REED, Inv. Dep. WESTROM and Sher. HAGGETT.

Tr. BUREAU also produced clothing which was left at the HENKEL residence which Tr. BUREAU was going to use for scent. The clothing belonged to SARAH CHERRY which was in a brown paper bag consisting of sneakers, socks and a jacket. Tr. BUREAU advised that SARAH did not have any shoes on when she left the residence.

0120 - Tr. BUREAU and I ran track with his canine unit from the Toyota pickup truck. The first track was run in the wooded area from where the Toyota pickup truck was located. The canine went into the woods, came back out of the woods and crossed onto the roadway. Another track was run across from the pickup truck was located across the road. The dog scented the area and ran across a deer track at which time started following the deer track. Tr. BUREAU thought he was chasing a deer when we heard a noise in the woods and pulled the dog off. The dog then was taken back to Tr. BUREAU's cruiser.

0200 - Tr. BUREAU called S P Augusta at my request to have the State Police Wrecker come to pick up the 1981 Toyota pickup truck.

0205 - I received the keys that belonged to the 1981 pickup truck from Dep. WESTRUM who advised that these keys were found underneath the seat of one of the cruiser in which DENNIS DECHAINE was being interviewed. These keys were found underneath the seat after DENNIS DECHAINE advised he had not had the keys on his person but had left them in the truck.

0240 - I arrived at the intersection of the Lewis Hill Road and the Dead River Road where I spoke to DENNIS DECHAINE. See attached Summary of Interview.

While sitting with DECHAINE in the back seat of the cruiser, I noted that his pants were wet, sneakers were wet and that there was a bruise on his left arm, on the bicep. It's a round bruise and when I inquired from

Page 3

Report of Deputy Sheriff Daniel Reed

When they arrived with Dennis Dechaine, I Read him his Rights and proceded to question him.

Q: Where is your Truck Dennis?
A: I parked it in the woods so as to go Fishing, While I was Fishing, I got lost in the woods and was unable to locate my Truck.
Q: Did you catch any thing?
A: ;
Q: Where is your Fishing Gear?
A: Once I realized I was'nt able to locate my Truck, I ditched my pole.
Q: Have you been on this Road (pointing to the Lewis Hill Rd.) today?
A: No;
Q: (Showing him the items that were found in the Drive Way) Are these yours?
A: Yes they are;
Q: Do you carry these items in your Truck?
A: Yes (maybe) - I went fishing —
Q: Where in your Truck do you keep these?
A: Passenger seat —
Q: How could these have been found in a Drive Way off the Lewis Hill Rd. If you havent been on this Road today?
A: I dont know
Q: An individual saw your Truck heading in this direction this afternoon.
A: I think I did go down this Road once looking for a Fishing Hole.
Q: Did you enter anyons Drive Way?
A: I remember turning around in one.
Q: Do you remember anything about this DriveWay?
A: It was a long Drive Way with a House that set back from the Road. NO I said I never saw a house
Q: Did you drive all the way in?
A: No, All I did was turn around, I met two older people and asked them for directions to a Fishing Hole. They told me to follow this Road to the end and take a right.
Q: How did these items end up in that Drive Way?
A: Probably when I got out to take a PISS, they must have fallen out.
Q: You just told me that all you did was turn around.
A: NO: I told you it I stopped and took a Piss (ANGRILY)
Q: Do you always take a Piss in some ons Drive Way, in the middle of the day?
A: It wasnt in the middle of the day, I worked at the Farm until 5:00 and then I came out to Fish, and I didnt Piss in the Drive Way, I went off to the woods.
Q: If you dropped these items at the end of the Drive, How did they get up to the house?
A: Who ever grabbed the Girl saw them and placed them in the Drive Way to set me up.

Afte Questioning the Individual I turned my information over to State Police.

END OF REPORT

Daniel L. Reed
Sag S.O.   7-7-88

*Statement concerning false allegations by
ex-prosecutor Eric Wright*

**TRIAL AND ERROR P.O.
Box 153 Madawaska, ME
04756**

June 2004

William Stokes
Deputy Attorney General
State House Station
Augusta, ME 04330

Dear Mr. Stokes:

On September 1, 1994, there was a meeting about the Dennis Dechaine case with Attorney General Mike Carpenter, Assistant Attorney General Eric Wright and Phil Dechaine, Don Dechaine, Senator Judy Paradis, Representative Doug Ahearn, his father, Dan Ahearn, and Carol Waltman.

At that meeting, many aspects of the arrest, trial, conviction and imprisonment of Dennis Dechaine were discussed, but two are presented here for your consideration.

We requested several documents and at the top of the list were the handwritten notes of Mark Westrum, which he referenced at the trial. We were told by Eric Wright that those notes were "unavailable". [As we now know, with the August, 2003 opening of the files to the public, those notes were faxed by Mark Westrum to Eric Wright on the same day. In those notes, Mark Westrum recorded "How could I kill her?" with the words "How could" crossed out and replaced with "Why did".]

Toward the close of the meeting, we were told by Eric Wright that Dennis had confessed to the state psychologists and that the confession was recorded on videotape. Judy Paradis's strong recollection is that Eric Wright made that statement while looking directly into her eyes. After this shocking revelation, the meeting adjourned with Dennis' supporters and brother severely shaken by this seemingly authoritative representation by Eric Wright. [To our current understanding, no statements by Dennis on the tape, also made available in August, 2003, of his interviews with the psychologists come close to a confession.] When asked for a copy of the tape, Eric Wright replied, "Ask the defense lawyer for one".

We affirm by our signatures below the truths stated above.

Sincerely,

_____ _____ _____
Doug Ahearn   Don Dechaine   Phil Dechaine

_____ _____ _____
Judy Paradis   Dan Ahearne   Carol Waltman

Report of Maine State Police expert regarding tire tracks

MAINE STATE POLICE	Case No: LC-88-203
	Cross File: L88-309

LAST NAME FIRST MIDDLE	SIGNATURE AND RANK	CODE NO
CHERRY, SARAH	Det. John C. Otis JCO Det. Ronald K. Richards RKR	3632 APPROVED 7/21/88
OFFENSE: Homicide	PLACE OF OCCURRENCE TOWN: Bowdoin COUNTY: Sagadahoc	CASE STATUS

Page 12

The left front tire of the vehicle is a Bridgestone Skyway Wide 78 deluxe tubeless tire with four plyrating 2 polyester, 2 nylon. Treadwear 80, Traction B, Temperature C. E-78-14-5BD V1 DOT ENLS BDD 291 BS

The right front tire is a Trison Steel belted radial 778 standard load P20 5/75 R 14 tubeless, Traction A, Temperature B DOT H2AD YP5 463.

The tires were sprayed with "Pam" lubricant and rolled on clean cardboard strips. These impressions were then dusted with magnetic fingerprint powder and marked L88-309-111 and L88-309-112.

7-18-88

The tire impressions cast at the HINKEL residence (L88-309-1, L88-309-2 and L88-309-3) were examined and found to have visible class characteristics. No accidental/individual characteristics were observed. In order to determine if a specific tire made the impressions, sufficient accidental/individual characteristics would have to be present.

A comparison of the casts (L88-309-1, L88-309-2 and L88-309-3) against the rolled impression of the left tire, L88-309-111, disclosed that there are similar class characteristics between the casts and the left front tire of the vehicle. The impression seen in the casts could have been made by the left front tire, however, this does not exclude any other tire with a similar tread design.

A comparison of the casts (L88-309-1, L88-309-2 and L88-309-3) against the rolled impression of the right front tire, L88-309-112, disclosed that the class characteristics are not the same.

Rolled impressions were not made of the rear tires of the vehicle as a visual comparison of the cast impressions L88-309-1 through L88-309-3 against them disclosed that the casts and the rear tires contained obvious dissimilar class characteristics thus excluding the rear tires as having made the impressions seen in L88-309-1 through L88-309-3.

Evidence submitted will be retained by the Lab at this time.

Enclosures: None

Copies: Attorney General's Office
Det. Alfred Hendsbee
Crime Lab

Report of Detective Hendsbee regarding no need of key to lock truck

CONTINUATION REPORT

LC 88-0203
DET. ALFRED HENDSBEE, cl
Page Three

1215 - I met with A.A.G WRIGHT at the A.G.'S Office.

1430 - A.A.G. WRIGHT and I arrived at the West Gardiner Beef Company and conducted a pretrial interview with SHARON GILLEY.

1530 - A.A.G. WRIGHT and I arrived at Wright's Farm Supply Company in Litchfield and did a pretrial interview with RICHARD and RAYMOND KNIGHT.

1615 - I arrived at the A.G.'S Office and called THOMAS CONNOLLY in reference to showing him the evidence as well as determining whether or not he had found any keys with a knife on them at the DECHAINE residence. CONNOLLY advised that he found a second set of keys for the truck, however, there was no knife on them. The keys for NANCY DECHAINE'S keys for the truck.

3-3-89

0945 - I called ERIC WRIGHT at his request and discussed the case with him.

1040 - I called ARTHUR ALBIN at his request. ARTHUR needed more information for the diagram.

1045 - I met with JOHN OTIS at the Lab in reference to having the evidence for this case available to be taken to court next Monday.

1230 - DR. McLAIN from A.M.H.I. called advising that he has paperwork for me at A.M.H.I. in reference to DENNIS DECHAINE.

1410 - I conducted a pretrial with TR. THOMAS BUREAU.

1500 - I met with DR. McLAIN at A.M.H.I. and received his records on DENNIS DECHAINE.

1530 - I arrived at Headquarters and tested the locks on DENNIS DECHAINE'S pick-up truck. The truck can be locked without a key by holding the latch inward and can also be locked with the key.

1645 - I spoke with THOMAS CONNOLLY via telephone in reference to him viewing the evidence. CONNOLLY advised that Monday, 3-6-89, would be okay for him.

Final report of state psychlogist MacLean

Re: Dennis J. Deschaine   8   November 3, 1988
Docket No. CR-88-244

defendant eventually obtained a four-year degree from Western Washington University in French literature. The defendant was married in 1983 and presently resides in the Bowdoin-Bowdoinham area. The subject is presently self-employed and alleges a long history of substance abuse, since his teenage years, which he describes as periodic. The subject is negative for psychiatric history and has a prior arrest, as a teenager, involving a drug offense.

A mental status examination indicated no present psychosis on the part of the defendant. Psychological testing indicated that the defendant was functioning in the high average range of intelligence, and that mental retardation was not indicated. A screening test for organic brain syndrome indicated low probability of OBS. Personality testing indicated that the defendant was not psychotic, but was extremely defensive in personality structure and exhibited an unrealistic view of himself and an over-evaluated sense of self moral worth. A comprehensive assessment aimed at determining competency on the part of the defendant resulted in a finding which inferred competency.

With respect to the defendant's state of mind at the time of the alleged offenses, it was determined, through the subject's statements and recollections concerning his activities concerning the time frame in question, that while he states he had difficulty determining the passage of time because of alleged substance abuse, he nevertheless, was in a conscious state and recalled the specifics of his behavior within the time frame. It was the defendant's position that he was alone on the day in question and was not responsible for the charges alleged against him. There was nothing seen, as a result of the examination process, which suggested that the defendant was unable to differentiate between right and wrong at the time of the alleged offenses.

                                                 Respectfully,

                                                 Neil MacLean, Ed.D.
                                                 Chief Psychologist

dn

cc: District Attorney
      Attorney of Record

Medical Examiner's Report

REV. 3/87 — STATE OF MAINE — CASE # ML 88-568

REPORT OF INQUIRY AND EXAMINATION BY MEDICAL EXAMINER

ML 88-568

- **DECEDENT:** SARAH CHERRY   **AGE:** 12   **SEX:** F   **RACE:** W
- **ADDRESS:** MEADOW RD   BOWDOIN   **M W S D:** S
- **NOTIFIED BY:** F. LAROCHELLE   **DATE AND TIME:** A.G. office 7/8 12:51A
- **POLICE INVESTIGATOR:** MSP   **DEPT.:**
  Write None if Applicable
- **INFORMANT:** Including Relationship to Deceased
  MSP
- **PLACE OF DEATH:** WOODS — HALLOWELL RD   BOWDOIN
- **SCENE VISIT:** (DATE AND TIME OR NONE) 7/8/88 — APP. 2:30 PM
- **PLACE BODY EXAMINED:** SCENE and KVMC   **DATE AND TIME:** 2:30 PM ; 3:40 PM

IMMEDIATE CAUSE
(a) ASPHYXIATION DUE TO LIGATURE STRANGULATION WITH
DUE TO, OR AS A CONSEQUENCE OF:
(b) MULTIPLE STAB WOUNDS OF NECK and CHEST.
DUE TO, OR AS A CONSEQUENCE OF:
(c)

OTHER SIGNIFICANT CONDITIONS:

ACCIDENT, SUICIDE, etc.	DATE & TIME OF INJURY	HOW INJURY OCCURRED
HOMICIDE	FOUND 7/8/88	STABBED and STRANGLED BY ASSAILANT

AT WORK?	PLACE OF INJURY	LOCATION
NO	WOODS	OFF HALLOWELL RD BOWDOIN

- **DATE AND TIME OF DEATH:** FOUND 7/8/88
- **DATE AND TIME FOUND:** 7/8/88 — APPROX NOON   **LAST SEEN ALIVE:** 7/6/88
- **AUTOPSY AUTHORIZED BY:** R Roy (Name and Title)   **PATHOLOGIST:** R Roy
- **BODY RELEASED TO:** _____
- **TOXICOLOGY OR OTHER STUDIES PENDING:** _____

I hereby declare that the information contained herein regarding this death is true and correct to the best of my knowledge and belief, as is the information contained on the death certificate if signed by me.

8/16/88   SAGADAHOC   _Ronald P. Roy_
Date   County of Death   Signature of Medical Examiner

Typed or Printed Name of Medical Examiner: Ronald P. Roy, M.D.   (203)
ORIGINAL TO BE FILED WITH CHIEF MEDICAL EXAMINER, STATE HOUSE STATION 37, AUGUSTA ME

Analysis of leaflet distributed by Rev. Dorr at the Democratic Convention

---

Dennis Dechaine
Guilty of Murder
Keep Him In Jail

What Trail and Error isn't telling you:

1. Dennis admitted that he stopped "to urinate" in the drive way of the home where Sarah Cherry was babysitting.

2. The rope that tied little Sarah's hands and was wrapped around her neck was cut from the roll of rope in Dennis Dechaine's barn. Item # L88-309-94A and # L88-309-94B

3. On the night Sarah disappeared, while Dennis Dechaine was sitting in the Sheriff's car, he claimed he left the keys in his truck and it was unlocked. Fact: After he got out of the Sheriff's car the keys to his truck were found under the back seat of the Sheriff's car. The truck was found to be locked.

4. Found in Dennis Dechaine home between his mattress and box spring: White "Blossoms" underpants. Item # L88-309-92 These are little girls panties.

5. Also found in home, Loose "Fruit of the Loom" label, size 2. # L88-309-95

None of this can be explained away by accusing someone else. Dennis Dechaine was found guilty by a jury of his peers after they heard testimony and examining evidence while under cross examination. Trial and Error can not erase this evidence and much more that is on record.

Talk to your representative about making sure Dennis stays in prison for the crime he has committed.

Robert Dorr
Waldoboro, Me.

1. False! This allegation is disproved by the July 7, 1988, written report of Deputy Daniel Reed, Sagadahoc County Sherrif's Department, and by Deputy Reed's sworn tesstimony in court.

2. False! The Maine State Police Report identifies both these items as found in Mr. Dechaine's barn. Maine State police Laboratory Examination Report, page 14, states: "Item L88-309-94A, rope: This item consists of a coil of yellow plastic rope. It is dissimilar in morphology to the rope from the scene—Item L88-309-16 and L88-309-106. Item L.88-309-94B, rope: This item consists of an approximately 2'9" yellow plastic rope. It is dissimilar in morphology with the rope from the scene —Item L88-309-16 and L88-309-106." (Item L88-309-16 was the rope binding Sarah Cherry's wrists; Item L88-309-106 was a piece of rope found in the woods near the victim's body.)

3. False! According to Maine State Police reports, this truck was not locked; the rear window of the cab was open. *But the condition of the truck has no relevance to the crime.* State Police technicians who chemically swabbed and vacuumed this vehicle, and microscopically examined its contents, found that there was no trace that the victim had ever been in the truck. The police dog, given the victim's clothing to sniff, detected no scent of her in the truck.

4. False! Maine State Police Laboratory Examination Report, page 14, states: "Item L88-309-92: This item consists of a size 7–large woman's underpants. Chemical and microscopic tests for seminal fluid were negative in the crotch area of this item."

5. Irrelevant and misleading! This is a label from a garment for a toddler, age 1–3. Maine State Police laboratory Examination Report, page 15, states: "Item L88-309-95, label: This item consists of a label containing the following information: 'All cotton Made in U.S.A. RN13765 700 Machine wash warm tumble dry medium Do not bleach colored garments Fruit-of-the-Loom Size 2'"

Robert Dorr, the author of this pamphlet fails to mention the evidence concealed from the jury and fails to specify any evidence connecting Mr. Dechaine to the murder of Sarah Cherry. He was formerly associated with the Office of the Attorney General. Official documents prove every one of his allegations to be untrue.

If truth would serve his purpose, why would he be utilizing falsehoods?

American Bar Standards for Prosecutors

AMERICAN BAR ASSOCIATION
Criminal Justice Section

Standards

Standard 3-1.2 The Function of the Prosecutor

(a) The office of prosecutor is charged with responsibility for prosecutions in its jurisdiction.
(b) (b) The prosecutor is an administrator of justice, an advocate, and an officer of the court; the prosecutor must exercise sound discretion in the performance of his or her functions.

(c) The duty of the prosecutor is to seek justice, not merely to convict.

(c) It is an important function of the prosecutor to seek to reform and improve the administration of criminal justice. When inadequacies or injustices in the substantive or procedural law come to the prosecutor's attention, he or she should stimulate efforts for remedial action.
(d) (e) It is the duty of the prosecutor to know and be guided by the standards of professional conduct as defined by applicable professional traditions, ethical codes, and law in the prosecutor's jurisdiction. The prosecutor should make use of the guidance afforded by an advisory council of the kind described in standard 4-1.5.

Standard 3-1.5 Duty to Respond to Misconduct

(a) Where a prosecutor knows that another person associated with the prosecutor's office is engaged in action, intends to act or refuses to act in a manner that is a violation of a legal obligation to the prosecutor's office or a violation of law, the prosecutor should follow the policies of the prosecutor's office concerning such matters. If such policies are unavailing or do not exist, the prosecutor should ask the person to reconsider the action or inaction which is at issue if such a request is aptly timed to prevent such misconduct and is otherwise feasible. If such a request for reconsideration is unavailing, inapt or otherwise not feasible or if the seriousness of the matter so requires, the prosecutor should refer the matter to higher authority in the prosecutor's office, including, if warranted by the seriousness of the matter, referral to the chief prosecutor.

Standard 3-3.11 Disclosure of Evidence by the Prosecutor

(a) **A prosecutor should not intentionally fail to make timely disclosure to the defense, at the earliest feasible opportunity, of the existence of all evidence or information which tends to negate the guilt of the accused** or mitigate the offense charged or which would tend to reduce the punishment of the accused.
(b) (b) A prosecutor should not fail to make a reasonably diligent effort to comply with a legally proper discovery request.

(c) A prosecutor should not intentionally avoid pursuit of evidence because he or she believes it will damage the prosecution's case or aid the accused.

Attorney General Rowe's assignment to committee to investigate

October 23, 2004

Honorable Eugene W. Beaulieu
United States Magistrate (Retired)
311 Woodlawn Avenue
Old Town, ME 04468

Charles H. Abbott, Esquire
Skelton, Taintor & Abbott
P.O. Box 3200
Auburn, ME 04212-3200

Marvin H. Glazier, Esquire
Vafiades, Brountas & Kominsky, LLP
P.O. Box 919
Bangor, ME 04402-0919

    Re: Sarah Cherry Murder Case

Dear Magistrate Judge Beaulieu, Mr. Abbott and Mr. Glazier:

  There have been allegations of prosecutorial and law enforcement misconduct concerning the trial of Dennis Dechaine for the 1988 murder of Sarah Cherry.

These allegations are that:

• Following their initial investigation, law enforcement officers altered their notes and/or reports to falsely attribute incriminating statements to Dennis Dechaine.

• Prosecutors misled the jury with respect to Sarah Cherry's time of death.

• At the time of trial, prosecutors and law enforcement officers had information about an alternative suspect which they should have shared, but did not share, with defense counsel.

• In 1992, law enforcement officers, with the approval of prosecutors, inappropriately destroyed physical evidence to include a rape kit as well as hairs and fibers discovered at the scene where Sarah Cherry's body was found.

• Prosecutors inappropriately failed to notify the court and defense counsel of a consultant's opinion regarding the reliability of an outside laboratory and DNA tests conducted in 1993.

  I have no reason to believe that these allegations are true. However, in order to ensure continued public confidence in the Office of the Attorney General as well as other law enforcement agencies in the State of Maine, I request that you conduct an independent and impartial review of these allegations and provide to me a report of your findings, which will be made public, to me. [sic]

I pledge the complete cooperation of my office during your review. State investigative and prosecutorial files regarding this case are public documents subject to 16 M.R.S.A ss 614 and will be made available for your review and copying at a time and place of your choosing. State personnel who investigated and prosecuted this case will also be available for interviews by you at a mutually convenient time and place.

You are asked to investigate these allegations only. Obviously, the guilt or innocence of Mr. Dechaine is for the courts.

Please provide your questions and requests for information directly to me. Thank you for your willingness to undertake this very important public service.

Sincerely,

G. Steven Rowe /s/

G. Steven Rowe
Attorney General

GSR/dp

Letter to AG Rowe requesting results of year-long study

JAMES P. MOORE
WRITER
POST OFFICE BOX 1032, BRUNSWICK, ME 04011
HTTP://WWW.SUSCOM-MAINE.NET/AUTHOR/

NOVEMBER 25, 2005

G. Steven Rowe, Attorney General
Office of the Attorney General
6 State House Station
Augusta, Maine 04333-0006

Dear Mr. Rowe:

It's been a year since you announced your assignment of three distinguished attorneys to review allegations of improprieties in the investigation and prosecution of Dennis Dechaine.

Considering the qualifications of these attorneys, it would be less than diligent for them to have dawdled along for this length of time in completing their assignment. Based on this conclusion, I assume that they have completed their inquiries and submitted their report to you.

Since your original announcement promised to make that report public, and unless you are awaiting some politically propitious moment to release that report, I request that you make the results known now and/or furnish me a copy.

Sincerely,

James P. Moore

Response from AG Rowe

G. STEVEN ROWE
ATTORNEY GENERAL

Telephone: (207) 626-8800
TDD: (207) 626-8865

STATE OF MAINE
OFFICE OF THE ATTORNEY GENERAL
6 STATE HOUSE STATION
AUGUSTA, MAINE 04333-0006

REGIONAL OFFICES:

84 HARLOW ST., 2ND FLOOR
BANGOR, MAINE 04401
TEL: (207) 941-3070
FAX: (207) 941-3075

44 OAK STREET, 4TH FLOOR
PORTLAND, MAINE 04101-3014
TEL: (207) 822-0260
FAX: (207) 822-0259
TDD: (877) 428-8800

128 SWEDEN ST., STE. 2
CARIBOU, MAINE 04736
TEL: (207) 496-3792
FAX: (207) 496-3291

December 9, 2005

Mr. James Moore
P.O. Box 1032
Brunswick, ME 04011

Mr. Moore:

This is in response to your November 25th letter wherein you requested that I release the results of the review by Judge Boulier, Attorney Abbott and Attorney Glazier into allegations of improprieties in the investigation and prosecution of Dennis Dechaine.

I do not have the results of the review. As soon as I receive the report containing the results, I will make it public.

Respectfully,

G. STEVEN ROWE
Attorney General

GSR:djp

Photographs

A young Dennis helps a friend install a furnace in 1988.

Seated, brothers Don and Phil Dechaine. Standing, Dennis Dechaine and his brother Frank, in 2003.

Above: Carol Waltman (right) addresses the crowd assembled at the State House. Below, friends and supporters of Dennis gather that same day for a telephone call to Dennis via speakerphone at the State House.

Above: Supporters march in Augusta in the snow. Below: supporters Libby Harmon and Bill Bunting find a way to wish Dennis "Happy Birthday" in the prison visiting room.

❖

If you are interested in more background on this case, the Trial & Error website
www.trialanderrordennis.org
contains a wealth of information, including trial transcripts, briefs, affadavits, and other documents related to the trial, hearings, and motions.

❖

JIM MOORE's twenty-five-year career with the Bureau of Alcohol, Tobacco and Firearms (ATF) included two years with the U.S. Justice Department's Organized Crime and Racketeering Strike Force, and two years with INTERPOL, where he directed international investigations of murder, terrorism, and other violent crimes. After retiring as ATF's agent-in-charge for Maine and New Hampshire, he worked briefly as a contract investigator for DEA, U.S. Customs, and the Department of Defense. His books include *Very Special Agents*, a nonfiction history of ATF; and a suspense novel, *Official Secrets*.